JANET AND COLIN BORD

Alien Animals

A worldwide investigation

PANTHER
Granada Publishing

Panther Books
Granada Publishing Ltd
8 Grafton Street, London W1X 3LA

This revised edition published by Panther Books 1985

First published in Great Britain by
Granada Publishing 1980

Copyright © Janet and Colin Bord 1980, 1985

ISBN 0-586-06469-9

Printed and bound in Great Britain by
Collins, Glasgow

Set in Baskerville

Contents

Acknowledgements   7

Why *alien* animals?   11

1 Elusive lake monsters   13

2 Cats that can't be caught   49

3 Mysterious black dogs   80

4 Giant birds and birdmen   109

5 Man or manimal?   136

6 Animals that aren't: following where the evidence leads   169

Appendix 1: A few hints for monster watchers   197

Appendix 2: A listing of 300 lake monsters around the world   199

Bibliography   205

Notes   209

Index   239

Acknowledgements

Our grateful thanks go to the following people for their help in providing data and answering questions about their own research: Ivar Anderson (Sweden), Alan Berry (USA), Don Boyd (Australia), Ivan Bunn (England), Bill Chalker (Australia), Peter Costello (Ireland), René Dahinden (Canada), Bertil Falk (Sweden), Lucius Farish (USA), David Fideler (USA), Rex Gilroy (Australia), John Green (Canada), Phyllis Hall (New Zealand), Rip Hepple (England), F. W. Holiday (Wales), Chris Holtzhausen (South Africa), Norman O. Josephsen (USA), Anders Liljegren (Sweden), Mary Moon (Canada), Norman Oliver (England), Revd Dr W. D. Omand (England), B. L. Owens (Australia), Tapani Rasila (Finland), V. I. Sanarov (USSR), Ron Schaffner (USA), Doc Shiels (England), Pushkar Singh (India), Jan-Ove Sundberg (Sweden), Jun-Ichi Takanashi (Japan), Jerzy E. Wielunski (Poland), Rocky Wood (New Zealand), Don Worley (USA), Joseph W. Zarzynski (USA). Also we acknowledge the contribution made by all the authors of books and editors of magazines listed in the Bibliography and Notes, and those magazine contributors whose material we have used. Our especial thanks go to R. J. M. Rickard for opening the voluminous files of *Fortean Times* to us, and being in himself a mine of valuable information.

Our thanks also to the following picture sources: Associated Press, 2; Gösta Blomquist/International Magazine Service, Stockholm, 3; Janet & Colin Bord, 11, 12, 16, 17, 18; Peter Costello, 1; British Library, 15, 26; René Dahinden/Fortean Picture Library, 25, 27; *Flying Saucer Review*, 21; Fortean Picture Library, 4, 5, 6, 7, 8, 9, 10, 13, 19, 20, 22, 24, 28, 29, 30; *Nottingham Evening Post*, 14; Royal Geographical Society, 23.

Fortean Picture Library is collecting pictorial material on Fortean topics of all kinds, including alien animals, and in this way plans to build a useful and authoritative picture source. It is always glad to hear from people who have illustrations which they feel might be relevant. Please write to them at the address given on page 198.

Grateful acknowledgement is made to the following for their kind permission to reprint copyright material:

George Allen & Unwin (Publishers) Ltd for an extract from *In My Solitary Life* by Augustus J. C. Hare.

Anchor Press/Doubleday and Hodder & Stoughton Ltd for an extract from *The Romeo Error* by Lyall Watson. © 1974 by Lyall Watson.

Ivar Anderson, for extracts from letters to the authors.

Charles Bowen, Editor, for extracts from *Flying Saucer Review*.

A. C. Buchan, Editor, for material from *The Western Times & Gazette*.

Ivan Bunn, for extracts from his black dog research published in *Lantern*.

J. T. Carter, Editor, for material from *The Western Morning News*.

Cheam Publishing Ltd, for extracts from Albert Ostman's abduction story quoted from *On the Track of the Sasquatch* by John Green.

David Clarke, for an extract from his article 'The Myth & Mystery of Morgawr, the Helford Monster' published in *Cornish Life*.

Coward, McCann & Geoghegan, Inc. for an extract from *In Search of Lake Monsters* by Peter Costello. Copyright © Peter Costello 1974.

Curtis Brown Ltd, for an extract from *Days of Our Years* by Pierre van Paassen.

René Dahinden, for an extract from his interview with Verlin Herrington, published in *Sasquatch* by Don Hunter with René Dahinden.

Tim Dinsdale and Routledge & Kegan Paul Ltd, for an extract from *The Leviathans* by Tim Dinsdale.

Futura Publications Ltd, for an extract from *The Monsters of Loch Ness* by Roy P. Mackal.

Affleck Grey, for extracts from his book *The Big Grey Man of Ben MacDhui*.

Robert Hale Ltd, for an extract from *The Ghost Book* by Alasdair Alpin MacGregor.

Mark Humphreys, Editor, for material from the *Falmouth Packet*.

Jove Publications, Inc., for extracts from *Abominable Snowmen: Legend Come to Life* by Ivan T. Sanderson, Copyright © 1961, 1968 by Ivan T. Sanderson.

Revd Dr W. D. Omand, for extracts from a letter to the authors.

Olle Petrini, Associate Editor, for material from *Expressen*.

Christine Shiels, for an extract from a letter describing her sighting of Morgawr.

Doc Shiels, for an extract from 'Words from the Wizard', and letters to the authors.

Sidgwick & Jackson Ltd, for an extract from *The Dragon and the Disc* by F. W. Holiday.

Colin Smythe Ltd, for extracts from *The Middle Kingdom* by D. A. MacManus.

Souvenir Press Ltd, for an extract from *Magic and Mystery in Tibet* by Alexandra David-Neel.

Ken Waddell, Editor, for material from *The Falkirk Herald*.

Mrs Myrtle Walton, for William Roe's 1955 Bigfoot sighting report.

Warner Books, Inc., New York, for extracts from *Creatures of the Outer Edge* by Jerome Clark and Loren Coleman. Copyright © 1978 by Jerome Clark and Loren Coleman.

R. Martin Wolf, Managing Editor, for extracts from *Pursuit*, including passages from his article 'Coherence in Chaos'.

We have made every effort to contact all copyright-holders of material we have quoted, but this has not proved possible in every case. Full bibliographical details of material quoted can be found in the Notes. Any errors or omissions brought to the publisher's notice will be corrected or included in future editions.

Why alien *animals?*

This book is about impossibilities. It contains reports of unidentifiable animals and of known animals seen where they should not be. The reports come from ordinary citizens from all levels of society who are puzzled or alarmed by what they see and feel they should report it to the police. When organized searches are made, the animals are strangely elusive and can rarely be found and never caught. In fact much of the behaviour of both the identified and unidentified creatures is uncharacteristic of 'normal' animals. Therefore we have named them 'alien animals'. A classic example is the Loch Ness Monster. Seen by literally thousands of people and convincingly photographed, this creature still remains an outsider, its very existence questioned by people who should be excited beyond measure at such a discovery. The many other lake monsters of the world (described in Chapter 1) are also treated by most authorities as if they did not exist.

The alien animals we are concerned with are of five main types: 1. lake monsters, 2. out-of-place big cats, 3. large black dogs, 4. giant birds and birdmen/women, 5. hairy anthropoids such as Bigfoot and Yeti. Our data is not solely a collection of unsubstantiated newspaper reports, but is often based on personal communications with Fortean* researchers throughout the world (see Acknowledgements) who have made first-hand investigations into reports of alien animals. We have few photographs of these creatures with which to illustrate this book because alien animals are elusive, and when they do appear, the witness is almost invariably taken by surprise. Few people habitually carry cameras; and even when photographs are taken, other problems can arise, as we shall describe in Chapter 1.

Despite man's belief that with the invention of instantaneous communication he has become master of the planet, it seems that there may well be many species of animals, even large ones, which

* The word 'Fortean' derives from the late Charles Fort, an American who spent a major part of his life collecting and analysing many thousands of notes on a wide range of strange and anomalous phenomena, enigmatic objects and controversial subjects of all grades of probability.

are still to be discovered, or rediscovered. Fascinating though such speculation is, we do not feel that many of the creatures we describe in this book come into that category, and we would direct interested readers to Heuvelmans' *On the Track of Unknown Animals* for a highly readable account of the evidence, including a convincing case for the likely survival of the Siberian mammoth. Our preoccupation is with those types of animals, listed above, that behave strangely and are not accepted by Science – *but which have been seen by thousands of reliable people*. Our interest over many years has been in the more esoteric side of life – so-called paranormal phenomena, unidentified flying objects, Forteana, earth mysteries – and rather than attempt taxonomical and zoological discussion, fields in which we are not qualified, we shall concentrate on the weirder aspects of alien animal sightings. We hope to bring our relevant experience to bear on the main question generated by the data in this book: What *are* these animals? In our last chapter we shall give some possible answers.

1

Elusive lake monsters

When Duncan MacDonnell and William Simpson headed their motor cruiser home after a day's fishing on Loch Morar in Scotland they expected an uneventful journey across the calm water to their moorings. It had been a hot summer day, 16 August 1969. MacDonnell was steering the boat and Simpson was boiling the kettle for tea. In his taped interview with author Elizabeth Campbell, Duncan MacDonnell told what happened:

I heard a splashing or disturbance in the water astern of us. I looked up and about twenty yards behind us this creature was coming directly after us in our wake. It only took it a matter of seconds to catch up on us. It grazed the side of the boat, I am quite certain this was unintentional. When it struck the boat it seemed to come to a halt or at least slow down. I grabbed the oar and was attempting to fend it off, my one fear being that if it got under the boat it might capsize it.[1]

The impact had upset the kettle and extinguished the flame, and Bill Simpson leapt to the cabin to turn off the gas. He came on deck and saw MacDonnell unsuccessfully trying to get the creature away from them with the oar. When that snapped he felt it was time for more drastic measures and grabbing his rifle he quickly loaded it. He fired at the creature and watched it slowly sink away from the boat.

During the brief moments in which they had struggled to prevent the possible overturning of their boat, the two men had had a close view of a creature some 25 to 30 feet long, with a rough, dirty brown skin. It had three low humps that stood 18 inches above the surface of the water, and MacDonnell saw a large brown snake-like head 18 inches out of the water and about a foot wide at the top. Although both men were sure that the collision was accidental, the huge size and strange appearance of the water creature had unnerved them, as has happened to so many other witnesses worldwide who have had a similar close sighting of an inexplicable creature. Later in the interview, Bill Simpson said: 'I don't want to see it again – I was terrified.' The two men did not publicize their story other than to tell their families, but a relative told the press and within days it appeared in many newspapers, often with wildly inaccurate details. By then the men, who were long-distance lorry drivers, were off on their journeys and could not be contacted.

The report caused some members of the Loch Ness Investigation Bureau to take a renewed interest in Loch Morar and in 1970 researchers teamed up with biologists from London University to form the Loch Morar Survey. The biologists planned a detailed study of the loch's ecology, while others in the team conducted watches from the camera sites set up on shore and interviewed witnesses who had seen 'Morag', as the loch creature is sometimes called. This study provided some useful information for the biologists and two brief sightings for the camera crews, but no photographs. The most interesting result came from the researchers who traced and interviewed eyewitnesses. They gathered thirty-three good reports covering the period from 1887 to 1971. Loch Morar is an inaccessible stretch of water in a sparsely populated area of western Scotland and is one of a group of lakes which includes Arkaig, Shiel, Lochy and Quoich. They are south-west of Loch Ness and from all of them sightings have been reported of unknown creatures similar to those which are frequently reported at Loch Ness.

There can be very few people in the Western world who have not heard of the Loch Ness Monster. Probably most of them accept the conventional view which is presented by the media each time a new report comes to its attention: that it is all rather a joke, good for a bit of light relief, and was probably started by the canny locals as an additional tourist attraction. Some better informed individuals realize that the phenomenon is now being studied seriously by a few reputable scientists and technicians, but the majority of scientists have accepted the conventional Establishment view without any question and refuse to consider any other. Briefly, this view is that the reports are misidentifications of boats' wakes, mats of rotting vegetation which rise to the surface, or conventional wild life such as otters, seals, and water birds seen under unusual circumstances, compounded with a certain amount of wishful thinking. Anything which can't be explained in any of these ways must be a hoax, because such a creature as the witnesses describe is unknown to zoology and therefore could not exist. So we find that the eminent zoologist Dr Maurice Burton, who has written much on the impossibility of the existence of a 'monster' in Loch Ness but has apparently done very little field investigation, receives approval from the officials of the British Museum and the Zoological Society of London, neither of which bodies has made much attempt to investigate the reported phenomena nor study the puzzling movie and still photographs that have over the years been produced by witnesses at the loch side.[2] If 90 per cent of the 10,000 known reported sightings of the Loch Ness Monster which have been made over the years[3] were shown to be misidentifications of known phenomena, that would still leave 1,000 inexplicable reports, plus all the photographic evidence and also the anomalous sonar results, surely enough to afford scientists an opportunity to extend their knowledge of the natural world and plumb more of its mysteries.

But the Scottish lochs do not stand alone as locations for inexplicable phenomena. There are a number of other lakes in the British Isles where similar sightings have been made. These lakes sometimes have legendary and historical reports as well as contemporary accounts from reputable eyewitnesses. Some of these waters are considerably smaller than Loch Ness, and in fact are so small that it is inconceivable that a large creature could exist in them. There could hardly be enough food in such lakes to support it or them (a continuous line of reports from historical times to the present day suggests a breeding colony rather than an isolated individual – if the creatures are in fact *physical*, a point we return to later). Some of the most intriguing reports come from the west of Ireland in the region of Connemara. Here there is an area of peat bogs dotted with small lakes interconnected by streams. One of the lakes is Lough Nahooin and on 22 February 1968 a local farmer named Stephen Coyne, his wife and their five children stood for some considerable time and watched a 12-foot-long creature swim round the lake, at times coming as close as 20 or 30 feet.[4] F. W. Holiday, investigator of and writer on the Loch Ness phenomenon, has also investigated reports from the Irish lakes and here is his account of the report given to him by Stephen Coyne when he was interviewed at his home not far from Lough Nahooin in July 1968.

At about seven on the evening of 22 February 1968, Stephen Coyne went down to the bog by the lough to bring up some dry peat. With him he took his eldest son, a boy of eight, and the family dog. Although the sun had set it was still quite light. On reaching the peat-bed beside Nahooin he suddenly noticed a black object in the water. Thinking it was the dog he whistled to it; however, the dog came bounding along the shore from behind. On seeing the object it stopped and started barking.

He then saw that the object was an animal with a pole-like head and neck about nine inches to a foot in diameter. It was swimming around in various directions. From time to time it put its head underwater; two humps then came into view. Occasionally, a flat tail appeared. Once this came out near the head which argued length and a high degree of flexibility. The thing was black, slick and hairless with a texture resembling an eel.

The dog's barking seemed to irritate the monster and it began to move inshore, its mouth open. However, when Coyne strode over to support his dog it turned away and resumed swimming around the little lough. At about this point the little boy ran home to bring his mother to see the strange beast. When Mrs Coyne and the children returned the Peiste [an Irish name for water monsters] was still busily patrolling the tiny lake.

Both Mr and Mrs Coyne agreed that the creature was about twelve feet long and both agreed that they saw no eyes. Mrs Coyne told us that she noticed two horn-like projections on top of the head. Whereas she thought the thing approached as near as four to five yards, her husband felt that the nearest point was about nine yards. Both agreed that the mouth was underslung in relation to the snout and neither of them saw any teeth. Coyne described the mouth-interior as 'pale'.

To and fro before the seven members of the Coyne family strutted the Nahooin dragon. As dusk was settling they finally left it and made their way home over the bog.[5]

Recording this report was only a preliminary to the operation that had been planned by the group of researchers of which F. W. Holiday was a member. During the following days they proceeded to stretch weighted nets supported on the surface by buoys across the lake in various places. This was not an impossible task as Lough Nahooin is only 100 yards by 80 yards and generally about 20 feet deep – quite a different proposition to Loch Ness which is approximately one mile wide, 24 miles long, and has sides shelving steeply down, in places, to a depth of 900 feet. But the Irish lakes have the same impenetrable peaty murk as has Loch Ness. The hope was that the creature could be caught in one of the nets, and to this end a fish stunner and 'monster rousers' were operated, but they had no success. Any creature that may have been in the lake refused to co-operate and the hunters, all of them people with numerous other calls on their time, had to pack up with nothing proven. Stephen Coyne told Holiday that he had seen the creature once before, twenty years earlier, when he was with his brother. Other reliable witnesses report having seen many such strange sights in other Irish loughs which are of a comparable size to Nahooin. The wonder is how such large creatures could remain unknown in so many lakes and how they could find sufficient to feed on where there is only a small trout population.[6]

The water monster phenomenon is not confined to the British Isles, but is worldwide. Canada's lakes are especially rich in water monsters, and for frequency of sightings and sheer volume of reliable eyewitness reports the creature or creatures often seen in Okanagan Lake in British Columbia must rival those of Loch Ness. The reports and legends existed in Indian lore when the first white settlers arrived in 1860 and from then up until the present there has been a continuous stream of eyewitnesses who have reported the presence of Ogopogo, as the creature has been named. (The most complete listing we have seen is in Mary Moon's excellent book *Ogopogo*.) The reported appearance of Ogopogo is in general similar to that of the Loch Ness Monster. In one description the creature is said to be from 30 to 70 feet long with a dark, sleek body 1 to 2 feet thick, and with a head that has a horse-like shape. When Mr and Mrs R. H. Miller and Mr and Mrs Pat Marten with their son Murray saw it on 17 July 1959 they reported a snake-like head with a blunt nose. Mr Miller, who was editor of the *Vernon Advertiser*, first noticed the creature swimming in the wake of their motor cruiser as they were returning home one evening (note the similar circumstances to our first report from Loch Morar). It was about 250 feet behind them and steadily gaining. Mr Marten was steering. He turned the boat and headed towards the creature so that they could get a better view. For about three minutes the group observed the creature through binoculars as it approached them, but it did not seem to like the appearance of the boat broadside on to it and gradually submerged. At its closest it was within 175 feet, which is quite close enough to avoid misidentification of a known creature, especially when using binoculars.[7]

In 1968 five young people had a very close view of the creature's body. It was Tuesday, 23 July 1968 at approximately 5.45 P.M. when Willie Walls, Bruce and Gwen Johnson, Rennee Bliss and Sheri Campbell, whose ages ranged from fourteen to twenty-one, were water-skiing on the lake. Sheri Campbell saw 20 feet of Ogopogo floating on the surface with no head or tail visible. (This 'basking' attitude is typical of many reports worldwide.) In her alarm she dropped the ski tow-rope and had to tread water while the boat circled to pick her up. By then Ogopogo had begun to move. 'His blue-green-grey scales glistened like a rainbow trout as the sun shone on him,' said Sheri. The group decided to try for a closer look and got within 'five feet' before the creature submerged and made off at high speed. 'When he swam beneath the surface, he made waves which streamed behind him in vee shapes.' They chased the creature in their motor boat but at 40 mph could not keep up with it.[8]

On the far side of the American continent lies Lake Champlain which straddles the American/Canadian border, and also has the New York/Vermont state border running through it. This lake is named after the French explorer Samuel de Champlain who was the first to record a sighting of the resident monster, now appropriately known as Champ. In 1609 he described what he saw as being a serpentine creature, 20 feet long, thick as a barrel and with a head like a horse.[9] Since then it, or they, has been frequently seen. In 1945 Mr and Mrs Charles Langlois of Rutland, Vermont, came close enough in a rowing boat to 'whack it with an oar'.[10] Whether this is simply an expressive phrase to indicate close proximity or a report of their actions, we are not told. Either way it sounds a hazardous undertaking! There was also a mass sighting of the monster in 1945 when the passengers and crew of SS *Ticonderoga*, who were spectators of a bridge-opening ceremony, saw a strange head raised above the water.[11] In 1971 Mrs Robert A. Green with her mother and a friend saw a snaky head and three black humps gliding through the waters of Lake Champlain and called the hotel bartender over to provide another witness. He took one incredulous look and quickly returned to his bar, stating: 'I'll never say I saw it.'[12] Champ was photographed in July 1977 by Sandra Mansi, who was visiting the lake with her husband, and Dr Roy P. Mackal, a professor of biochemistry who has analysed the photograph, believes that it shows a kind of zeuglodon, primitive serpentine whales thought to have been extinct for 25 million years. Lake Champlain is 105 miles long with the northern end lying inside Canada, and its maximum width is 12½ miles. Sixty species of fish have been recorded in it, the largest of these being the sturgeon,[13] so there would seem to be enough space and sufficient food for a whole colony of water monsters. Since the 1970s their existence has been actively explored by a team calling themselves the Lake Champlain Phenomena Investigation, headed by school-teacher Joseph W. Zarzynski.

In western United States, Flathead Lake in Montana also has its monster. Once again we find that the local Indians had their lake monster legends; with the arrival of the white man in the area first-hand reports started to be made and have continued ever since. The US *Grant* was the first steam boat to operate on the 188 square-mile lake, and in 1885 James Kern, the skipper, thought he saw another boat coming towards him. As it came closer he realized it was no boat but a large animal similar to a whale. A passenger fired at it, whereupon it submerged. In 1919, fifty passengers on the *City of Polson* saw an object that at first appeared to be a log swimming away from the path of their vessel. During the following years numerous fishermen and tourists reported the humped back of a large, partially submerged creature, usually about 20 feet long. On a Friday in September 1960 the Zigler family were enjoying the lakeside air at the Polson country club when they decided to investigate why the waves were crashing against the shore. They walked to a nearby pier and saw 'something' rubbing itself against the pilings, rather as a cow scratches against a gatepost. Mr Zigler went off for his rifle and Mrs Zigler moved closer. The thing raised its head from the water and she reported: 'It was a horrible looking thing, with a head about the size of a horse . . . and about a foot of neck showing.' This caused her to scream and her husband ran back just in time to see the monster swim away at a 'great rate of speed'. Mr Zigler, who says he knows a sturgeon when he sees one, says that it was not any sort of sturgeon. In the following week it was seen again several times, including another sighting by Mr and Mrs Zigler, once more at the country club.

Flathead Lake is the largest in the north-west United States, its length being 27 miles and its width 15 miles, and it is fed by rivers of glacier water. This causes the water to be low in micro-organisms and the fish population is not prolific. The salmon, for example, are not over 5 pounds in weight. Sceptics suggest that people are seeing a giant sturgeon. These fish are reported from Seton Lake, British Columbia, to be 22, 28 and 35 feet long! And on the Volga River in Russia a sturgeon of 26 feet in length was said to have been taken.[14] But the record shows that there has only ever been one sturgeon caught in the lake, in 1955, and he was a puny 7.5 feet long. Also there is a suggestion that this one was brought in specially to boost the interests of the tourist fishing trade.[15]

Over the Rockies now to Lake Elsinore in California where the first report of a water monster was made in 1884. During the winter of 1970 Bonnie Pray, who lives on the lakeside, saw the creature twice and described it as snake-like, about 12 feet long and 3 feet thick, moving through the water with an 'undulating' motion. This up and down mode of progress is often noted in water monster reports and differentiates them from misreports of water snakes which progress through the water by 'weaving' from side to side over the surface.[16] After Bonnie Pray's sightings three officials of Elsinore State Park were in a boat when the creature appeared only 50 feet from them. Although they didn't agree on the details, they do know that they saw something very unusual. What makes this lake of particular interest to monster researchers is that in 1951 it dried up, and did so again in 1955. On neither occasion was any 'monster' carcase reported.[17] One possibility is that these creatures could be amphibious, and so could leave the lake before the water level became dangerously low. There are reports of the Loch Ness Monster having been seen on the shore, and crossing the lochside road. Another suggestion is that not all lake monsters are physically solid in the generally accepted sense of the term. We will be considering these possibilities and others later.

It would be remarkable if in the vast wilderness of Russia's Siberia there were not also mysterious denizens in isolated lakes, and although very little information on our subject comes from that huge continent, researchers have been able to obtain a few reports. Tim Dinsdale has spent more than twenty years investigating the reality of the Loch Ness Monster and in April 1960 he shot the now famous four minutes of 16-mm cine film at Loch Ness which has been exhaustively analysed and possibly shows the moving body of a large unknown creature in the loch.[18] He has been able to make contact with Dr S. K. Klumov of the Moscow Institute of Oceanography and exchange information on the subject. Dr Klumov told him of a sighting in 1953 made by geologist V. A. Tverdokhlebov who was the leader of a group doing prospecting by Lake Vorota, which lies in eastern Siberia near Verkhoyansk and is north of the Arctic Circle. Geologist Tverdokhlebov and a companion observed a creature swimming rapidly towards them; it was some 32 feet long and over 6 feet wide. They could see eyes, light-coloured patches on the side of the head and a dark grey body. Along its back was a 20-inch-high fin. It moved forward in leaps and at 100 yards from the shore it stopped and sent up a great cascade of spray before diving out of sight.[19] The lakes of that area are said to have an evil reputation among the local hunters and fishermen, and many of them have seen the creatures. The largest lake there is Lake Labynkyr which is about 9 miles long and 200 feet deep, and so for size stands midway between the small loughs of Ireland and the huge inland seas of the American continent, examples of all of which contain water monsters.

In 1963 and 1964 expeditions visited both lakes Labynkyr and Vorota and saw enigmatic humps swimming close to the shore for several minutes.[20] A much more impressive sighting occurred at some unspecified date during 1964 and was reported in the 21 November edition of *Komsomol'skaya Pravda* of that year. At Lake Khaiyr in the same eastern Siberia area, a biologist, N. F. Gladkikh, was at the lakeside early one morning when he saw a creature on the shore eating grass. It had a small head, a long gleaming neck, and a huge bluish-black body with a fin along its spine. Although Gladkikh was a biologist, this creature was quite unknown to him and he rushed back to wake his chief. Members of the biology unit quickly armed themselves with guns and cameras and went to the lakeside, but of course the elusive monster had disappeared, the only trace left being the trampled grass. Back at camp, Gladkikh made a sketch of what he had seen, probably at the same time cursing himself for not always carrying a camera. But the existence of a strange creature in the lake did not have to rest on his testimony alone. Later the leader of the scientific expedition and two members of the biology group saw a head appear in the middle of the lake with the dorsal fin also showing, and to convince them that it was not just a mat of rotting vegetation, 'The Monster was lashing the water with its long tail and sending out waves all over the lake.'[21]

Another Russian scientist who was prepared to do some physical research on the subject rather than be an armchair theorist was the geographer Anatoly Pechersky. Being interested in the legend of the 'huge snake' which the locals in the Karakystak Valley talked of but denied ever having seen, he and Volodya, his son, spent a holiday in 1975 beside Lake Kok-kol which is in the Dzambul area of Kazakhstan in Soviet Central Asia. In his letter published in *Komsomol'skaya Pravda* he said that about 25 feet away the lake was covered with ripples which turned into zigzags as the great beast surged up from the depths. Its snake-like body was 50 feet long, its massive head 3 feet across and 6 feet long. He was terrified as he scrambled up the steep bank to get his gun, calling to his son who had also seen the creature from a short distance away. When they returned to the shore the beast submerged in a swirl of water. It was only then they recollected they had both a still and a cine camera, but during the experience had given them no thought (an interesting point to which we shall return later).[22]

For those who gather reports of water monsters, one of the best known lakes is Storsjö in mid-Sweden. But before we relate a few of the incredible happenings there, let Ivar Anderson, who lives in Ulvaboda in southern Sweden, tell of his own experience at the lake Slagesnässjön in 1965.

This lake must have been a volcano way back in time. It's round and formed like a crater. Very deep and surrounded by steep hills.

It happened in the summer of 1965. A fishnet had been lost and Emil and I were rowing around the lake with a drag, trying to find it. Suddenly Emil's face turned white. He hollered out aloud: 'I have a beast on the drag!' The boat went out in the middle of the lake with good speed. A big whirl came up to the surface and the boat slowed down and stopped.

I saw nothing. Emil is used to breaking in wild horses. I asked him if the 'beast' was as strong as a horse. 'Ten times stronger,' answered Emil.

Emil is that type of a person you only meet once in a lifetime. He can endure all kinds of hardships and is very close to nature.

Ivar Anderson's father had a sighting too:

It may interest you to hear about a monster my father, Sven Anderson, used to talk about long ago.

He was born 1851 and when 12 years old, he was fishing perch in a lake called Lilla Källsjö. It was a calm and sultry day. Thunder could be heard from a far away distance.

Lilla Källsjö is a lake in the deep woods. It resembles a wilderness lake in northern Scandinavia or Canada. The water is all around surrounded by a belt of quagmire. You can't get out to open water without hightop boots or with bare legs.

As the boy watched the float a commotion occurred in the middle of the lake. A monster, looking like an enormous bull, came to the surface, about 100 yards away. It churned the water to foam and made an awful noise. The boy threw away the fishingpole and ran home as fast as his legs could carry him. Next day a grown man went with him to the lake. They saw nothing. No cattle, not even a moose could make his way through the quagmire out to open water, without getting stuck in the mud.

The lake has for centuries had a bad reputation as a 'stamping ground' for ghosts and spooks. As a little boy I used to listen to old people tell tales about this lake. A very old man, born before 1820, claimed he had in his youth seen big waves on the lake, when there was no wind at all.

Mr Anderson also told us of a water monster in Lake Myllesjön, which is about 5 miles west of Slagesnässjön. There have been many sightings over the years, and on one occasion

Two men living close to the lake decided to capture the monster. A blacksmith made a big hook which was fastened to a cable tied to a plank. Another cable was fastened to the plank and tied to a big oak. A dead hog was used as bait. The monster swallowed hog and hook. The oak was uprooted and dragged out in the middle of the lake. The monster disappeared for some time. In 1968 it showed up again. A man saw a log floating on the water. After a while the monster dived and was gone. Another big hook was made and a dead calf was used as bait, but the monster didn't show up.[23]

There are probably thousands of other experiences like these in Scandinavian lakes which are never reported. But from Lake Storsjö there are many reports; this lake is probably the Swedish equivalent of Loch Ness. It is in mid-Sweden, 6° further north than Loch Ness, at latitude 63°N. In fact scientific interest and the recording of sightings began at Storsjö long before such efforts started at Loch Ness. In 1898 there were a number of reported sightings which aroused the curiosity of the local zoologist, Dr Peter Olsson. He collected all the reports he could from trustworthy witnesses, and found some twenty-two between 1820 and 1898. They reveal the same characteristics of behaviour that are reported from Loch Ness and the other lakes worldwide: the 'upturned boat' shape which silently drifts or moves with great speed, the line of humps, the log-like shape which moves against the wind, and the strong surge of waves evidently caused by a powerful creature swimming below the surface. A detailed close sighting occurred on 10 July 1898. P. E. Asen with five other people thought he saw an upturned boat about one kilometre from the shore. He rowed out to get closer and found a creature some 15 feet long moving north against the wind. Its head and neck were visible below the water and were 5 feet long. Mr Asen was able to observe warts on the slimy, scaly body which was a cinnamon colour, and green 'things' which were thought to be either weed or a mane hanging from the vertebrae. On top of the creature's head its 'ears' were white and laid back.[24] These 'ears' are a distinctive feature and have been noted by a number of observers. In a letter to Tim Dinsdale, the curator of the Jämtlands läns Museum at Östersund wrote: 'It has great fins on the back of the head, possibly ears, described as little sails, which can be laid tight on the neck.'[25] Asen watched it for about half an hour, and then out on the lake a steamer whistled. The animal pricked up its ears and sank out of sight.

Five years earlier, in October 1893, two sisters, Marta and Karin Olsson, aged eighteen and twenty-one, watched a creature which swam about in the lake in front of them for one and a half hours while they were washing clothes. Karin was interviewed by the editor of the *Östersund Post* and from her detailed description Peter Costello prepared this summary of the creature's appearance.

The animal's head was round like a dog's. The eyes were as large as saucers, and dark in colour. They stared without blinking. The mouth was wide and open, the interior dark red like a fish's, with a tongue which flicked in and out. The eyes were set about 6 to 8 centimetres apart. The head was 3 feet wide and equally as long. The neck was about 8 or 9 feet long, with the back being 14 feet long. There were no forefeet, more likely fins. On the head two big ears which were laid back along the neck.[26]

After a time Karin threw some stones at the creature which then turned and swam towards them. This caused her to run up the bank while her sister climbed a tree. The animal churned the water, dived, and then surfaced again before swimming away and finally diving. In their community they were considered to be truthful girls and close questioning did not cause them to alter the details of their story. As Storsjö is such a northerly lake it freezes in winter, but this does not seem to trouble the Storsjöodjuret, as the Swedes term their monster. Again in 1893 A. M. Johannsson and his wife were crossing the lake by a bridge to the island of Froso when the ice below was broken up and the creature's head shot up about 2½ feet and then quickly sank back. The witnesses thought that it appeared to be as surprised to see them as they were to see it![27]

More recently, a young couple had an alarming experience while on a fishing trip. We quote from a report in the Swedish newspaper *Expressen* (30 July 1976).

'I have always laughed hilariously at all the stories about the monster, so I cannot be angry if people do not believe me now,' said Rolf Larsson, aged 35, who was out on the lake fishing with Irene Magnusson, 20. The great lake was as smooth as a mirror when Rolf and Irene went fishing. Rolf told me: 'We were about 500 metres from land and we were going home when we passed a buoy. Suddenly some waves rocked the boat. 50 or 60 metres from us between land and the boat we saw something that moved under the surface. Then it came up to the surface, not with a splash but with smooth waves. The part of the body we saw above water was not more than 20–30 cm high and about 1 metre long, but from the amount of water it displaced we could see that it was a large object beneath the surface. I would like to compare it with an upside-down boat, you only see the keel of it. We could see it quite close. We had plenty of time to look at it. We had shut off the motor because we were fishing. The thing was swimming in half circles around our boat. From the beginning I stood completely still without really understanding what was going on. After some minutes I started the motor but then Irene who had been quiet all the time shouted that I should immediately return to land. She was as pale as a corpse. When we made for the shore the animal followed us for a time. We were doing perhaps 10 knots but the creature kept up with us. We returned to land and we could see the wake of the creature for 5 or 6 minutes, as the water was so calm.' Irene admits she was really shaken: 'It's true I was pretty scared, you know. We were so far away from land. At first I just sat and stared but when Rolf started the motor it was as if I woke up again. I thought he intended to go closer to the animal so I became frantically scared. I think I'm a little bit more of a coward than Rolf.'

A few years earlier, on 2 August 1973, 73-year-old Ragnar Björks had had a hair-raising experience on Storsjö which changed him from a sceptic to a convinced witness. He said:

As I am the fisheries officer in this area I was out checking to see that all anglers had their valid permits. But instead of anglers I saw something peculiar, a big tail that was 0.5 metre high just above the surface. At first I thought it was a piece of driftwood. But when I got closer I saw a colossal fish whose tail was out of the water. My rowing boat is 3.8 metres long and I estimate that the fish was 2 metres longer than my boat. When I was by the side of this monster I took my oar and hit it straight over its back. I shouldn't have done that for in the same moment the animal slapped the water with its tail so that the boat was thrown 3 or 4 metres into the air. Strangely enough, the boat came down again on its keel but I had to balance it. I believe that God was with me then. It's true that once I could swim, but I don't know how I would have reacted if I had had to try, because later I was suffering from shock. When I finally landed I had to lie on the grass for twenty minutes before I could walk home. The creature was grey/brown on top and yellow underneath and was 5½ to 6 metres long. I think it was a *marl* [possibly the wels (*Silurus glanis*), a voracious, predatory fish that grows over 16 feet long in some countries]. Yes, it was a real experience and many people will think that this Storsjöodjuret is a mere fake, but I've seen it with my own eyes and I'm not afraid to talk about it. And what could I gain by hoaxing in this case? At first I didn't believe that there was any monster in the Storsjö. Some years ago my wife saw it. It had two humps and was slowly moving forward. I didn't believe her but now I am convinced.[28]

We only have space to briefly review some of the more impressive reports of lake monsters seen throughout the world. The bibliography gives details of books where more reports can be found. As our list in Appendix 2 shows, there are dozens of other lakes where strange creatures have been seen, and hundreds of competently investigated reports exist as well as the visual evidence of cine and still photographs and sonar traces. So why is it that academic science refuses to acknowledge the existence of the problem and is content to dismiss the evidence as worthless? We do not have a complete answer to this complex question, but we can present some observations which may help to illuminate the situation. Contrary to the current ethos of our age, men are instinctively aware that they are frail creatures in an environment about which they know little. Science is an attempt to categorize and assimilate the knowledge which they do obtain about their environment. It is the rationalists' means of holding at bay a natural fear of the unknown. Unfortunately science is now limited by the basic materialism of its adopted viewpoint and any individual who, however unwittingly, attempts to enlarge the boundaries of accepted knowledge by introducing facts which cannot be accommodated within a rational materialistic framework is immediately discredited and attacked by the accepted authorities and indeed by all 'right-thinking' men. Often the first means of attack to be employed is laughter, and so the initial reaction of the media to reports of unidentified lake monsters or for that matter unidentified flying objects is to turn them into a joke, and then to ridicule those who continue to report such anomalies. Fear of ridicule is strong in children and adults. Dr Jacques Vallee, astronomer, computer scientist and ufologist, has said that in 1961 while he was working at a major observatory in Europe as a member of a team which was tracking satellites, some of the points of light which they observed did not behave in any way that could be identified as a satellite, and they definitely should not have been there. One night the team obtained eleven data points for one of these objects and they planned to run the tape through a computer to obtain an orbit for the object and try to see it again. The respected astronomer who was in charge of the project confiscated the tape and erased it. Vallee asked him why they didn't send it to America, where all the results of worldwide observations were being co-ordinated. He was told: 'The Americans would laugh at us.' Vallee observed: 'You must realize that the fear of ridicule is just as strong or even stronger among professional scientists, than it is among the general public.'[29]

The same fear of ridicule is evident in the reaction of the bartender at Lake Champlain, mentioned earlier in this chapter, whose words 'I'll never say I saw it' epitomize the attitude of hundreds of witnesses to anomalous physical objects, be they water monsters, BHMs (big hairy monsters), or UFOs. Dr Maurice Burton, an eminent British zoologist who was until the early 1960s a proponent of the Loch Ness Monster, believed that it was 'probably a plesiosaur-type animal'.[30] But between then and 1962 he reversed his opinion and on 30 April 1962 wrote in a letter: 'I am now very resentful of those who, wittingly or unwittingly, have misled us and have caused me to spend so much time and effort needlessly, and to *make me look ridiculous.*'[31] (Our emphasis.) Dr Burton is now so sensitive about the subject that he will not allow fellow scientists to view the three minutes of 16 mm cine colour film of the Loch Ness Monster taken on 29 May 1938 by South African tourist, G. E. Taylor, which he has in his possession.[32] Peter Costello tells us that Dr Burton refused to send him stills from it, and refused to let the Loch Ness Investigation Bureau view the film.[33] Burton did publish one still from it in his book *The Elusive Monster*, which Dr Roy P. Mackal, professor of microbiology at the University of Chicago, considers to be 'positive evidence'.[34] The fact that there have been known hoaxes has done nothing to lessen the fears of the academics, and has also encouraged the media to treat the whole matter in a ribald manner.[35] Probably one of the worst cases of a newspaper getting its fingers burnt occurred in 1933 when the *Daily Mail* hired a big-game hunter and a photographer to track the animal down. They quickly found some large unidentified footprints on the shore, and jubilant headlines in the *Mail* announced the Monster to be a fact. Plaster casts of the spoor were duly sent to the British Museum of Natural History, who on 4 January 1934 issued a report which said that the tracks had been made by a dried-up hippopotamus foot. It seems that two youngsters had borrowed the family's Victorian umbrella stand, made from a hippo foot, and with a sense of fun manufactured a crude hoax that shouldn't have fooled anyone familiar with animal tracks.[36] This sort of incident naturally gives added fuel to those armchair critics who wish to dismiss all the reports as hoaxes and hallucinations, and enables the British Museum of Natural History to write in 1956, in a booklet on 'Scientific Research', that the phenomenon was 'one of waves and water currents'.[37]

When ridicule is not a sufficiently effective weapon to silence a witness, the opponents of truth can resort to threats and violence. There are a surprisingly large number of paranoiacs in our society who are ever ready to issue threats and to act violently against anyone endangering their feelings of security. This applies particularly in the case of some UFO witnesses in the United States who have been publicly jeered at, harassed, attacked, and have had their property destroyed. They have found it impossible to get employment and their children have been unable to continue at school. Families have had to sell up and disappear into other localities in order to continue to be able to live a reasonably civilized life. All this simply for having reported an enigma that they witnessed! When Arthur Grant, a 21-year-old veterinary student, was travelling from Inverness to Glen Urquhart on his motorbike about one o'clock on the morning of Friday, 5 January 1934 he saw in the moonlight a creature rapidly cross the road and plunge down the bank into Loch Ness. He reported:

It had a head rather like a snake or an eel, flat at the top, with a large oval eye, longish neck and somewhat longer tail. The body was much thicker towards the tail than was the front portion. In colour it was black or dark brown and had a skin rather like that of a whale. The head must have been about six feet from the ground as it crossed the road.[38]

The Provost of Inverness, an outspoken sceptic, confirmed that Mr Grant was perfectly sober when he left Inverness. Mr Grant, who as a student vet would not be completely unfamiliar with animals, estimated the total length of the creature to be 15 to 20 feet. Nevertheless some distant experts were later able to identify the creature as an 'otter'. Unfortunately this sighting occurred just after the 'hippo foot hoax' mentioned above. The ridicule and pressure of opinion brought to bear on Mr Grant became so insupportable that he had to miss a term at college.[39]

Professor Roy Mackal too refers to the 'disparagement amounting almost to hate mail'[40] to which some press and TV publicity gave rise, though he also notes the 'expressions of intense interest' from those with a more flexible mental attitude. Although the critics so often cry 'no scientific evidence', when it is provided they are equally able to ignore it. This was shown when Tim Dinsdale's 16 mm cine film showing a large object moving across the loch was analysed by the Joint Air Reconnaissance Intelligence Centre. This branch of the Royal Air Force analysed and interpreted films taken over enemy territory during World War II and were able to pinpoint such activities as the building of the V1 and V2 launching sites, many of which were destroyed before the full impact of these weapons could be unleashed against the population of London. Many times they had proved that they could accurately interpret the size, shape and speed of an object that was only a minute area on a movie frame.[41] When given the opportunity to apply their skills to Dinsdale's cine film their report concluded that: 'the object was most probably an animate object initially projecting 3.0 to 3.7 ft out of the water and moving at speeds up to 10 mph. The length at the waterline was at least 5.5 ft.'[42] After filming the animate object Dinsdale had wisely arranged to have a motor boat travel the same route, which he also filmed from the same viewpoint for comparison. The photo interpreters of JARIC estimated that the boat was 13.3 feet long with a speed of 6.5 mph. In fact it was 15 feet long and moving at 7 mph. This illustrates that their results had a high degree of accuracy.[43] Although JARIC's findings were stated in a properly cautious manner and refer only to 'an animate object', the opposition would still not admit that there was anything to merit scientific study in the loch, preferring instead to believe that JARIC's interpretation was wrong.[44]

Other positive results achieved by the use of scientific instrumentation have been similarly attacked. In 1968 sonar equipment was successfully used in Loch Ness. Sonar is similar to radar in principle, but instead of transmitting radio waves through the air, the equipment beams sound waves through the water. When they meet a solid object underwater they are reflected back. The equipment measures the time taken for the waves to return and can plot the size and distance of the object. A permanent record is made which can later be studied and interpreted. All rather too accurate and irrefutable for opponents of the unknown. In 1968 Professor D. Gordon Tucker, chairman of the Department of Electronic and Electrical Engineering at the University of Birmingham, with two colleagues Dr Hugh Braithwaite and Dr D. J. Creasey, in collaboration with the Loch Ness Investigation Bureau, used two types of sonar in a field test and obtained 'echoes' which conclusively established that

a number of large (6 metres [20 feet] long), animate objects are swimming in Loch Ness at up to 17 mph and diving at rates up to 5 mph. The acute angles of descent and ascent, plus the speed and size involved, rule out any of the fish with closed swim bladders which are known to inhabit the loch.[45]

His paper was published in the *New Scientist* of 19 December 1968 after having first been accepted, then later refused, by the editor of *Nature*. On 28 December 1968 *Nature* retaliated by publishing an unsigned editorial attacking Professor Tucker's professional ability with an unfounded statement that his sonar equipment was unreliable. Fortunately Professor Tucker was well known as a leader in the field of sonar research and his scientific integrity was supported by a letter from Dr Peter F. Baker of Emmanuel College, Cambridge, which *Nature* published on 11 January 1969.[46]

From 1968 to 1970 sonar equipment was used in the loch with varying success by a number of different groups. In 1972 an American, Robert H. Rines of the Academy of Applied Science, Boston (Massachusetts Institute of Technology) teamed up with the Loch Ness Investigation Bureau to set up underwater sonar that was linked to a camera with a powerful flashlight which was designed to operate only when a large moving object came into photographic range. It was set to take a picture once every 55 seconds so long as the object remained within range.[47] They obtained some remarkable pictures in the early morning of 8 August, which if anything, served to deepen the mystery and increase the curiosity of those engaged in the chase. The colour photographs showed a close-up of a diamond-shaped paddle or flipper (4 to 6 feet long) of which Henry Lyman of the New England Aquarium (Boston, Massachusetts) said: 'General shape and form of flipper does not fit anything known today', but Roy Mackal points out that it is similar in configuration to other aquatic animals including sharks and dolphins, and considers 'that these photos very likely show the pectoral limb of one of the large animals in Loch Ness.'[48] In 1975 Robert Rines and his colleagues were again at Loch Ness with similar equipment as before but deployed in a different way with the expectation of obtaining superior results. On 20 June, again in the early morning, one of their cameras recorded an indistinct shape which has been interpreted as a 20-foot-long body with two appendages and with a head on a long neck. But as it was photographed through 25 feet of peaty murk in the loch, the scientists did not obtain a detailed image. Later that morning the cameras and strobe light operated again and this time on one of the frames was recorded an object that has been interpreted as possibly being the head of a creature, although a certain amount of 'imaginative' interpretation must be used to see it as such.[49]

What makes Rines' photographs particularly interesting is that the cameras were operated only when the sonar recorded an object with a cross section of 4 to 5 feet entering the beam at a distance of less than 40 feet.[50] And with the 1972 photographs there is a sonar record that quite independently records the presence of a large moving body. True to form, the senior zoologists of the Natural History Museum in London were not moved from their past attitudes and in a statement issued on 20 November 1975 dismissed the photographs, first suggesting that a hoax could have been perpetrated on Rines and his team, and finishing with vague references to 'small gas bubbles' produced by 'the larvae of phantom midges', admitting at the same time that they had no data on this subject.[51]

The Academy of Applied Sciences, in the person of Robert Rines with his American/British team, has continued to be active at the loch and has greatly increased the scope and sophistication of its equipment. In the late 1970s the team introduced underwater slave strobe lights (developed at MIT by Harold E. Edgerton, the 'father' of electronic flash equipment) which are similar to those used by high altitude photo reconnaissance aircraft and which can fire at 3-second intervals. Batteries have been eliminated by running cables from the shore and the functioning of the equipment can be monitored from the shore. Only when the instruments show that the cameras have been triggered need they be hauled to the surface and the film removed.[52] Other recent developments include the use of video equipment, and a 1983 project to obtain tissue samples. A grid of floating sonar devices covering an area of 6,400 square feet and a depth of 100 feet was moored offshore, the idea being that when a large creature came into range, its presence would be monitored and a biopsy dart fired to obtain a small tissue sample without harming the animal. Two American scientists, Rikki Razdan and Alan Kielar, were behind the project, but had no success in 1983.[53]

It is clear to students of the Loch Ness phenomenon that the inspiration and finance for research with sophisticated and expensive equipment has all come from outside Britain and has been instigated and conducted by overseas scientists. This is in no way a reflection upon the efforts of those dedicated researchers who in the first place gathered sufficient data to arouse the interest of those scientists, and who have whenever possible assisted in the operations at the loch side. But although the scientists with their computerized equipment have had some limited success, the best sightings are still obtained by the ordinary citizen, such as Bill Wright, who was fishing in the loch early on the morning of 17 June 1978 when the big beast surfaced 30 yards in front of him. He told Frank Thomson of the *Falkirk Herald*:

I was fishing at the side of Urquhart Castle near Drumnadrochit Bay just after 3 A.M. as dawn broke when, suddenly, from out of the water only 30 yards away rose this large arch-shaped body, not unlike an upturned rowing boat. It was black in colour, and seconds later the creature's round brown head and long brown neck appeared. It was absolutely fantastic. I could hardly believe my eyes but there it was all right.

Bill said he hastily ran over the pebbly beach to find a better viewpoint, but the noise frightened Nessie who 'suddenly slid its bulk under the water and disappeared.' On reflection Bill said: 'I don't think I'll ever get that picture out of my mind. It was really something worth seeing, believe me, because what I've told you is certainly no fairy story.'[54]

Another lakeside visitor who had the picture in his mind also had the foresight to have his 35-mm SLR camera ready with a telephoto lens and loaded with fast colour film. When the monster suddenly surfaced in Urquhart Bay he was able to secure two pictures which are undoubtedly the best still photographs ever taken of the beast. The photographer was Tony 'Doc' Shiels who had been alerted to the monstrous phenomenon by reports of Morgawr, the water monster that has been frequently seen in Falmouth Bay, Cornwall, near where Doc lives. He became an avid investigator of monster reports and a hunter of the elusive beasts, and eventually saw Morgawr himself. Making the long journey from Cornwall to Loch Ness, Doc (who is a wizard and professional psychic entertainer) arrived at the lochside on 19 May 1977. His vigil was rewarded on 21 May at 8 A.M. when he was with some other watchers – his wife, Mr and Mrs Richard Smith of Carharrack, and a young couple from

Bolton. They saw three black humps gliding through the mirror-like waters of Borlum Bay. Later Doc and others saw long wakes on the far shore from below Castle Urquhart. But the best sighting, and the one which provided the photographic opportunity, occurred at 4 o'clock in the afternoon of 21 May. Doc was standing on Urquhart Castle when a sleek head broke the surface

rather less than a hundred yards away . . . the part of the neck showing above the water-line must have been around 4 or 5 feet long . . . The colour of the animal was greenish brown, with a paler underside. Skin texture, smooth and glossy. The animal was visible for no more than 4 or 5 seconds. It held itself very upright, very still, except for a turning of the head and a straightening of the neck before it sank very smoothly, below the surface. It had powerful neck muscles.[55]

During those few seconds Doc reacted quickly and fired off two frames of high-speed Ektachrome. His transparencies are impressive when projected on to a large screen and show a detail of structure and colour never before achieved in a picture of the creature. This has caused critics to doubt that these photographs show the Loch Ness Monster, the sad truth being that the sharper and more detailed a photograph of any anomalous phenomenon, the less likely people are to believe it is genuine. This is perhaps understandable, but it is nevertheless illogical. No evidence should be rejected because it looks too good; but neither should it be uncritically accepted.

The records of sea monsters are, like those of lake monsters, worldwide and cover a long time span from ancient legends to contemporary reports, many made by ships' officers of unimpeachable integrity. It is a vast subject and some excellent books (see Bibliography) have been devoted to it. We have decided in this book to limit our review to reports of lake monsters only, as being that much less explicable than are unknown creatures in the oceans. There are, however, two locations on the British coast from which a number of strange and little-known reports have come, along with some interesting photographs, and we cannot ignore them. One of these locations is Falmouth Bay where the creature known as Morgawr (meaning 'sea giant' in the ancient Cornish language) has frequently been seen and occasionally photographed in recent years. The latest spate of reports started in September 1975 when Mrs Scott of Falmouth and her friend Mr Riley were at Pendennis Point.

They saw a large, lumpy creature with stumpy horns, and a long neck which had bristles down the back. (An interesting point is that a little more than two months later, Rines' Loch Ness pictures were published, one showing what could be described as a close-up of an ugly head with stumpy horns!) It suddenly dived beneath the waves and immediately re-emerged with a conger eel in its mouth. During the early months of 1976 various visitors saw the traditional humped back and snake-like neck of the water monster, familiar to investigators through worldwide reports. Then on 5 March the *Falmouth Packet* published on its front page two photographs of Morgawr and a letter from the photographer which had been sent to their office. The writer gave no address and signed herself Mary F., so in effect the photographs were submitted anonymously and as such are not admissible evidence. But having examined first-generation copy prints which provide greater tonal detail than do the newspaper reproductions, we feel that these photographs could well be genuine. They are virtually silhouettes and as Mary F. writes: 'The pictures are not very clear because of the sun shining right into the camera and a haze on the water. Also I took them very quickly indeed.' Mary F.'s comments in her letter (see photo caption) are also convincing, for these are consistent with other little-known worldwide reports, and so suggest that hers was a first-hand observation.

On Friday, 9 July 1976 the *Western Morning News* published the account of two fishermen, John Cock and George Vinnicombe, who had been fishing 25 miles south of Lizard Point. The report reads:

There was visibility for several miles and a flat sea when they had their first sighting. 'It looked like an enormous tyre about 4 feet up in the water with a back like corrugated iron. We came up towards it and must have woken it up because a great head like an enormous seal came out of the water. It just turned its long neck and looked at us and very slowly submerged. The body was black and the head was grey and we saw a total length of about 22 feet.' Mr Vinnicombe thought it weighed several tons and that if they had not reversed engines they would have been right on top of it. 'It had a big rounded back and there were humps on the top like prehistoric monsters have. We always thought the Loch Ness Monster was a tourist attraction. Now I have my doubts; what we both saw was there.'

George Vinnicombe added: 'Some people think we were nuts but I've been fishing for 40 years and have seen nothing like it. I am convinced there is something out there.'

It was about this time that Doc Shiels had his own first sighting of

Morgawr. With his wife Christine and four of their children, he was sunning himself on Grebe Beach on Sunday morning, 4 July. Three times he thought he saw 'something' out in the estuary and each time he brought his binoculars to his eyes the object disappeared. He then told the others, who started to scan the water. The youngsters were the first to see it, with cries of 'There it is . . . the monster.' Christine Shiels, whose letter was published in the *Falmouth Packet*, Friday, 9 July 1976, wrote: 'my husband is unwilling to write to you himself, saying you wouldn't believe him and that he's not sure if he believes it.' She found that:

It was at the edge of my vision, and when I tried to focus on the image it simply and suddenly wasn't there. After two or three frustrating attempts to get a clear picture of the thing by staring straight at it, failing each time, I decided to allow it to be coy, to stay in the 'corner of my eye' so to speak. This worked. For several seconds, I saw a large, dark, long-necked, hump-backed beast moving slowly through the water, then sinking beneath the surface.

Having finally encountered Morgawr, Doc was no less shaken than the numerous other witnesses and at first suggested that perhaps they had all been hallucinating, due to the unusual heat and strong sunlight of that long, hot, dry summer of 1976.

Throughout that summer a variety of holiday-makers and local residents saw the creature from the shore and at sea, and their reports were published in two local papers, the *Falmouth Packet* and the *West Briton*. The national press did not report the events other than to print a few slighting references which suggested that the monster reports were part of a silly season tourist campaign. On Sunday, 12 September 1976 Allan and Sally White, a brother and sister on holiday from Gloucestershire, took an early morning walk on Grebe Beach and caught a momentary glimpse of something long (15–20 feet) and brown sliding off the beach into the water. It took them by surprise and was gone so quickly that they were unable to see any details. Eighteen-year-old Allan said: 'I've certainly never seen anything like it before.'[56] It was on 17 November 1976 that Doc Shiels had his second sight of Morgawr and obtained his photographs. He was walking near Parson's Beach, Mawnan, with David Clarke, editor of *Cornish Life*, who was taking pictures of Doc for a magazine feature. Doc noticed an object halfway across the estuary, 'a small dark head poking out of the water', as David Clarke wrote later.[57] As it moved closer to within 70 or 80 feet, they could see that the greenish black head was supported on a long arched neck, more slender than that of a seal. In the wave-troughs at least 4 or 5 feet of the neck were visible . . . at one point a gently rounded shiny black body broke the surface . . . The head was rounded with a 'blunt' nose and on the top of the head were two small rounded 'buds'.

Doc's description was as follows: 'The animal we saw was small by monster standards . . . no more than fifteen feet in length. The head . . . had *horns*, stumpy little things, which Dave saw clearly. through his viewfinder . . . the head was extremely ugly, like a big snail's head with those odd little stalks.'[58] The two men excitedly jumped up on to a rock to get a better view. David had fitted a telephoto lens to his 35-mm camera and could see a magnified image through his viewfinder as he made several exposures on black and white film. Doc was using his trusty old Rolleiflex and Kodacolor film. Later when the films were developed David Clarke was frustrated to find that his camera had failed to wind on the film correctly after each exposure and all his pictures were partially double- or in some instances triple-exposed. The detailed image which he had expected to see on the negatives was blurred with double-exposed waves. Doc was luckier, his commercially processed colour film showed what he had seen in the viewfinder, but due to his camera's slightly wide-angle lens the important images were very small and could not show any fine detail when enlarged. As always with photographs of the elusive monster, the results were inconclusive, though tantalizing.[59]

All these occurrences did not seem to interest the national press, and neither did the strange sequence of events which had happened in another scenic holiday area a year earlier. These were centred around Barmouth, once a busy fishing port and now a holiday centre on the west Wales coast overlooking Cardigan Bay. It was here that on 2 March 1975 six local girls, all twelve years old, were walking on the beach at dusk when 200 yards away a creature rose up and made towards the sea. Carys Jones and Julie Anderson described what they saw as: 'about 10 feet long, with a long tail, a long neck and huge green eyes.' Its 'feet were like huge saucers with long pointed protruding nails . . . Its skin was black, patchy and baggy – it was not like anything we have seen before.'[60] As they ran away the girls could still see the eyes above the surface of the sea. Mr R. A. Anderson, a coastguard and the father of Julie Anderson, said that his daughter was extremely disturbed by what she had seen, and the coastguard to whom they had reported the sighting also said that they were extremely upset. The girls were all pupils at Ysgol Ardudwy, Harlech, and art teacher Colin Palmer made a drawing based on their descriptions, which tallied. When this was later published, other witnesses revealed that they also had seen this creature, usually in the sea. In 1971 Mrs R. Griffith of Colwyn Bay had been walking on the beach at Llanaber, just north of Barmouth, when she and her companion saw 12–18-inch diameter footprints at the water's edge. They felt a little apprehensive but decided there was no animal on land or sea in that area that could make prints that size and so thought that someone had been playing around, even though the prints did look very convincing.[61] In December 1975 Mr Holmes of Dolgellau wrote to Colin Palmer to say he had recently seen footprints deep in the soft sand at the Penmaenpool toll bridge. He wrote: 'the footprints were a little larger than a good-sized dinner plate and you got the impression that they were webbed.' Even though the tide had been in and out several times the impressions still remained.[62]

Further north, the crew of a fishing boat was off Bardsey Sound in calm water when a few yards away a large creature surfaced. The men had a good view of the huge body and long neck and head. It submerged with amazing speed and within the next hour resurfaced three times more. When Colin Palmer showed them his drawing he says 'there was instant recognition'. 'These fishermen are very experienced in these waters, and being professionals, not given to exaggeration.'[63] During the summer of 1975 Marjorie and Vernon Bennett were sailing their 30-foot sloop *Mala* in Cardigan Bay and were near Harlech about 5 miles from Mochras Point. It was a sunny day with a very calm sea when half a mile ahead they saw something in the water which looked like a seal playing in two motor tyres. Mrs Bennett said:

As we drew closer we thought it was a huge turtle, but it turned out to be unlike anything we'd ever seen. It had a free-moving neck, fairly short, rather like a turtle's, and an egg-shaped head about the size of a seal's. Its back had two spines, which were sharply ridged, and it was about 8 feet across and 11 feet long, although the ripples on the water when it dived indicated that it was probably about twice that length.[64]

Vernon Bennett dashed below to find a camera, as they had both still and cine cameras on board, while his wife circled the boat around the creature, apprehensive that it might upset their craft. As Mr Bennett climbed on to the cabin roof and focused his camera, the creature sank below the surface. Later Marjorie Bennett said: 'I didn't sleep properly for two nights after we'd seen the thing.'[65] The Bennetts had not heard of any earlier reports of a water monster, though they had been spending their sailing holidays in that area for the past twelve years.

Such reports were not really new to that area, nor in fact to other parts of the Welsh coast. In 1883 *Nature* published a letter from Mr F. T. Mott of Leicester in which he told how a group of worthy citizens including W. Barfoot, a JP from Leicester, and F. J. Marlow, a solicitor from Manchester, stood on Llandudno pier on Sunday, 3 September 1882 and for two minutes watched a large black snake-like creature travel across the mouth of the bay towards the Great Orme. They estimated its speed as 30 mph and its length as 200 feet. Although water monsters are reported to have incredible turns of speed, the length of 200 feet seems quite excessive even for these large aquatic creatures. They estimated it to be a mile distant, but if in fact it were closer than that, it would also be smaller than their estimate and travelling at a slower rate. Various correspondents wrote in to explain the sighting as a flock of birds or a shoal of porpoises, but Mr Barfoot came to Mr Mott's support and wrote that although he had seen everything from flocks of sea birds to whales at sea, what they had seen that day could not be accounted for by any such creatures.[66]

Llandudno is on the north coast of Wales, and a few miles further west is Red Wharf Bay on the north-east coast of the island of Anglesey. It was here that employees of the Minydon Hotel on several occasions saw a large creature swimming up the main channel of the bay. This was during February 1975 but Phillip Wendel, the hotel barman, said that it was first seen before they had heard of the Barmouth girls' experience, which also occurred during February that year. On one occasion five people saw a black symmetrical form about 12 feet long and showing 1 foot above the water with a square-cut, prominent tail following, 30 feet away in the channel. 'Explanations' included a basking shark, a dolphin and a mini submarine on a secret exercise. But Mr Wendel said: 'It was too weird and rather frightening' to be any of these.[67]

When the huge number of eyewitness reports is considered we wonder yet again at the refusal of scientists to acknowledge that there is anything unknown which requires to be investigated. Perhaps this refusal is due to a number of factors. A principle method of science is the examination of physical evidence, preferably a living creature, otherwise such remains as corpses, fossils, skeletons, samples of skin or hair, footprints, or excreta. Lake monsters leave none of these (or at least, none has ever been reliably found) and zoologists find it impossible to believe that herds of huge creatures could be breeding in lakes worldwide without leaving some traces for examination. It is true that there have been a number of unidentifiable carcases washed up on beaches in various parts of the world. But the zoologists who might have welcomed an opportunity to examine a possibly unknown denizen from the depths have usually preferred to explain what the remains were without actually have seen them.

Another reason for doubting the existence of water monsters is the impossibly small or shallow lakes from which they have sometimes been reported. We have already written of the loughs in western Ireland, which are often less than 100 feet each way and in which large creatures have been observed. Also we mentioned Lake Elsinore in California which periodically dries out and yet still maintains at least one large unknown creature within its depths. One explanation could be that these creatures are amphibious. Arthur Grant, veterinary student, saw a strange creature cross the road and plunge into Loch Ness (as described earlier in this chapter) at night, and Roy Mackal lists 17 reported land sightings at Loch Ness, from 1879 to 1963.[68] During the night of 30 September 1965 on the A85 road between Perth and Dundee in Scotland, two drivers independently saw a 20-foot long creature 'humped like a great caterpillar' moving slowly on the road verge, not far from the River Tay.[69] And we have already mentioned the Russian scientist who observed an unknown creature on the shore of Lake Khaiyr apparently browsing on the grass. It is known that eels can travel up to 20 miles across land,[70] and it is conceivable that water monsters could also leave their lakes and travel overland to another body of water, though if this were the case it is puzzling why they have not been seen and reported doing this more often. In fact the elusiveness of the water monster is one of its most noted characteristics amongst monster hunters and this is only one of the many similarities that all the alien animals which we describe here have in common with the ubiquitous unidentified flying objects, a point we intend to examine later.

The annals of monster hunting also contain numerous examples of missed photographic opportunities. Both UFOs and water monsters, and other alien animals, are peculiarly evasive when it comes to being photographed, and on the few occasions when they have been, the image which the camera has caught is blurred and indistinct, providing very little evidence and serving simply to compound the enigma and increase the argument. Organized attempts to photograph the Loch Ness Monster have had a phenomenally low success rate. In 1965 the Loch Ness Investigation Bureau set up a camera platform near its headquarters at Achnahannet and installed a 35-mm cine camera fitted with a 36-inch telephoto lens and synchronized with two cameras with 20-inch lenses which would take stereoscopic still frames. One reason for choosing this site was that the previous year there had been two excellent sightings from there with multiple witnesses, but after the installation of the camera no further sightings were made. During 1965 a camera located on a platform near the Clansman Hotel had to be removed for servicing. On the following morning the hotel staff watched a hump moving about in water close inshore below the unmanned position. On another occasion F. W. Holiday, a veteran monster hunter, played a hunch and kept a close watch from Strone Point on Urquhart Bay by the castle. Just before 6 P.M. the Loch Ness Investigation Bureau observer-photographer he was with decided to call it a day and packed up his gear. Just after he had left a monster was seen by Holiday near the castle.[71] On another occasion in 1968 he had spent several days watching at the lochside and had been joined by a Yorkshire schoolmaster and his family. On the morning of Monday, 26 August he started watching from first light and continued through breakfast. About 9.30 he strolled 50 yards across the grass to have a chat with his camping friends, leaving behind his binoculars and camera fitted with a 14-inch telephoto lens. As he talked he noticed a large black object ploughing through the water near the opposite shore, and although it was a mile away it still looked huge. Shouting 'Watch it while I get the camera' he made a dash back to his equipment, and as he reached it his friends saw the creature submerge.[72] On Loch Urabhal two local teachers Ian McArthur and Roderick Maciver were fishing when 45 yards away they saw a hump appear and 6 feet away from that a head. It appeared and submerged three times and by then McArthur had his camera ready for a picture, but the creature did not reappear.[73]

This apparent awareness of monsters of the presence of cameras or other recording equipment is not confined to Scottish lochs. As far away as Malaya, the aboriginal Semelai have legends of the great serpent which closely resembles the Loch Ness Monster even to having small soft horns on its head. This is said to live in the remote Tasek Bera, part of a great lake. Stewart Wavell, jungle explorer, anthropologist, radio producer and author, made a trip to the area in 1957 with a recorder and waited to hear the strange, unearthly cry of the creature, of which the natives had spoken. Suddenly there was 'A single staccato cry from the middle of the lake . . . more like a bellow – shrill and strident like a ship's horn, and elephant's trumpet, and sea-lion's bark all rolled into one. I was momentarily petrified then frantically switched on the recorder and waited for the next cry – but it never came . . .'[74]

Tim Dinsdale (whose 16-mm film we wrote of earlier) is another veteran of Loch Ness who has experienced the strange inertia which causes watchers to just miss capturing the phenomenon on film. During a period of calm weather, when sightings are more likely to happen, he was watching from the western end of the loch and although he had intended to take his boat out on to the water on the morning of 14 October 1972 in order to have the sun behind him, he delayed and eventually stayed on land. The next day on his way home he made contact with the Loch Ness Investigation Bureau at Achnahannet and learnt that 'my failure to use the boat the day before had cost the opportunity to film an adult head and neck, at close range, and with the sun behind me.'[75] Perhaps a similar spell was upon Wilfred H. Gibson, a photographer from Victoria who with a group of others saw a strange animal sporting among the log booms in Mill Bay on Okanagan Lake, British Columbia. He ran with the others to get a closer look and completely forgot the camera left in his car.[76] Similarly in 1975 when Russian geographer Anatoly Pechersky and his son saw a huge, 15-metre-long body in Lake Kok-kol (referred to earlier). After the sighting they remembered they had both still and cine cameras back at camp.

Once again the phenomenon had a joke at the expense of a witness, this time Alan Butterworth who in 1970 was a student of zoology and a member of the Loch Morar Survey for that year. On 4 August he was on camera watch and was viewing the opposite shore-line with his 10 × 50 binoculars. As he made his sweep he saw the rocky islet which was almost opposite his position, but as he continued he saw the islet again. Swinging back to the first object he studied it and saw that it was in fact a regular-shaped hump 15 feet long and 3–4 feet high. He ran to the camera but by the time he had reached it the object had submerged.[77]

All too often cameras malfunction just at the time when they should be securing valuable evidence. When Hugh Gray took his now famous photograph of the Loch Ness Monster on 12 November 1933 he did in fact take five shots but four were blank.[78] Another famous photograph was that taken by R. K. Wilson, FRCS, on 1 April 1934 which has become known as 'The Surgeon's Picture'. He took four shots on his quarterplate camera fitted with a telephoto lens and had them developed immediately at Inverness by a local chemist. This time two of the plates were blank.[79] During 1970 the team from the Academy of Applied Science led by Robert Rines was using sonar equipment in the loch. In October a four-minute sonar contact was made with a large animate creature, but the camera which should have recorded the image on the sonar screen jammed during this time so there was no record available for later study. Similarly, an automatic underwater camera, set to take pictures when the sonar equipment detected a large moving body, was unsuccessful when an opportunity arose in the winter of 1976–7. It was found that a crack had developed in the casing of the electronic flash unit which caused it to fail.[80] We wrote earlier of the frustrating experience of David Clarke, editor of *Cornish Life*, who, having thought he had secured pictures of Morgawr in Falmouth Bay, found that his 35-mm precision reflex camera had at that moment failed to wind on the film properly and had presented him with a series of double and triple exposures.

Why should there be so many camera failures when witnesses attempt to photograph water monsters? Perhaps the proportion of failures is no higher than in ordinary circumstances, say when families take snapshots of homely events. But it does seem that for the number of people who actually try to photograph water monsters, a high proportion fail for some reason to do with the working of their cameras. A possible explanation suggests itself. *If* water monsters are some kind of psychic phenomenon rather than being solid, physical creatures, and *if* they are more readily seen by psychic individuals who somehow can tune in to the same wavelength on which a monster is appearing, then perhaps that person at the same time initiates some kind of involuntary telekinetic effect* on the equipment he is operating, simply because at that moment of 'linking in' with the monster his psychic sensitivity is heightened and likely to operate in any number of different ways, unknown to and uncontrollable by the witness. Or it may be that the energy from which the monster is formed also 'reaches out' and affects physical objects at a distance, in this instance cameras. All this presupposes that the monster is a non-physical entity, an idea that will be considered more fully in Chapter 6.

Another strange effect that some witnesses experience is a refusal to admit to themselves during the period of the sighting that what they are observing is in any way unusual, and in fact their minds will very often provide a conventional explanation which on later reflection they readily acknowledge to be ridiculous. Researcher F. W. Holiday noticed this in himself when in 1965 he had chased down the shore of Loch Ness a large yellowish object that was swimming in mid-channel, watched by witnesses on the opposite shore. He wrote in the Loch Ness Investigation Bureau report: 'It could have been a boat.' Later he explained in one of his books:[81] 'Yet manifestly it was not a boat as I could see through my 10× binoculars; nor did I believe it to be a boat.' In July 1968 Dr Kenneth McLeod of Cortland, New York, saw a grey-black object about 15–20 feet long and 3–5 feet high speeding down Loch Ness in the same direction as his car. His father was on the other side of him and did not see it. At no time did he mention to his father what he had seen, neither at the time nor later when they were having tea in Fort Augustus, though that evening he did note the sighting in his dairy.[82] This inertia was also experienced by Mr and Mrs R. Jenkyns whose house stands on the shore of Loch Ness. On 30 September 1974 they viewed the monster for half an hour through binoculars. It appeared 50 or 60 feet long with a trailing tail or neck. Although a loaded camera was nearby, neither of them thought of using it, nor did they think to telephone any neighbours. Even stranger is the fact that during the sighting Mr Jenkyns sat on a sofa and went to sleep for a few minutes.[83]

The 'fading away' or disappearance of substantial evidence is another strange characteristic of both the UFO and monster fields of

---

* Telekinesis = the ability to move objects and affect events by 'mind power', not always intentionally.

research. Of the two colour pictures which Doc Shiels took on 21 May 1977 the second was mailed to a fellow researcher in the United States, Max Maven, later that year: he received the envelope but not the picture! It seems to have disappeared somehow from a sealed envelope en route.[84] Between the years 1933 and 1936 an unidentified creature swimming in Loch Ness was filmed on three occasions by researchers with cine cameras. These films, which could, under analysis with modern techniques, be of great interest, are now all missing, 'presumed lost'.[85] Perhaps the most enigmatic and tantalizing of the missing films are those which F. W. Holiday learnt of during his investigations at Loch Ness. These were taken by Dr McRae, a retired London physician, in the mid-1930s. Dr McRae had since died and the films were held by a group of trustees. This arrangement had been made because of the derision which had been heaped upon any individual who made a serious report of the creature, and because of the doctor's distaste for the commercial exploitation which would inevitably follow if his films were made public. F. W. Holiday spoke at length with one of the trustees who gave him a detailed description of the content of the two lengths of film, one taken at Loch Ness showing the creature at a range of 100 yards and the second of a similar creature in Loch Duich on the Scottish west coast where Dr McRae had his home. Judging from the conversation reported by Holiday in his book *The Great Orm of Loch Ness* the films must show greater detail than any others yet made, and are quite definitely of the same type of creature that many other eyewitnesses have reported seeing in the loch and elsewhere in the area. Another film which is said to be 'legally locked away "until such time as the public takes such matters seriously"' was made by James Currie, a London banker, in 1938 and shows the head, neck and humps.[86] However, these films are still guarded and have never been seen by any of the researchers who have devoted so much time and energy to the mystery of Loch Ness, and so in effect they are lost to research.[87]

The wisdom of Dr McRae and Mr Currie's decisions to avoid public disbelief and ridicule is perhaps emphasized by the experience of Arthur Folden, who in August 1968 used his 8-mm movie camera to film a monster in Okanagan Lake, British Columbia. Using a telephoto lens he recorded a creature between 50 and 70 feet long which changed direction, moved fast enough to create a bow wave and dived and surfaced three times. Mr Folden was in no

hurry to publicize his movie and for eighteen
to family and friends. His brother-in-law pe
local mayor of Kelowna and other dignitarie
long before the press published the story and
ridicule was showered on Mr Folden, who th
the film' and all contact with him has been los

In some cases, might cameras be forgotten
the witness realizing it; and might photographs and negatives be
mislaid or destroyed in the same way? To see a water monster is to
have one's belief structure disorientated, which most people find an
unpleasant experience. To minimize the disruption, the unacceptable intruder must be banished, and one way to do this is to make
sure that no evidence of his visit remains. We think this motivation
is rarely conscious, but it may sometimes account for lost data or lost
opportunities.

On some occasions failure to capture a monster on film can
certainly be attributed to sheer bad luck – or can it? Marcelin
Agnagna was the leader of an expedition in the summer of 1983
whose aim was to track down Mokele-Mbembe, the sauropod
dinosaur believed to be still living in the Likoula swamps of the
Congo. At Lake Telle he and his companions actually saw the
creature for twenty minutes or more, but although Agnagna had a
cine camera, no film of the creature was obtained. He knew that he
had only a short length of film left in the camera, and he began to
wade closer to the creature, filming as he walked. Then he realized
that in the excitement the camera setting had been left on 'macro'.
He changed the setting and continued filming, unsure whether there
was any unexposed film left. His fears were confirmed: when
processed, the end of the film was black and did not show Mokele-
Mbembe. The result was that Agnagna had no proof to support his
momentous claim, a claim potentially of great scientific importance.
It does sometimes seem as if there is a jinx on would-be photographers of monsters and other anomalies.[89]

Those who see water monsters often regard them as something
repugnant and intrinsically evil. The earliest reports, which reach us
as legends, stress that these creatures were even then considered
unnatural. In an old epic poem relating the deeds of an Irish dragon
slayer named Finn, a number of lake monsters which the hero
successfully slew are named and are referred to as phantoms.[90] A
translation of a Welsh legend first published in English in 1921

the wyvern of Cynwch Lake (a wyvern is said to be a two-
... agon) would come on land and 'At times one could see it
... ng with hateful, stealthy movements, here and there upon the
... le slopes of Moel Offrum, jerking its cumbersome form into
uncanny humps as it made its way in quest of food, and leaving a
slimy trail behind it.'[91] The mental image this description produces is
very much like the descriptions of the witnesses who saw the unnamed
creature at the roadside on the A85, written of earlier in this chapter.
In Canada the monster of Okanagan Lake, British Columbia, known
since 1926 as Ogopogo, was known to the Indians as Na-ha-ha-itkh,
which translates as the 'lake demon'. This beast was treated with the
greatest respect by the Indians;[92] and the same attitude exists across
the world in Russia.

Among the local inhabitants – hunters and fishermen – the lakes of the
Sordongnokh Plateau, and particularly the biggest of them all, Lake
Labynkyr (about 9 miles long and 200 feet deep) have an evil repute. They are
convinced that some Monster lives there, which they call a 'Devil'. Many a
time this 'Devil' has carried off their dogs when these have jumped into the
lake to retrieve ducks that have been shot. Once the 'Devil' chased a
fisherman's raft and the man was able to see that the animal had an enormous
mouth and was of a dark-grey colour. In short many local inhabitants have
themselves seen it . . . [93]

The same has always been true of the Scottish lochs where the
locals have deemed it wiser to hold their tongues when strangers came
asking questions about water monsters. The third Earl of Malmesbury was favoured one day by a rare confidence from his stalker John
Stuart of Achnacarry, of whose account of his sighting the Earl wrote
in his Memoirs in 1857. He also noted that the locals considered the
creature had a diabolical element in its nature, for when he observed
that he wished he could get a shot at it, John Stuart remarked
'Perhaps your Lordship's gun would misfire.'[94] Rather, we imagine,
as so many cameras have misfired in more recent times.

The Australian name for lake monsters, 'bunyip', is derived from
the aboriginal and means a 'devil' or 'spirit'. William Buckley, an
escaped convict who lived with the aboriginals for thirty-two years,
told his biographer John Morgan in the first half of the nineteenth
century:

We lived very sumptuously and in peace for many months at this place
(Kironomoat) and then went to the borders of another lake called Moode-

warri (Lake Modewarre); the water of which was perfectly fresh, abounding in large eels, which we caught in great abundance. In this lake, as well as in most of the others inland, and in the deep water rivers, is a very extraordinary amphibious animal, which the natives call Bunyip, of which I could never see any part except the back, which appeared to be covered with feathers of a dusky grey colour. It seemed to be about the size of a full-grown calf, and sometimes larger; the creatures only appear when the weather is very calm and the water smooth. I could never learn from any of the natives that they had seen either the head or tail, so that I could not form a correct idea of their size; or what they were like . . .

Here [on the Barwon River (Victoria)] the Bunyip – the extraordinary animals I have already mentioned – were [*sic*] often seen by the natives, who had a great dread of them, believing them to have some supernatural power over human beings, so as to occasion death, sickness, disease, and such like misfortunes. They have also a superstitious notion that the great abundance of eels in some of the lagoons where animals resort, are ordered for the Bunyip's provision; and they therefore seldom remain long in such neighbourhoods after having seen the creature.

. . . When alone, I several times attempted to spear a Bunyip; but, had the natives seen me do so, it would have caused great displeasure. And again, if I had succeeded in killing or even wounding one, my own life would probably have paid forfeit – they considering the animal, as I have already said, something supernatural.[95]

This reaction of dread is also experienced by many witnesses of water monsters today and has been noted by both Tim Dinsdale and F. W. Holiday when interviewing them. Holiday wrote to Dinsdale: 'When people are confronted by this fantastic animal at close quarters they seem to be stunned. There is something strange about Nessie that has nothing to do with size or appearance.'[96] And he later wrote that his personal feeling was 'a mixture of wonder, fear and repulsion'.[97] One witness, who with her twelve-year-old son had a very close sighting from the shore, later admitted she had been 'paralysed with fear'. 'It was horrible. I never want to see it again,' she told F. W. Holiday. Her son, who until then had enjoyed fishing, gave it up entirely.[98] Mr George Spicer, who with his wife in 1933 saw a monster cross the road in front of his car and make for Loch Ness, told a reporter: 'It was horrible – an abomination.' We wrote earlier of Dick Jenkyns who from his lochside home had a protracted view of a creature very similar in shape to George Spicer's. He commented: 'I felt that the beast was obscene. This feeling of obscenity still persists and the whole thing put me in mind of a gigantic stomach with a long writhing gut attached.'[99] Georgina

Carberry, a librarian at Clifden in western Ireland, had a similar reaction to the creature she and some companions saw swimming up Lough Fadda in 1954. She said that the whole body had movement in it, and when asked by F. W. Holiday what she meant by 'movement' she explained: 'wormy. You know – creepy. The body seemed to have movement all over it all the time.' Miss Carberry, an expert angler who was very familiar with the bays and loughs of her area, was much affected by her sighting. As the group left the lakeside she watched apprehensively in case the creature was following them. Later she experienced recurring nightmares for many weeks. She did not return to that isolated lake for six or seven years, and then never alone.[100] We have told the story of Mary F. who photographed Morgawr in Falmouth Bay. In the letter she sent with the photographs to the *Falmouth Packet* she wrote: 'As a matter of fact the animal frightened me. I would not like to see it any closer. I do not like the way it moved when swimming.'

Judging from all the foregoing descriptions, and from the vast number of reports of water monsters which are on record but which we have not been able to include here, it seems that there must be more than one type of unknown water creature, though many reports have similarities which also suggest that in these cases people are seeing the same animal. One of the most popular identifications, especially for the creature or creatures in Loch Ness, is the plesiosaur, a reptile that lived on earth 65 million years ago. Other suggestions have included giant eels, an unknown type of long-necked seal, an unknown type of amphibian, a huge aquatic worm,[101] and a giant form of the fossilized *Tullimonstrum* (a segmented invertebrate only a few inches long) found near Chicago in 1958.[102] Other identifications such as sturgeon, whales, seals and otters have also been suggested. The only problem is that none of them satisfactorily fits all the evidence produced by the eyewitnesses and the scientists. Sometimes water monsters exhibit strange characteristics in common with the other alien animals we still have to describe. The truth might, indeed, be even stranger than the discovery of a plesiosaur, fantastic as that would be.

2

Cats that can't be caught

The puma is not indigenous to the British Isles; neither is the lion . . .
Yet both of these animals have been seen roaming the streets, fields
and gardens of Britain and extensive searches have been organized to
find and trap them. These mysterious visitors are never caught, and
rarely leave the normal traces of excreta or the remains of kills that a
hunting 'big cat' would be expected to leave. But sometimes they do
leave footprints, and some of these are excessively large. The obvious
answer is that these creatures have escaped from zoos. Why the
people who collect and study such reports find the obvious answer
unacceptable should become clear during this chapter. When the
police receive a flurry of reports they naturally check with local zoos to
see if there are any animals missing, but there never are. But, say the
defenders of rationality, these animals must therefore have escaped
from private zoos and were smuggled into the country, bypassing the
quarantine regulations; or perhaps the owners do not wish it to be
known that they are so careless with their animals and perhaps be
held responsible for their depredations; or perhaps they have been
turned out of the house by owners who find their growing pets are
getting too hungry and energetic.

Let us consider some of the reports from the massive collection
that has accumulated over the years. The term 'the Surrey puma' is
an all-embracing phrase that covers a series of sightings of big cat-
like creatures dating from August 1962 until the present. Like other
handy terms coined by the press, it is not entirely accurate in so far
as the creatures seen are not invariably or necessarily pumas, nor do
the reports come only from Surrey. Bob Rickard, an indefatigable
Fortean researcher, author, and editor of *Fortean Times*, has recorded
well over a hundred puma reports from south-east England and says
that many others have slipped through the newsclipping net provided by his readers,[1] quite apart from the incidents that are never
reported due to the not unreasonable expectation of ridicule that
many of the witnesses have. One of the largest collections of puma
sighting reports has been compiled by the Godalming police force in
their Day Book. For the two years between September 1962 and

August 1964 they have 362 sightings listed of animals which are alien to the countryside of Britain, and which have been provisionally identified as pumas.[2] A situation similar to that found with the Loch Ness Monster exists here: there are historical reports of alien animals from various countries, but it is only in recent years that the phenomenon has been publicly acknowledged and detailed records are now being kept by researchers.

The current documentation began in 1962 when from August until the end of the year a light, sandy-coloured animal with a flat face and large paws was seen on a number of occasions by water board officials in the vicinity of Heathy Park Reservoir in Hampshire. As it was not a newspaper that carried these reports but the house journal of the Mid-Wessex Water Company, the reports did not receive widespread attention. Ernie Jellet, who first saw it, said it looked 'like a young lion cub', 'definitely not a fox or a dog', and it stood 18 inches to 2 feet high. Later that year, it was seen again by Mr L. Noble, station superintendent for the southern area.[3] Nothing more was reported until 18 July 1963 when David Back, a long-distance lorry driver, stopped at 1 A.M. on Shooters Hill in south-east London to help what looked like an injured dog at the roadside. He said: 'I walked over to it – and then it got up. I knew then it wasn't a dog. It had long legs and a long, pointed tail that curled up. It looked as if it had a mouthful of food. It ran off into the woods.' Very soon afterwards a police patrol car went to the area, which consists of woods and open common land and is used for public recreation. The 'cheetah', as this alien animal was later called, obligingly jumped over the bonnet of the police car and the hunt was on. Later that morning other reports were made in the vicinity by motorists and pedestrians. A police check showed that no zoo or circus had reported any escapes. Extra police were drafted in from nearby divisions, and also police dogs and their handlers. Chief Superintendent of Police John Harper deployed his searchers by stringing them out across the woods, and walkie-talkie sets kept him in contact with his far-flung forces. Systematic beating was carried out until late afternoon. Nothing was heard or seen of a cheetah, but a set of large footprints was found in a muddy stream bed. They were much larger than the tracks of the police dogs and the marks of claws were clearly visible.[4] It should be noted that the cat family, with the exception of the cheetah, all walk on their pads with their claws retracted, unlike dogs which do leave claw marks.

During the following week the police received various reports from people who had seen a strange animal prowling through the woods which are surrounded by the heavily populated area of south-east London. Before dawn on Tuesday, 23 July 1963 Jim Green, head groundsman of a sports club, was woken by a 'loud snarling noise'. 'It sounded like a fighting cat, only much louder,' he said. He called the police who rushed five police cars to the sports ground at Kidbrooke, 2 miles further west than the original reports. At the nearby Royal Air Force base a security sergeant and constable heard snarls and saw a big dark animal silhouetted against a cricket screen. The police made a systematic search of the area but again the 'cheetah' had disappeared. The following weekend the fine summer weather and the news reports brought hundreds of sightseers to the woods at Shooters Hill, but there was no further sight or sound of the 'cheetah'.[5]

The next beast to hit the headlines appeared over a hundred miles north of Shooters Hill in East Anglia on 19 February 1964. At East Runton near Cromer, Norfolk, various people had seen a large animal on the railway embankment. There was a search with thirty police dogs and appeals on television for further information. The animal, which different witnesses described variously as a tiger, a lion, a puma, and a cheetah, again mysteriously vanished. As the four animals listed do not look alike, there must either have been a menagerie charging around East Runton on the night of the 19th, or the witnesses were shaky on their identifications. One thing that all the descriptions had in common was that all the animals described belonged to the big cat family.[6] Interestingly, this report also produced a prime example of the rationalizer, debunker or explainer-away. It is rarely possible for a mystery to remain unexplained without someone attempting to rationalize it by presenting an explanation, and these are sometimes as incredible as the original report. Thus witnesses of UFOs who observe large craft of solid appearance with flashing multi-coloured lights and brilliantly glowing windows, hovering for minutes overhead, are assured by Air Force officials that they have been looking at Venus. And at East Runton, the witnesses were assured that they had seen a fox.

At this time there had been few reports from Surrey and the term 'Surrey puma' had not been heard. But in August 1964 there were a great number of reports from the Farnham and Odiham areas on the Surrey/Hampshire border, and enquiries revealed that there had been many sightings of mystery animals for the previous two years which had received no publicity. The apparent centre of this activity was Bushylease Farm, covering some 300 acres between Ewshot and Crondall. The farm manager, Edward Blanks, said that the puma had made periodic appearances during the past two years, but during the severe winter of 1962–3, when there had been some heavy snowfalls, there had been a complete absence of the tracks by which he had hoped to trail it. During its visits certain characteristics of behaviour had been noted and these he outlined to Charles Bowen, the editor of *Flying Saucer Review* magazine who in the following October had gone to interview him. When the animal was known to be around the property, the farm dogs, normally quite fearless, had been unleashed but had strangely refused to follow the scent and appeared to be quite terrified. Mr Blanks had also noticed a strong smell with an ammonia tang when the mystery creature was around. Strong odours are sometimes reported by witnesses of other types of alien animal, especially BHMs (see Chapter 5). Zoologists state that a strong odour, described by some witnesses as 'almost suffocating' and 'musty like rotting wood', is not typical of a puma. The people at Bushylease Farm knew when the 'puma' was near by the 'screaming' and yowling noises it made, usually when crossing open ground, and though its visits were usually made at night, sometimes it appeared during foggy days. Mr Blanks, his wife and son would catch occasional glimpses of it, in their car headlights at night or by torchlight as it disappeared behind a tree. Its footprints were 4 inches long and it left claw marks on tree trunks. In the nearby woods the many foxes seemed as terrified as the farm dogs when the 'thing' was near. During one fortnight Mr Blanks shot eight foxes in the open after they had been scared out of cover. Perhaps the oddest phenomenon he observed was the lights that sometimes shone upon the roofs of the farm buildings at night. There was no apparent source for them in this isolated area and every time they were seen, the alien animal was seen to be in the area shortly afterwards![7]

The matter received the attention of the national press when on 30 August 1964 a 4-hundredweight Friesian bullock was found badly mauled but still alive. On the night of the attack the mystery animal had evidently been around: the herd had stampeded and smashed a fence down in three places. The missing steer was found lying in a pool of blood in the undergrowth with vicious claw marks on its neck, shoulders and flanks. It was still alive and recovered after veterinary treatment. Pumas are usually very efficient at despatching their prey and normally will feed on part of the carcase and cover the rest with leaves and undergrowth in order to return later. Ministry of Agriculture officials pronounced that the strange droppings which were found near the mauled steer were clots of congealed blood and the wounds were lacerations caused by barbed wire. The animal continued to appear near the farm at about five-day intervals. During these visits Mr Blanks waited and watched from tree hides but never saw the beast. However, strange droppings, as were found beside the mauled steer, were found on these occasions.[8] Another time Edward Blanks found the remains of a 90-pound calf which had been dragged over three and a half fields from a neighbouring farm. He said: 'A fox couldn't do that.'[9]

On 17 August 1964 a dairyman driving his mini-van near the village of Crondall at 3.30 A.M. ran over a strange cat-like animal. The number plate was bent and there was a loud thump as the creature hit the underside of the van. It then jumped over a hedge into a barley field and was lost from view. The front-wheel drive mini has a flat, solid bottom and a ground clearance of only 5 inches, not nearly enough space for a puma.[10] At nearby Marsh Farm, Crondall, Leonard Hobbs often heard what were presumably this creature's screams and once caught it in his headlights' beam. He has farmed for eighteen years and was born and bred in the country, the son of a gamekeeper, so is no stranger to the normal sights and sounds of the countryside. Christabel Arnold of Crondall mistook the mystery animal for a dog and spoke to it. It left the dead crow it was eating, hissed at her, and wriggled under a gate. She described it as about 3 feet high with lynx-like eyes.[11]

September saw the start of a period of intense activity on the part of both the puma and the police, who were planning to trap it. They had their puma-hunting headquarters at Godalming Police Station where the dozens of puma reports were entered into a book and the reported positions marked on a map. They had also borrowed a strong cage from the London Zoo in which they hoped eventually to house the puma once caught. Perhaps the mystery puma too had heard of their preparations, because it turned up again on 7 September at Munstead, one mile south-east of Godalming. A large unidentified animal was seen near the racing stables and huge paw-prints were found in a stretch of sandy earth used as a gallop. They were variously reported as running for half a mile to 1½ miles and finished by leaping a 5½-foot fence and disappearing into the undergrowth.[12] The prints measured 6 inches across and were half an inch deep. The police took plaster casts, one of which is illustrated later. Again on 7 September George Wisdom came face to face with it when picking blackberries on Munstead Heath. While they eyed each other, Mr Wisdom noted that it was 3 feet high, 5 feet long, and dull gold in colour, with a long tail and large paws, and it had a fierce, cat-like face. He said it hissed at him and disappeared into the bushes.[13] On 23 September a dead roe deer was found with claw marks and a broken neck (typical of a puma's kill) at Cranleigh in Surrey.[14] Also on the 23rd, builders and police at Hascombe in Surrey watched a large animal 600 yards away lying at the edge of a wood. Two police officers approached but as they drew near the creature made off into the woods, leaving a partly eaten rabbit.[15] On 24 September at Hindhead Common, Surrey, a heifer was found badly clawed but still alive.[16] The next day a puma ran across the road in front of a car at Dunsfold. It was 5–6 feet long, 3 feet high, and a gingery colour.[17] At Hascombe Place a roe deer was savaged near a waterhole.[18] All these reports came from a limited area to the south of Godalming.

The avalanche of sightings continued throughout October. At Farley Mount west of Winchester, Hampshire, a gamekeeper shot at a 'black slit eyed animal'. There were reports of a 'wounded puma', but a police search found nothing.[19] Another gamekeeper reported seeing the 'puma' on two occasions at Kings Somborne, 7 miles west of Winchester, and by 28 October there were several reports coming in from the area of Crondall, near Bushylease Farm, which is where we first picked up the trail.[20] On 12 November an alien animal was seen by two policemen at Stoke Poges, Buckinghamshire, a short distance from the churchyard by the poet Thomas Gray's memorial. This is 30 miles and more north of the September/October area of activity and separated from it by two motorways and the densely populated west London suburbs. It is known that in the natural state a puma may have a hunting territory of 15 to 30 square miles and can travel 20 to 30 miles a day with ease. That is of course in the wild; an urban area is a completely different situation. After an appearance at Littleworth Common near Wing, Buckinghamshire, on 18 November,[21] two days later a mystery animal was seen 30 miles south-west at Nettlebed, Oxfordshire.[22] On 13 December an

80-pound ewe was killed, dragged 200 yards and partially eaten at Northchapel, West Sussex.[23] On 16 December another ewe, weighing 110 pounds, was killed and partly eaten in the same area;[24] and in between these two events the puma was reported seen at Ewhurst, Surrey.[25] Again on 18 January 1965 an in-lamb ewe weighing 150 pounds was killed near Cranleigh, Surrey.[26] Early in February 1965 Michael Lewis, a gamekeeper, with his brother David found large footprints which they thought might be a puma's, at Farley near Salisbury, Wiltshire, and photographs and plaster casts were sent to London for identification.[27]

It was about this time that the flood of reports caused Ron Ware, the ranger of Hurtwood Common, Surrey, to issue a public warning, saying that a puma was believed to be wintering on the common land (which is a well wooded area) and that 'a pony could easily rear in fright at seeing this animal and a child could be thrown.'[28] On 4 February 1965 police were warning tourists in the New Forest, Hampshire, to look out for a 'leopard like' animal, which had sprung out of the bushes in front of 17-year-old Felicity Whiteway as she was cycling home near Ashurst. The police search as usual found no wild animal nor any signs of dead prey.[29] 1965 was a quiet year for puma reports, or else newsdesk editors felt the story had had sufficient exposure and were reluctant to print more. But the 'puma' at last made the society columns when on 17 October 1965 it leapt over the head of the daughter of Viscount Chelmsford at Hazelbridge Court, Chiddingfold, Surrey, as she was attending to some horses.[30]

Having looked at so many reports labelled 'puma' and with plenty more to consider, we might now relate what is known of the puma in its natural state. It is only found on the American continent and has adapted to the various climates from the southern areas of Canada through to the southern parts of South America. It is also known as the panther, cougar, mountain lion, catamount, and Indian Devil, but we will stay with the name 'puma' (*Felis concolor*). Of the big cat family it is one of the smaller members, an average length being 6–8 feet (including tail), a height of 2½ to 3 feet, and weight of rather more than 150 pounds. Its colour ranges from a dark brown through to light brown and tawny reddish, and some have a smoky grey tint. It has no spots or stripes when adult, though the 'kittens' do have dark spots on their backs. Those who have studied the creature in the wild say that black pumas are very rare, which fact should be remembered when we come to examine some of the reports from the United States. It is thought that the number of pumas still surviving in the eastern states of North America is less than a hundred,[31] and in the western states it is a similarly rare animal and is becoming a protected species as more people realize the value of the fast-dwindling wildlife. Pumas do not normally attack humans. When puma and man meet, pumas often exhibit curiosity tempered by caution, but meetings between humans and pumas are rare. These big cats are well aware when humans are in the vicinity and choose to keep out of sight. The puma is in fact one of the most rarely seen animals. Their natural diet is deer, which they hunt at night and in the early morning. They will also eat fish, rabbits, grouse and similar prey. They have been known to steal meat from campsites and eat bread left by picnickers. When a deer has been killed they will, after eating, scrape leaves and similar debris over the carcase and return to it later.

'Puma' reports (the quotation marks should be understood for the rest of this chapter) continued to be made from Hampshire and Surrey throughout 1966. On 4 July a group of police, Post Office engineers and villagers watched through field glasses as a puma stalked a rabbit and ate it. Motor-cycle patrol officer Constable Robin Young said: 'It was ginger coloured and had a long tail with a white tip and a cat like face. It was just walking casually round the meadow. I had a good look at it through binoculars from 60 yards away.'[32] On 1 September a 'lady farmer' walking through a thistle patch at Chiddingfold, Surrey, stepped on a puma's tail. It retaliated by scratching her cheek, so she hit it with her stick. The puma, which probably had not wanted to get involved in the first place, ran away and climbed a tree. When the lady returned with assistance the puma had of course gone. Some hair was found by a Ministry of Agriculture and Fisheries official.[33]

It would be repetitive and take too much space to relate every report during the ensuing years, so we continue by selecting a few that demonstrate some special feature of the phenomenon.

In June 1969 an unusual animal was closely observed during daylight hours prowling in the lanes of Devon. Colonel W. A. C. Haines of Brushford was driving near Witheridge, some 10 miles west of Tiverton, when he came upon the creature by the roadside. For three minutes he was able to watch it in brilliant sunlight from 15 feet away. He said:

I have seen many leopards in Malaya, and it was exactly like one, but smaller, although it was the size of a calf. At first I thought of a Great Dane or fox gone wrong, but it was far bigger than a fox. I am nonplussed: I just do not know what it was.

It had a brown head, large, black, prominent eyes and a nose extraordinarily like a pug. Its left ear was pricked, but the other hung down as if torn. Its ribs were a bright, pale chestnut, turning to a sort of dirty gingery brown, and its hindquarters were darker still.

On its hindquarters were three black spots about the size of a penny and along its spine was a ridge of hair, about 2 inches in length which waved in the breeze. Its body was smooth-haired and thin. Its tail, long and thin, looked like a piece of dirty rope. Its legs were very long for its body, and pale fawn in colour.

This description is quite unlike a puma and it does not sound a great deal like a leopard either. It is another version of the hybrid alien. The same area had in 1967 already produced a series of alien animal reports and the colonel contacted some of those witnesses and found that their descriptions tallied with his.[34] In 1983 the spotlight again shone on Devon, when for several months the 'Exmoor Beast' was terrorizing southern Exmoor around the Devon/Somerset border. It killed great numbers of sheep, in a cat-like manner, but people who saw the large black or dark brown creature said it looked more like a dog, and its tracks, 3½ inches across, were dog-like, with claw marks visible. At one point the Royal Marines were called in, but despite extraordinary efforts, the animal was not killed or caught. The depredations suddenly stopped, and the Beast had gone.

On 27 January 1970 Freda Siggers and a neighbour were walking their dogs in the early morning on Ash Ranges near Aldershot, Hampshire. The dogs growled and were uneasy, so they turned for home. Then they heard a terrifying scream and an animal crossed the path 20 yards away. Mrs Siggers had a clear view of the creature and gave an accurate description of a puma. This was followed a few days later by a report (published on 10 February) which said that Bill Richards who had shot a fox in his chicken run near Ash Ranges believed he had ended a 'five year mystery'. Referring to Mrs Siggers' sighting, he said: 'I think it could very well have been this fox that she and other people have mistaken for a puma.' He added: 'It was unusual to see a fox out in broad daylight, especially in a built-up area such as we are in.' He didn't appear to question why a fox should leave the cover and invade the town during daylight hours.[35] Another 'end of the mystery' report had been published in the *Daily Express* on 25 November 1969. Large prints had been found on a golf course at Bramley near Guildford, Surrey. Police made plaster casts which were sent to the Zoological Society of London. The owner of an Old English Mastiff called Simba, which weighed 224 pounds and had a 5-inch-wide pawprint, claimed that they had been made by her dog and a check with the dog's foot confirmed this. The report went on to say: 'But despite the Simba stumer, people in the area are still keeping a wary watch for the puma said to have been prowling in the Surrey countryside for two years or more.' More like seven in fact, and there was no mention that the reports had come from a far wider area than Surrey: from Oxfordshire to the north-west, from Hampshire to the south-west and Devon to the far south-west, and from south-east London to the east.

There were frequent sightings throughout 1971 and on into 1972 on both sides of the Hampshire/Surrey border, centred around Odiham, and also in the New Forest area of Hampshire. In late June 1972 Edna Hughes of High Street, Bagshot, Surrey, looked out of her bedroom window early one morning and met the eye of something that 'slowly walked up and down, staring at me'. 'It was white and about 3 feet high when it sat up,' she said.[36] During September 1972 a strange animal was seen frequently at Fleet Station, Hampshire, often by commuters arriving home from the City. Dennis Long of Fleet said: 'We looked across the lines to the up platform and saw it behind the railings . . . It was very much like a big cat. It had a black head and a brown body with grey markings.' Railwayman Vic Carr watched it and gave a similar description. It was often seen in the overgrown garden of the once station master's house, behind the up platform. While her reporter husband watched the garden, Joan Deverell sat in their car, parked in the station car park. As she waited, the puma came by and 'It went in and out between the cars carrying a fish in its mouth. It threw back its head and tossed the fish up, made a purring noise and caught it, and went on out of sight.'[37] The large Fleet pond adjoins the car park, which fact probably explains the fish.

This concentration of close-up sightings over a short time produced the inevitable reaction. This time it was Keith Hopson of Tavistock Road, Fleet, who announced that what everyone was seeing and mistaking for a large prowling puma was in fact a Siamese cat. He had seen it twice, first on Monday, 11 September, and again the next day about 6 P.M. as his train pulled into Fleet

Station. On Wednesday he took his camera with him and photographed something running into the undergrowth. Whatever it was he had photographed, the picture was not good enough for the *Aldershot News* to print.[38]

About this time something was also active in the New Forest area of Hampshire. During September 1972 three young brothers, 12-year-old Stuart Cron, Andrew (10) and Donald (6), of Lower Bartley Road, Woodlands, which is some 5 miles west of Southampton, saw a creature creeping through the grass on the edge of the forest near their home. Andrew, who got closest, said, 'It was larger than an Alsatian dog but looked like a cat. It had a big head with stick-up ears, like cat's ears, and its eyes looked fierce.' At first it looked black, but a closer look showed that it was a tawny brown. When he slapped his dog's lead against his leg it bounded off 'in big leaps'. When the boys ran off, their Alsatian, which normally chased anything that moved, ran away with them. Later Andrew identified a picture of a puma as the animal he had seen. The boy's mother, Mrs L. M. Cron, had earlier seen large pawprints with claw marks showing in the clay on the edge of a ditch.[39] Early in February that year Mrs H. P. Short of Tatchbury Lane, Winsor, not far from Woodlands, had seen huge pawprints in her garden which also showed 1½-inch long claws, far bigger than her Alsatian dog's.[40] Again may we remind the reader that members of the big cat family (except for the cheetah) retract their claws and walk only on their pads.

1973 started with a sighting at Alkham, Kent, midway between Folkestone and Dover. Fred Arnold of Bridge Street, Folkestone, saw a large animal bound across the road in front of him as he drove from Capel to Alkham early in January. A gamekeeper and Tony Jepsom of the RSPCA inspected the large tracks and thought they might have been made by a puma.[41] Later in the month Peter Cookson of Berwick Manor, Lympne, Kent, told a *Folkestone Herald* reporter that in the previous June he had seen a large cat-like animal bound across the road when he was driving between Canterbury and Lympne at 3.30 A.M.[42] During January pumas were seen again in the New Forest, Hampshire. In late March 1973 Charlie Christopher of Cove Road, Farnborough, Hampshire, was on an early morning bike training ride when the 'puma' ran across the road in front of him. Having seen plenty of foxes at such times he knew this was something different. Afterwards he said: 'Now I am a confirmed believer in the puma. The way it whipped across the dual-carriageway and then turned round and stared really startled me.'[43] In June 1973 an alien animal was seen by two policemen in the Queen Elizabeth Park, in Farnborough, Hampshire, at 4.20 A.M. at a distance of 10 yards. PC Anthony Thomas (eight years in the force) said:

It was in the early hours of the morning but the light was good. It stood about ten yards from me. It was three or four times the size of a cat with a long tail and pointed ears. It definitely was not a dog or a fox. But I'm not saying it was definitely a puma.[44]

Four months later an alien animal made an appearance at Branksome, Dorset, in the heavily populated area between Bournemouth and Poole. At 3.30 A.M. on 7 April 1974 Joan Gilbert saw it loping across Western Avenue. She said: 'It had stripes, a long thin tail, and seemed to be all grey, though it might have had some yellow on it. It was thin and definitely not a fox.' She later identified the creature from an illustrated book. The animal that best fitted her description was a Tasmanian marsupial wolf, or thylacine! These animals, native only to Tasmania, are so rare as to be once thought extinct.[45]

On 15 January 1975 a lorry driver saw two lion cubs romping in the rubble of a council tip. The council's rat catcher, Bill Crane, was asked to investigate but he found nothing. This was at Langham, Norfolk.[46] During March 1975 pumas were active around Horsham, West Sussex. Two girls who were horse-riding near Brooks Green, south-west of Horsham, were thrown when their mounts were startled by a large cat-like animal which crossed their path. Two days later, and on the other side of Horsham, at Pease Pottage, a woman saw a puma sitting by the M23 motorway.[47]

The overwhelming volume of reports of wild cats at large precludes the possibility that they have all escaped from captivity. Where there are known escapes the chase and recapture period are normally brief. On 4 May 1975 an eight-month-old puma escaped from Jeff Day's garden shed in Medstead, Hampshire. After roaming the village gardens for four hours, Sheba was cornered, tranquillized and driven off to a zoo.[48] Four lions, frightened by fireworks on 5 November 1975, escaped from their circus cage at Gainsborough, Lincolnshire, with tragic results. Three were recaptured almost immediately but the fourth was at large for over an hour. During that time it badly mauled ten-year-old Stephen Jackson-Parr who was watching the firework display, and fifteen days later he died in hospital.[49] In August 1975, a Clouded leopard escaped from Howletts Park near Canterbury, Kent, and lived for eight months at large in Kent. In April 1976 it was shot by a farmer whose lambs it had been killing. The owner of Howletts, John Aspinall, said he was surprised the leopard had survived for so long.[50] In September 1976 three lions escaped from a circus in Epsom, Surrey. One attacked a horse, but all were soon recaptured.[51] A few days later three lion cubs were soon recaptured after escaping at Stevenage, Hertfordshire.[52] In October of the same year a pet cougar escaped at Blackley, Manchester. After four hours police with dogs recaptured it.[53] In Georgia, USA, six lions escaped from a zoo at Ringgold on 25 October 1976. They were all shot by order of the owners, four within a few hours, the other two on the two following days.[54] The lion that escaped from its cage in a Belfast, Northern Ireland, theatre in January 1977 tasted freedom for only two hours before police and circus staff cornered and tranquillized it.[55]

The foregoing reports suggest that escaped animals are usually not too difficult to find and with an organized effort are soon recaptured or killed. The arguments against large wild predators roving the English countryside were cogently put by naturalist Dr Maurice Burton in an article he wrote for *Wildlife* magazine in November 1966.[56] Dr Burton, who has for some years taken an interest in the 'Surrey puma' reports, has usually argued against the puma's existence (as he has, of later years, argued against the existence of the Loch Ness Monster). He points out that the frequent kills for food that one or more pumas living in the countryside would have to make are absent. Deer, their normal prey, are plentiful in the Surrey and Hampshire countryside. Victor Head, writing in *The Field* in 1965,[57] quotes American authorities when stating that a puma needs about 300 pounds of meat a week. 'As this is five times the average weight of a British roe deer a fully grown puma would need each year to kill 250 of them to live comfortably and free in Surrey.' Nothing like this scale of attacks on the roe deer has been reported, and farmers have had relatively few attacks on farm animals. No food caches, such as are normally left by pumas, have been found either. But in 1965 Victor Head wrote[58] that the London Zoo authorities, having examined a plaster cast of one of the pugs of the 'Munstead Monster', are '99 per cent certain that the creature is a puma'. And hairs found after sightings have been identified as being similar to hairs from puma tails. The zoo authorities have their own file on the 'puma' too which they do not publish, and it looks as though they have other evidence which convinces them that the reports probably refer to a puma.

Although in the wild pumas may have a hunting range of some 30 miles, the wide spread of reports in England from Dover to Devon to Norfolk and the distance apart of some simultaneous reports are not consistent with the idea of one puma loose. Many pumas loose is an even less tenable suggestion. Soon we shall detail reports from the Midlands and northern Scotland! Known in their native habitat for their elusive habits, pumas are rarely seen and will always avoid people. Compare that with the reports of the alien animals leaping over police cars and a young woman who was grooming horses, and also jumping across the path of girls who were riding on bicycles. It almost looks as if these creatures are trying to attract attention to their presence! Later in this chapter when we come to look at reports from the United States, there are cases with even more untypical behaviour. Dr Burton further points out[59] that the reported calls that the animals make, variously described as snarl-like, yowling, and like a woman screaming, are not in accord with known descriptions of the voice of a puma. The descriptions of the animals' appearance vary widely too. In the early 'sixties people in the Crondall area were seeing creatures they described as cheetah-like, monkey-like, and 'about the size of an Alsatian dog', though the plaster cast of the footprint at Munstead suggests a much bigger animal than this. Other reports speak of lions and tigers, while some witnesses report small animals that are partly striped but are not tigers. Whatever it is that is being seen, its appearance varies considerably from sighting to sighting.

To avoid creating the false idea that UK sightings of alien big cats are confined to the southern counties, we shall delve into our files once more and look at some reports from further north. For several days in July and August 1976 the Nottingham lion scare became national news. It started just after 6 A.M. on a Thursday morning (29 July 1976) when two milkmen on an early round at Tollerton 4 miles south-east of Nottingham saw a lion. David Bentley of Abbey Park, West Bridgford, saw it first and was joined by his mate David Crowther of Clifton, who said: 'We both saw together what certainly to us was a lion. It was 50 yards away, had its head down and its long tail had a bushy end. It was walking away from us but only very slowly.' David Bentley said: 'If I had been on my own I don't think I would have told anyone, because they wouldn't have believed it. But it was there and we both saw it together.' The police took the report seriously and toured the nearby villages of Ruddington and West Bridgford with loud-hailers warning people to stay inside and keep windows closed. Local people told the police how their dogs had been strangely restless during the night, and a farmer at Clipstone, near Cotgrave, reported strange pawprints on his land.[60] During the day armed police made an extensive search of the countryside using dogs and a helicopter. A police spokesman said, 'There are no zoos anywhere near here', and admitted that they were puzzled as to where the lion could have come from.[61] At the end of the day no lion had been seen and the hunt was called off. The publicity brought more reports to the police, eighteen that day, thirteen of which they treated seriously, and all of them were about sightings that had happened before the milkmen's report. From Norfolk came a report that two people had seen a lion at Lowdham a week earlier, but had not reported it for fear of ridicule. A false alarm occurred when a bus passenger reported seeing a lion over a garden wall, but a police check found that a Great Dane dog lived there.[62]

On the third day of the hunt, Saturday, 31 July, the police repeated the 'stay on your guard' warning to the public as reports continued to come in, but they were unable to find any trace of the creature themselves, and there were no reports of dead livestock or missing pets – so what was it living on?[63] John Dunthorne saw a lion on his farm and found tracks with a trail forced through the crops, believed by the police to be too wide to have been made by a badger, fox or dog. A check on owners of wild animals found nothing missing. On Sunday, 1 August the *Sunday Express* published a police warning to people living with 20 miles of Nottingham to lock up pets at night and to keep a close watch on small children during the day. On Sunday evening, 1 August 1976, Dr John Chisholm, deputy coroner for Nottinghamshire, saw the rear end of a lion breaking through some undergrowth to get to a stream in his garden at Normanton on the Wolds. He returned to his house and watched from an upstairs window with his wife and 18-year-old son until a police car arrived, the lights of which, Mrs Chisholm said, seemed to disturb the lion, which then left the area. Also during that Sunday, a woman watched through binoculars as a puma-like animal 200 yards away stalked wildfowl by a reservoir. This was at Nuthall, ten miles from Normanton and on the opposite side of Nottingham.[64] On the Monday, police, some armed, toured a three-mile radius around Normanton. In the expectation that the lion might be lying low during the day and would be more active at night, patrols were increased during the evening.[65]

On Tuesday, mounted police and police dogs joined the search parties as Dr Chisholm's sighting gave an added impetus to police interest. Chief Inspector John Smith, chief of operations, was reported as saying they were now 98 per cent sure that there was an animal in the area. Police expressed alarm at the lack of care being taken by the public. A spokesman said that when they went to investigate a reported sighting they found over fifty people including children in the field looking for the lion. The police stressed that there could be a real danger and that people should stay away from the area in which the animal had been seen.[66]

The Great Lion Hunt, as the press now called it, entered its sixth day with police still receiving sighting reports and still finding nothing when they got there. Chief Inspector John Smith said: 'We are almost totally convinced it is there.' He also commented: 'We haven't received reports of cats, dogs or rabbits being found dead and we would like farmers to make regular checks on their stock.' The search parties of men, dogs and horses were joined by motor patrols. A sighting at Ruddington on Tuesday night drew a blank from the searching policemen. The public made helpful suggestions: A man who had twenty lions offered to lend some as a lure; someone else suggested dead chickens should be strung from trees. Police said they were grateful for all advice but they had staff from three safari parks as advisers and didn't want to trouble anyone else. Ladbrokes the bookmakers offered odds of 3–1 against a lion being caught before midnight on Saturday.[67]

On Thursday, 5 August the hunt was a week old. A report was made of a 'sandy coloured animal, like a young lioness' in a field near Nottingham racecourse. Police searched the area and found nothing.[68] The next day the police announced that they no longer thought there was a lion on the loose. They had received 65 reports of sightings and immediate searches had all proved negative. On more than one occasion they had had reports of the animal being seen in two places at the same time. No farmer had reported any livestock being attacked. No lion escapes had been reported and an expert on the behaviour of lions, from a local safari park, had found no evidence of a lion in the areas being searched. One sighting, said the police, had been a large dog and another had been found to be a large brown paper bag.[69] That was, more or less, the end of the Nottingham lion. But not, of course, the end of the big cat sightings. The scene quickly changes to the little village of Thorganby, 8 miles south-east of York, and 70 miles north of Nottingham. On the evening of 9 August 1976 Alan Pestell, a 33-year-old electrical supervisor at a nearby frozen food factory, left home at 9.55 P.M. and was walking down the main street to call in at the pub. From the shadows into the moonlit street came a large animal. Mr Pestell said: 'At first I thought it was a dog and spoke to it, but then I realized it had a cat's face and a long tail . . . I was scared stiff. I froze for a few seconds and then decided to keep on walking to the pub. I thought if I turned and ran it might jump on my back.' He later described it as 3 to 4 feet long and nearly 3 feet high, and told how it sat and looked at him with its right paw lifted until he had passed. Then it vanished into the shadows again.[70] According to another report, Mr Pestell was able to identify the beast more positively as 'a large lioness'. Police with dogs immediately made a search of the locality but saw nothing that resembled a lion. The usual checks for escaped animals were made, and searchers also checked nearby houses for Alsatians or other large dogs which they thought could have caused the report. A police statement said: 'We have no reason to connect this report with the recent sightings of a lion in Nottinghamshire.' Why should they, indeed? Could a lion walk 70 miles across England in one or two days without being noticed?[71] The police, who evidently considered Mr Pestell a sober and reliable witness, continued to search next day but, as usual, drew a blank.

The similarity between this report and the traditional black dog story (see next chapter) has already been noted by other Fortean researchers.[72] It is also interesting to note that in 1975, only a year before, milkman David Bowlby saw what he described as a bear, about as tall as a 10-year-old child, on its hind legs, brown in colour and with black foot-pads, on Skipwith Common just down the road from Thorganby.[73]

Later in 1976, on 20 September, the police gave high credibility to Dr Alec Jamieson, the police surgeon of Skegness, Lincolnshire, when he reported 'a large sandy coloured cat about 5 feet long; definitely a cougar.' Police Constable Jock Gartshore also viewed it with him in the grounds of a sea-front convalescent home. Staff at the home who had seen it a number of times during the past weeks said they had assumed it was just a large and unusual dog. When the grounds were searched, pug marks 2½ inches by 3 inches were found, so a naturalist and an inspector from the RSPCA hid, ready with cameras. But, of course, nothing more was seen.[74]

On the other side of England alien animals have sporadically appeared in recent years in and around the city of Chester. During May 1974 an unidentified animal was frequently seen in Delamere Forest some 8 miles north-east of Chester. Thomas Marrington, owner of the Lakeside Café near Norley, twice saw it in his car headlights. It looked something like an Alsatian dog, but had a brush tail like a fox. His adult son Tom had also seen it twice and said, 'It was about 2 feet in height and had this big tail. I don't know what it was.' Both were sure it was not a fox.[75] On 23 October 1976 a lioness was seen in Deva Lane at Upton, Chester, about a mile from the zoo. The Chester Zoo did a check and found all theirs were indoors. Later it was seen twice more near West Chester Hospital. Police on foot and car patrols scoured the area but no trace of it was ever found.[76]

Big cat reports from Wales have been unexpectedly few, considering the huge numbers of sheep roaming the wild hillsides, but in recent years there has been sporadic activity. In 1980 there were several sightings in Powys, one by a district nurse who described an animal sounding remarkably like a lynx. In October a sheep farmer on a remote farm near Llangurig contacted the police to report that he believed he had a strange animal in his barn. Armed police kept watch through the night, using subtle tactics like hammering on the side of the building in order to flush their prey, but when next day they went inside, they found, not surprisingly, that the beast had flown. A year later, people were seeing large cats around Tonmawr in West Glamorgan, and naturalist Di Francis, who is making a special study of the British big cat and has written a book on the subject, managed to see and photograph one of the Tonmawr cats for herself. During 1982 and 1983 a large cat 'like a large ginger tomcat, but about the size of a medium sheepdog' was being seen regularly in the Brechfa area of Dyfed. It killed sheep, lambs and chickens, and then killed a sheepdog which had been tied to a chicken run to protect the birds.

There are some locations in Scotland which have drawn attention to themselves by the repeated sightings of alien animals, quite apart from the country's water monsters. There was much activity in 1974 in north Ayrshire. During the summer a puma-like creature was roving around the countryside south-west of Glasgow and was often seen. Hugh Gilmour of Barrmill was driving his lorry early one morning when a kind of lion 'bounded' across the road ahead of him. He said: 'Its body was 2½ to 3 feet from the ground, had heavy legs, fairly large paws and a long curled up tail.' John Jackson, also from Barrmill, saw it at close range when he was driving a taxi full of passengers to Beith at midnight. He said:

It was sitting on its haunches in the middle of the road and I was forced to stop. I was within a few feet of it and my headlights were full on – but it would not move. I waited for about five minutes, then drove round it. In doing so my car brushed against it and it growled.

The police thought both men were sensible and reliable and treated the reports seriously, but their investigations found 'nothing unusual'.[77]

When John Stewart found five of his geese dead on his farm at Ballageich Hill about 8 miles south of Glasgow, the deaths were unhesitatingly attributed to the mysterious cat-like animal which had been prowling the Renfrewshire and Ayrshire countryside since 1973. The dead geese were found in August 1976 and each one had 1½-inch-deep puncture marks on its body 4 to 5 inches apart. These were the only injuries. A six-foot wire fence had been ripped open and nearby cowered an Alsatian dog described as normally vicious. Deep tracks 'the size of a man's fist' were found by a stream and were identified by Richard O'Grady, director of Calderpark Zoo, Glasgow, as a 'puma'.[78] Although Mr O'Grady was satisfied that the puncture marks on the body were typical of 'how a puma kills', he is not reported as wondering why a puma, having killed five birds, should not feed upon any of them. This report suggests other unasked questions too. It says of the 'puma' that 'this is the first time it has left proof of its identity', which we read as meaning that no depredations of livestock had previously been discovered although it had been around the area for 'the last three years' and had been seen 'by hundreds of people including at least a score of policemen'. So what was this creature living on? Another unasked question was, why had large chunks been ripped from the wire fence? A 6-foot wire fence would not prove to be a barrier for an active house-cat; a puma can clear a 10- to 15-foot-high fence if it tries. If breaking through fences *were* typical of puma behaviour, the wire compounds in which many zoos keep their pumas would be far from secure. Note also that such compounds are completely roofed with wire to stop the animals climbing up and over the top, which they could easily do.

The 'normally vicious' Alsatian guard-dog which was 'beside itself with terror' is also untypical of dogs faced with pumas. Pumas normally behave to dogs as most cats do, they avoid them and if chased will climb a tree. Dogs can be trained to hunt pumas and do not normally cower in terror when facing them. The terror shown by dogs when in the vicinity of an alien animal has been noted in earlier reports; it may also be of significance to note that dogs are frequently reported as exhibiting the same reaction when they are in the vicinity of a UFO. We are also intrigued by the method of killing those geese. The puncture marks have more than a hint of vampirism about them. It would be interesting to know if an autopsy were performed upon the geese and if so, whether the expected quantity of blood was found or whether there was a remarkable lack of it. This gruesome thought is prompted by reports of depredations in May 1810 at Ennerdale in Cumbria, when sometimes seven or eight sheep a night were killed but not eaten, only the jugular vein being bitten open and the blood sucked. Similarly in 1905 at Great Badminton, Avon, sheep were killed and their blood taken but not the flesh. Neither mystery was satisfactorily solved, though dogs were shot and the mysteries were said to be solved.[79] We shall look further into the interest that alien animals apparently have in blood later in this book.

A few days before the killing of the five geese, an alien animal paraded before the amazed gaze of a Glenfarg, Perthshire, woman. When she went into her garden on the evening of Sunday, 9 August 1976 to find out why her terrier was barking, she found the dog shivering with fright and staring at a large cat-like creature which was sitting on top of the garden wall. It had long pointed ears with tufts on the tips and its eyes were a 'burning orange'. The animal was spitting and snarling at her and with commendable presence of mind she scooped up her dog and backed towards the house. As she did so, the cat-creature leapt off the wall and into the fields on the other side.[80] This happened about 60 miles north-east of the previous Scottish reports, but there was no suggestion that it was the same animal. The tufts on the ears suggest a lynx rather than a puma, although lynxes are no more native to Scotland than pumas. The burning orange eyes could have been caused by the normal reflection of the house lights in the cat's eyes; or they could have been more than this. In later chapters we shall find that many witnesses report that the alien animals they see have eyes which glow with their own internal light. This applies particularly to BHMs (big hairy monsters – see Chapter 5), and 'winged things' such as Mothman and Owlman (see Chapter 4). The traditional black dog phantom which we describe in the next chapter also often has glowing eyes.

A little more than a year later a lioness with two cubs was seen about 10 miles south of Inverness at Farr. This was on 27 September 1977 at 5.30 P.M. when John Jenkins from Inverness was within 20 feet of these creatures, together with his son and nephew. A few days later they were again seen near Inverness, at Culdethel. On 30 September the police mounted a hunt but found nothing.[81] It is worthy of note that the first report gave the exact sighting as being in a field at Crask near Farr. The Ordnance Survey map shows Crask as an isolated structure, probably a large house, and a mere 5 miles away to the west lie the brooding waters of Loch Ness. Boleskine House, in which, for a while, Aleister Crowley practised his magical conjurations, is only 12 miles south-west of Crask, by the side of Loch Ness. Not a long way as distances go in these wild, uninhabited hills.

During December 1977 armed men scoured the hills at Strathnaver near Bettyhill, Sutherland, on the northern coast of Scotland. They were searching for the feline predator that had killed and fed upon a sheep whose carcase had been found by its owner Thomas Todd, a crofter and store-keeper of Achneiskich, Bettyhill. Mr Todd recalled how a few days earlier he had found pawprints in the snow 3 inches in diameter, and two years previously he had found a dead ewe which had been badly mauled. There had in fact been periodic searches during the past two years, following the discovery that animals had been attacked. Veterinary investigation officer Scott Johnston was called in to examine the dead sheep and stated that all the details 'point to a feline predator'. On the evening after the carcase was found, Donald Mackenzie and his 15-year-old son James were shooting foxes at night using a spotlight. They saw a large animal swimming the River Naver a mile from Bettyhill and after chasing it across the fields in their Landrover Mr Mackenzie got a shot at it. The creature was hit but limped off in the darkness.

Police Sergeant Donald Bruce, who organized the search party, said: 'When I saw the carcase of the sheep I knew it was something different and the vet confirmed it was not a dog. We have searched the area but found nothing. It is vast and unfenced and the beast could be anywhere.' Other locals also related seeing a 'big cat' in the area. Alistair McLean of Skerray was hunting foxes in 1976 with Hugh Mackay, a crofter who had had sheep killed, when a large animal ran away from them across the moorland. He said: 'It was broad in the back, strongly-built and very fast. I thought it was a dull rusty colour. I was convinced it was big game.'[82]

Early in 1978, on 30 January, Helen Fitch of Bishop Kinkell, Conon Bridge, saw in a field 100 yards away from her house 'a big cat – similar to a small lioness or puma'. She added: 'I have lived in Central Africa and seen animals like that before.' This was in Ross-shire about 10 miles directly north-west of Inverness. The police came and took plaster casts of the footprints they found, while an armed officer tracked the prints as far as he could, but found nothing. Seven days later John Henderson, who farms a mile away from Mrs Fitch, at Leanaig Farm, found large pawprints in the snow near his house. He said: 'They were three to four inches long and the pads and indentations of claws could clearly be seen.' If it was a big cat, it had no business leaving claw marks. As we mentioned earlier, almost all cats retract their claws when walking and leave only pad marks; and unlike the reports from the Bettyhill area there was no mention of any livestock being slaughtered.[83]

It was in January 1927 that Inverness-shire was struck by a wave of mystery predators. Strange footprints were found and sheep and goats were slaughtered. A farmer killed 'a large, fierce, yellow animal of unknown species.' The footprints and the slaughter continued; another animal similar to the first was shot, and then a third was trapped. 'The body was sent to the London Zoo, where it was identified as that of a lynx.' The lynx is not of course indigenous to Great Britain.[84]

Back to the northernmost shores of Scotland again where Sergeant Donald Bruce of Bettyhill was still waging his valiant campaign against the phantom killer. On 8 February 1978, after another mutilated sheep had been found, he said:

There now seems to be a pattern over a wide area which suggests there could be more than one animal. It is very difficult to find the animal because it kills at night. When we had the snow, tracks were found, but we were unable to follow them because we were busy digging people out of the snow.[85]

Sergeant Bruce, like his colleagues down south in the land of the Surrey puma, was receiving so many simultaneous and scattered reports that they couldn't possibly all refer to the same creature. And this not from jittery urbanites in the stockbroker commuter belt, but from stolid Scots farmers and crofters who had lived all their lives in the Scottish hills and knew the indigenous wildlife as well as they knew their own families.

These alien visitors from who knows where are not at all a modern phenomenon; there are examples to be found scattered throughout historical writings. But our present time is unique in so far as we have rapid communications and many places are far more heavily populated than they were a century or more ago, added to which, the zoologists are now far more certain which creatures are indigenous to a given area. This was not the case when the sixteenth-century chronicler Ralph Holinshed wrote: 'Lions we have had very many in the north parts of Scotland, and those with manes of no less force than those of Mauretania; but how and when they were destroyed as yet I do not read.'[86] Another relevant record has been found in an ancient document of the ninth century from Mesopotamia. This states that some time before 774 A.D. the people in the region of Abdin Rock were plagued by unknown creatures similar to wolves but with ears like a horse and a ridge of bristly hair along their spine. They had no fear of men and would turn to attack any who pursued them. They entered the houses in villages and carried off the children, and 20 to 100 people were devoured by them.[87]

During the winter of 1764–5 a fierce creature was at large in the region of Languedoc in France. It was described as being bigger than a wolf with large claws, many teeth and grey on the underside with reddish and black hair above. It attacked by springing for its victim's throat and by late 1764 it had killed and eaten at least 20 people, most of them being young women. It continued to elude troops who were organized to search for it and the reports of its existence and depredations were met with incredulity outside France. The *St James Chronicle* of 6 June 1765 published a summary of the story of 'The Wild Beast of Gévaudan', at the same time suggesting that it was a 'mongrel' cross between a tiger and a hyena. It also suggested that there were several of them, no doubt because of the number of simultaneous reports from widely separated locations (a characteristic of the recent British big cats too). On 20 September a hunter, Monsieur Beauterme, with the aid of a gamekeeper, succeeded in killing the beast and the body was sent to the king at Versailles, who had been taking an interest in the matter. It was dissected by a court surgeon and was found to be 32 inches high and 5 feet 7½ inches long including its tail, and with forty teeth. The surgeon thought it more like a hyena than a wolf.[88]

For a last historical encounter with an alien big cat we return to eighteenth-century England. It was in the grounds of the ruined Waverley Abbey near Farnham, Surrey, that traveller and essayist William Cobbett saw a strange cat when he was a boy. As he reported in his *Rural Rides*, in the section from Chilworth to Winchester dated Thursday, 27 October, the hollow elm tree into which he had seen a large cat, 'as big as a middle-sized spaniel dog', go, was still standing. He received a scolding and then a beating for insisting he had seen an unidentifiable animal, and adds: 'I have since many times repeated it, and I would take my oath of it to this day. When in New Brunswick I saw the great wild grey cat, which is there called a *Lucifee*; and it seemed to me to be just such a cat as I had seen at Waverley.' The 'great wild grey cat' to which he refers is of course the puma, which is native to the North American continent and in his time was well established in New Brunswick, though now it is in need of protection as an endangered species.[89]

The perceptive reader will have noted that the ruined Waverley Abbey, being only a mile south-east of Farnham, is in the heart of Surrey puma country.

Alien big cats are also seen in North America. It might be thought that, the States being the natural habitat of these big cats, any sightings of a puma would be almost an everyday event; but we shall show that this is not so. Although originally abundant in most of the states, the pumas have been so mercilessly hunted for the past three centuries that they are extinct in most states, and are known to exist only in very small numbers in the eastern states and over the border into Canada. In the Mid-West, which is a hotbed of alien animal activity, including big cats, particularly Indiana and Illinois, the puma has been declared extinct for over a 100 years, which puts the authorities there in the same difficult situation, when attempting to explain away the reports, as their British counterparts.[90]

Many of the reports speak of black pumas or panthers, but melanism, as the black coloration is known, is in fact very rare and, to quote from Bruce Wright's *The Eastern Panther*, 'No black panther or cougar has ever been killed in North America ... However, a black specimen has been shot in South America.' Wright says he was puzzled by the reports he received of black animals and after discussing a variety of explanations is left with 'no alternative but to accept the eyewitness accounts at face value.'[91] Possibly what the witnesses were reporting would in fact fall into the category of 'alien animals'.

The number of alien big cats seen in the States is overwhelming. The phenomenon has been recorded from the earliest settlers up to the present and in nearly every state. In 1877 a young couple were walking home one night near the village of Rising Sun in Indiana. As they skirted a thickly wooded region they heard a wild shriek among the trees. Mary Crane looked back and, seeing a pair of glowing eyes, the two started running wildly. This ambush was not entirely unexpected. A few days earlier another young man had been pursued at this point by 'some monstrous animal' and felt he had barely escaped with his life. The couple stopped their flight momentarily to look back. The creature was running rapidly towards them along the top of the roadside fence. As they continued to run, the animal, 'as big as a good sized calf, with a tail as long as a door', leapt to the ground and started to gain on them rapidly. At this the young man, choosing safety rather than chivalry, let go of Mary's hand and sprinted for the nearby village. The terrorizing beast quickly caught up with the girl and as she felt its claws in her dress she fainted and fell. Moments later she came to – and found herself pinned to the ground by the weight of the animal which was licking her face. She lay quite still and silently prayed. Soon she heard voices, the animal raised its head, listened, gave a piercing scream and made off into the woods. In the light of the following day, the 6- inch-wide footprints were tracked for half a mile until they were lost. A further hunt in the ensuing days failed to find anything more.[92]

In 1948 alien big cats were on the rampage in the area around Richmond, Indiana, where there were frequent reports. On the morning of 7 July two farmlads, Arthur and Howard Turner, were walking across the yard at 5.30 A.M. when they saw an animal not far away. Further off on a rise stood another. The first was large-headed, brownish and 'shaggy' as a lion; the other was black and looked more like a panther. Arthur whipped his gun up to his shoulder and fired at the 'lion'. It spun round, jumped a gate and was away. For the next two days others saw the two big cats together in the district. Police searchers found only tracks made by a five-toed animal of some 300 pounds' weight. Big cats only have four toes and more usually weigh up to about 200 pounds.[93]

During the 1950s there were sporadic outbreaks of alien big cat activity over the whole of the Mid-West. A book devoted to the subject would not be large enough to contain all the reports. When Sheriff Robert Shelton of Paradise, Indiana, was flooded with reports in January 1958, he is reported to have said: 'It seems there's more than one cat in the vicinity.'[94] A conclusion that was also reached by the Surrey and Ayrshire police forces in Britain.

Farmer Ed Moorman was leapt upon by a large tan-coloured animal which clawed his face and only ran off when he fired his rifle. This was in June 1962 in the Monument City area of north-east Indiana. The next incident was on the 26th of the month when Moorman found ten of his pigs dead. Blood had been sucked from their necks and their hearts and livers eaten. From witness descriptions and claw marks found on a wooden gate, the creature was identified as an 'African lioness'. Eventually Moorman and some other farmers were ready waiting for it with rifles near Huntington. There were also a couple of jittery television men there who opened fire before the animal was within range and so it made off.[95]

In August 1971 a 'cat of some kind' was creating havoc in the Michigan countryside. It slaughtered many farm animals and in Canton Township alone it killed 197 chickens and 55 rabbits. Glenn Brothers had a close look at it and chased it into a cornfield. The prints he found were like a cat's but they also had large claw marks.[96] The alien animal that was roving about Champaign County, Illinois, in the spring of 1963 was also one of the numerous cats which left footprints showing claw marks, untypical of felines. These simply caused arguments between those who had seen the creature and said 'cat' and those who had seen the prints and said 'dog'.[97]

An alien 'black panther' appeared at Stockbridge, 20 miles from Atlanta, Georgia, in September 1975. This cat was noted for its huge glowing eyes, screams at night, and a propensity for appearing out in the open on highways, in daylight hours. It attacked and killed a goat tethered next to a house, without disturbing the residents, and later killed two cows, again without disturbing the owners, asleep 100 feet away in a mobile home. They noted that their cats had been wildly trying to scratch their way out of the trailer that night. Organized search parties could never find any trace of the animal. The panther seemed to leave as suddenly as it had come, and there were no further reports. The nearby Seminole Indians have legends about the 'ghost panthers' which preyed on people and deer and could be killed only by spears blessed by the holy man.[98]

During the spring of 1977 something nasty was on the rampage in the Richland Township area of Ohio. Farmer Sherwood Burkholder had 57 sheep badly mauled in two days. Earlier, on 22 March on Elmer Nesbaum's 94-acre farm in the same area, most of his sheep which were penned in the yard near the house were badly mauled, and very few of them survived. The creature returned on 26 March, set off six steel muskrat traps, and ripped apart the gates in front of the sheep pen, leaving fang and claw marks on the wood. Again the sheep were badly clawed 'from the backbone to the stomach' on each side, but with no attempt made to feed off the flesh. Also fang punctures were found, two on each side of the neck. On the two nights a total of 20 sheep had been killed on the Nesbaum farm. The killer continued to rampage across the country and through April and May reliable witnesses were reporting seeing a big cat, 18 inches high and grey and black in colour. By mid-May it was held responsible for the deaths of 140 sheep and various birds and dogs. At 2 A.M. on a morning in late May, two police officers and two county officials had the cat in sight in a ploughed field a few miles from Lafayette. They spread out and using spotlights began to close in on it. When they were within 35 yards, it started to walk towards them 'like it was going to be a docile animal', but when it was only 20 yards away, it made a 150-yard dash for the woods. The police officer stationed there saw it flash by and disappear into the trees. This animal showed an unnerving intelligence when faced by a group of men, and its ferocious use of claws and teeth to reach its prey is very similar to the reports detailed earlier from Scotland.[99]

Researchers have called 1977 the most spectacular year for 'phantom feline' reports. One of the grimmer absurdities of that year came from near Bay Springs, Mississippi, where pigs were having their ears, and only their ears, eaten off. The attacks started in early January when Joseph Dixon's sow died after having its ears eaten. The next day two more suffered the same fate, with the same result. On 9 January Dixon saw the animal. He said: 'It was bigger than any German Shepherd [Alsatian dog], and it was longer than any dog, and it was jumping further than any dog could jump.' Next day another pig had half its ear removed, but it survived. Dixon noted that in all these cases there was also a 2–3 inch cut in the back of the animal's neck. About this he said: 'It's not a tear . . . it's a smooth cut . . . as smooth as you would cut with a pair of scissors.' On the 16th another farmer, Ollis Martin, found his 300-pound pig with both ears 'torn out by the roots'. One ear was lying nearby; the pig survived. And so the attacks continued through February and March. One of the weirder aspects of these reports concerns the occasions when the creature was face to face with men. Far from being scared, it turned on them and only with a measure of good fortune did they escape unscathed. Joe McCullough had a close look at this alien animal and said: 'If I was standing up beside him he would near about be up to my waist. The creature had a large head and very short ears. It was black and grey, slightly resembled a dog and had a long shaggy tail.' During these three months, alien big cats were also active in the states of Kentucky, Ohio, Michigan and Illinois.[100]

In the early hours of a snowy January morning in 1978, a security guard in the Zoological Park in Washington, DC, saw the rear end of an animal wriggling under the main gate and setting off northwards. It was too large to be a domestic cat, dog or fox so the cages were checked to see what was missing. In the cheetah's exercise yard were pawprints in the snow and the city police were alerted and started a search across the north-west section of the city. When zoo officials examined the cage, however, both of their cheetahs were still securely locked up inside and fast asleep. Nothing else was missing and the mystery still stands. What the prints in the snow revealed was not stated in the news report.[101]

Lest the reader think that the US reports describe rarely seen but quite 'ordinary' native pumas, we must emphasize that although we cannot prove this is not the case, the behaviour of the animals we describe is quite out of character. Also they rarely look like pumas; and indeed in several cases they are not even definitely identifiable as cats – they look something like a cat, and something like a dog, but not clearly either.

Now some really weird 'big cat' reports – as if the previous ones were not weird enough. On Friday, 10 April 1970 Mike Busby was driving to Olive Branch, Illinois. It was 8.30 P.M. and he was due to meet his wife. Driving along a little-used road alongside the Shawnee National Forest, his engine faltered and stopped. No sooner had he got out of his car to check the engine than a large black cat-like creature with greenish glowing eyes moved quickly towards him from the shadows. Even more surprising was that it walked on its two hind legs. Before the amazed Mr Busby could move, the black, 6-foot-tall animal hit him hard in the face with its two padded front feet and then grappled with him as they rolled over together on the ground. Busby, thinking that it would go for his throat, held its head back at arm's length, while the alien animal clawed at him with dull 2-inch claws, inflicting wounds on his left arm, chest and abdomen and shredding his shirt. The beast was disturbed when a lorry came by, and loped off into the forest. Busby staggered back to his car, which started without any difficulty. When he arrived in Olive Branch the lorry driver was there and confirmed that he had seen what looked like a big cat. In the ensuing days Mike Busby was frequently dizzy and once fainted.[102] Needless to say, genuine big cats never walk in an erect position, but these aliens apparently can and sometimes do. In 1948 at the Rice Hope Plantation, Santee River, South Carolina, manager Sam Lee and Troy T. Rogers were looking for poachers. About 10.30 P.M., while they were outside their car, they heard a noise which caused Lee to switch on his torch. They saw a large cat 'like a maneless lion' slowly rear up and stand on its hind legs. As it stared at them at eye level, the two men hastily retreated to their car.[103] In Canada, Herman Belyea had to run for his life as a 6-foot-tall black cat standing on its hind legs repeatedly charged him and then jumped aside each time he swung his axe at it. It only desisted when they neared the settlement Belyea was making for. This happened in Queens County, New Brunswick, on 22 November 1951.[104]

Perhaps the weirdest report of all came from Mr A. V. Hamm who with five other people was travelling by car near Pana, Illinois, on 19 September 1970. Suddenly, as though 'it just fell out the sky', a tan and grey puma-like animal was running alongside the car. At the time Mr Hamm was quite sure that it had suddenly materialized before his eyes, though on later reflection he tried to convince himself that it must have leapt from a clump of roadside bushes.

What could not be altered was the fact that only some of the car's occupants could see it, even though they were all in a position to do so. The alien animal looked at the travellers, then jumped a fence and was lost in the brush.[105]

Although the alien big cats are often shot at, and sometimes appear to be hit, this never seems to impair their ability to escape. In common with others of their ilk, whom we shall meet in forthcoming chapters, bullets have little or no effect upon them, even when fired at point-blank range. An account from a Boston newspaper of 1823 tells how two marksmen at Russelville, Kentucky, pumped 12 rounds into a 'tiger of brindle colour' from a distance of 50 yards without affecting it at all.[106] A similar occurrence took place in April 1958 near Atlanta, Georgia, when two patrolmen, who had been searching the woods for a 'black panther', were confronted by the yellow-eyed brute charging directly at them. They emptied their revolvers into it as it went by 'like a bullet', but without effect. Officer J. F. Porter said: 'Both of us were firing at point-blank range. I don't see how we could have missed it.'[107]

The Australian continent has always been a land of zoological wonders, but big cats have never been among its fauna. But since 1956 sheep farmers have been plagued with predations on a big scale and all the signs point to pumas. Perhaps the Australian equivalent of the Surrey puma is the Emmaville panther. Emmaville is in New South Wales near the border with Queensland and just over 100 miles from the coast. Since 1959 witnesses have been seeing a large black cat-like creature bounding across roads and behaving very much as our other mystery cats do. Clive Berry, who farms 4,600 acres west of Uralla, is convinced he is dealing with something that is neither dingo, dog nor fox. During 1956–7 it killed 340 of his sheep. He has spent many nights hunting for the killer, without success. He said that he had the feeling he was hunting something intangible. The usual massive hunts with fifty riflemen found nothing.[108]

Further south in western Victoria striped animals have been seen. These might be examples of the thylacine (*Thylacinus cynocephalus*), a kind of marsupial wolf thought by most authorities to be extinct though said by some still to survive in the remote regions of Tasmania. Recent sightings suggest that it may survive on both the mainland and on Tasmania. On the other hand, the sightings may be of something that just looks like a thylacine. Some witnesses report that the creature has stripes on its shoulders, whereas the thylacine is thought to have stripes only on its back and hind-quarters. The creature that Mrs Gilbert saw in her headlights in Bournemouth, described earlier in this chapter, fitted the description of a thylacine fairly well, but there is no conceivable way one could be running loose on the south coast of England. Perhaps a striped wolf-like creature is just another disguise that alien animals can adopt.

Down at the southernmost tip of Western Australia the sheep men have in recent years been having trouble with marauding big cats. Despite the fact that no big cat has ever lived on the continent, in recent years stockmen have had hundreds of sheep killed by 'phantom' cats, and farmers, hunters, and zoologists have seen them on numerous occasions. Mobile night hunters armed with strong spotlights and high-powered rifles now cruise the bushlands, firing at the large gleaming yellow eyes that shine back at them from the darkness. Sometimes traces of blood are found but no carcase; the wraith melts back into the darkness and the sheep depredations continue. For some while now the stockmen have been saying 'It's only a question of time' before one of these big cats is hit by their bullets, but as yet that time has not arrived. When the Western Australian Minister for Fisheries and Wild Life, Mr MacKinnon, said, 'Quite obviously from the reports I have received there is a phantom animal, or animals, of some kind plaguing stock in the south west', he was far nearer the truth than he could ever have guessed.[109]

3
Mysterious black dogs

The black dog has his roots deep in the folklore of Britain. He is an enigmatic creature, friendly in some places, an omen of death or disaster in others. But whatever the significance of the encounter, the people who have seen him are unlikely to forget the experience – a statement which can safely be made in regard to *all* the alien animals featured in this book. The black dog is generally thought of as peculiarly British, but we have accounts of him from Ireland, France, Italy, Croatia (northern Yugoslavia), Germany, Austria, Pomerania (northern East Germany and north-west Poland), the United States (Mississippi, Missouri and Pennsylvania) and Canada (especially Nova Scotia), and suspect that more research abroad would reveal him to have been seen even further afield. He is also usually thought of as a purely legendary creature, alive only in tradition and folklore, but this is far from the truth, as we shall show.

If we return to Britain, we find that there are few English and Welsh counties where he has not been seen. The black dog is known by different names in different parts of the British Isles, and here are some of them: Shuck/Black Shuck/Old Shuck – Norfolk; Skeff – Garveston in Norfolk; Old Shock – East Anglia; Shucky Dog – East Anglia; Scarfe – Suffolk; Gally-trot/Gallytrot/Galley Trot – Suffolk; Moddey Dhoe – Suffolk; Moddey Dhoo/Mauthe Doog – Isle of Man; Buggane – Isle of Man; Trash/Guytrash – Lancashire; Skriker – Lancashire and Yorkshire; Barghest/Barghaist/Barguest/Bargest/Barn-ghaist – Yorkshire Dales; Cappel – Westmorland; Padfoot – Staffordshire and the Wakefield area; Hooter – Warwickshire; Hairy Jack – Lincolnshire; Shag Dog – Leicestershire; Gwyllgi (Dog of Darkness) – Wales; Le Tchan de Bouôlé – Jersey. So far as Scotland is concerned, the *cu sith* or fairy dog of the Highlands is more common, though black dogs are occasionally seen. The *cu sith* is usually green, sometimes white; other fairy dogs are usually white with red ears. Non-black dogs are also quite widely seen in England and Wales too. Usually they are white, but sometimes grey, brown, or yellow; and in some reports, just to complicate matters, no colour is mentioned. As the behaviour and appearance of the non-white dogs is often the same as that of black dogs, we have decided that they belong in the same category of alien animals, so they too are included in this chapter.

How do 'alien' black dogs differ from 'physical' black dogs? the sceptical reader might ask. How does the witness know that the dog he sees is not a local labrador out for a stroll? The principal differences are those of size, eyes and behaviour. Many descriptions refer to the dog as calf-size; others vary from 'the size of a very large collie'[1] and 'bigger than any ordinary dog'[2] to 'almost waist-high',[3] 'table high',[4] and 'as tall as a mantelpiece'.[5] The dog's coat is often remarked upon, a word frequently used being 'shaggy', and the coat is sometimes compared to that of a sheep. An exception was the dog seen in Old Leys Lane, near Willoughton, Lincolnshire. His coat was described by the man who saw him several times as 'like a *pig's* skin rubbin' agen me, bristly, an' not like a dog's coat at all!'[6] The feature of the animal which usually makes the most impression during an encounter is its eyes. These are often described as 'as big as saucers', and, even more frequently, as 'glowing'. It has been suggested[7] that 'the "large blazing eyes" are a feature which has been added to older stories and legends to add a bit of weight and colour', but in fact the glowing or fiery eyes *do* occur in some modern first-hand accounts. The dog seen by author Stephen Jenkins near Bewdley, Worcestershire, in 1943 had eyes which 'glowed faintly';[8] an Irish black dog seen in 1928 (an encounter described more fully on page 91) had 'fearsome, blazing red eyes, which seemed like live coals';[9] and the black dog seen by a little girl in Bredon, Worcestershire, during World War II (full story on page 92) 'had very large, very red eyes, which glowed from inside as if lit up'.[10] This is a feature we cannot ignore when considering the black dog as a twentieth-century 'alien animal', especially as it reappears elsewhere in this book.

All the descriptions given so far have been taken from first-hand accounts. If we take the traditional stories into consideration (remembering that these too are very probably based on fact), other features emerge, for example *headless* dogs have been reported from Dartmoor, Cumbria, Sussex, Shropshire and Suffolk. This is not as impossible as it sounds – there is a photograph of a headless dog in this book. Sometimes black dogs seem to grin at the witnesses, showing 'large, long teeth'[11] as described by a Hertfordshire schoolmaster; and more than once the witness has been aware of the dog's breath. The dog which jumped up at a Great Yarmouth, Norfolk, woman in the nineteenth century had breath 'of noxious odour' which 'struck her face in hot blasts'[12] (compare this with the descriptions of smelly BHMs in Chapter 5); and when a black dog seen on Dartmoor yawned, 'a stream of sulphurous vapour issued from its throat'.[13] Foaming and slavering mouths have also been reported. Not only are the dog's eyes as big as saucers and glowing like fire – one-eyed dogs are on record,[14] and a headless dog with its eyes glowing in the expected place.[15] The Winsford Hill, Somerset, black dog vanishes slowly until only its glowing eyes are left.[16]

Sometimes the black dog can be heard as well as seen. The Trash of Lancashire is so called because of the sound of his feet, like heavy shoes splashing along a muddy road.[17] But the black dog seen one night near St Blazey, Cornwall, by several men and boys approached with a 'clatter of hoofs' which, until they saw the animal, made them think a horse was passing by.[18] However, a noisy approach is by no means the norm. Stephen Jenkins' black dog was noticeably silent: 'There was no click of paws on the metalled road in the profound stillness. My shoes were rubber-soled and heeled, so I was making no noise of any kind myself.'[19] Other witnesses, too, remark specifically 'It made no sound.'[20] A black dog seen at Snitterfield, Warwickshire, during World War II was even more insubstantial, for it ran across a dug garden and left no footprints.[21] The *cu sith* are the ones which leave footprints, especially on the beaches of the many small islands off the west coast of Scotland.[22] Not many black dogs growl or bark, and most of the reports we have which include a vocal aspect are traditional accounts, not first-hand. The Lancashire Skriker (another name for Trash) has this name because of his screams,[23] a sound also uttered by the great dog encountered by a woman one night near Laugharne, Carmarthenshire. She fainted when, 'about four or five yards . . . [away] it stopped, squatted on its haunches, "and set up such a scream, so loud, so horrible, and so strong, that she thought the earth moved under her." '[24] The black dog of Creag an Ordain, Sutherland, growled and then turned into a Devil-figure, finally disappearing with 'a diabolical peal of laughter'.[25] The dog-cross-human creature seen in the Vale of Glamorgan made 'unearthly howlings',[26] and very occasionally a black dog actually speaks, such as happened on the road to Woolpit, Suffolk, last century. A man was confronted by a black dog which told him, 'I shall want you within a week.' He died the next night.[27]

Occasionally the black dog is heard but not seen, as was a Barguest (black dog of Yorkshire) near Grassington, one night. The witness said that he 'heerd summat come past me – brush, brush, brush, wi' chains rattlin' a' the while, but I seed nothing'; and he knew it was a Barguest, an identification confirmed later, after the noise had followed him nearly to his home, when he actually saw the creature lying across his threshold – 'a grit thing like a sheep, but it war larger . . . it war woolly like'. The story is worth continuing. The man told the Barguest to 'Git up!', but it wouldn't, it just looked at him, and its eyes were remarkable: 'as big as saucers', 'they did glower' and 'First there war a red ring, then a blue one, then a white one; and these rings grew less and less till they cam to a dot!' The dog grinned at him as he exhorted it to move. The man's wife heard him and came to the door, whereupon the dog got up and walked away, 'for it war mare freeten'd o' t'owd wife than it war o' me'![28] More recently, in 1973, a man working on the marshes behind Blythburgh church, Suffolk, heard a dog panting right by his ear, but nothing could be seen.[29] This report is interesting, in view of the notorious visit to Blythburgh church by a black dog several hundred years before (described later in this chapter). All these accounts tell of the black dog making some kind of noise, but in many reports, no sound is mentioned, which suggests that none is made or heard. There are also a few instances where a dog was neither seen nor heard, only felt. The road up to Moortown Hall in Lincolnshire was haunted by a black dog which was sometimes seen, but sometimes he was only felt, 'brushing past one's legs'. Also in Lincolnshire, a man living near Willoughton had a strange experience which ended with him being forced back against his gatepost by something which felt like 'a large dog, as big as an Alsatian, with its front paws on his shoulders'. This happened in 1933, in an area where black dogs were often seen.[30]

Black dogs are usually – but not invariably – seen at night, and one would expect that, if it were not for their glowing eyes, they would be difficult to see. However, this is not so, and in fact one witness remarked: '"No matter '*ow* dark a night it is, *you can allus see the Dog* because 'e's so much blacker"'.[31] He has also been described as coal-black, and jet-black.[32]

The behaviour of black dogs varies considerably, but in many cases a person out in a country lane late at night is suddenly aware of a black dog trotting alongside him. (Later in this chapter we shall describe the locations most often frequented.) What happens next often depends on the witness's reaction. If they do not immediately realize that the creature is 'alien', they might reach out to stroke or pat it, only to recoil in alarm as their hand fails to make contact with anything solid. We have a number of first-hand accounts of this, including one from Buckinghamshire. About 1880 a black dog was often seen accompanying a farming family's dog cart between Stewkley and Soulbury, and on one occasion a lady bent over to stroke it, whereupon it vanished.[33] A nineteenth-century hiker on Dartmoor tried to pat the head of a large black dog which had joined him on his walk, but his hand passed through it;[34] and again from Dartmoor, but a modern report: the so-called 'white hound of Cator' disappeared when a lady reached out to pat it.[35] Such behaviour on the part of an apparently solid, friendly-looking dog (note that in these cases the dogs did not have large glowing eyes but looked like normal, albeit somewhat large, dogs) would be enough to disconcert even the most stolid of citizens, but Margo Ryan who encountered a black dog at midnight in County Wicklow, Ireland, in 1952 was not immediately alarmed. She just tried again to stroke the dog – and again! The full story is worth quoting.

She was carrying home a large can of buttermilk from a neighbouring farm and was walking along a quiet country road within a short distance of her house, which is near Redcross in County Wicklow. As she strolled on in the quiet of the country night, a quiet that town people and people in mechanized country districts can never know, she heard a soft patter behind her and the next moment an enormous jet-black dog ranged up alongside and walked quietly on in company with her. After a bit, as it seemed so peaceable and friendly, she put out her hand to pat it, without looking down. But she could not feel it; her hand seemed to miss it and touch nothing. She tried again, but again she could not touch it.

This puzzled Margo, so she looked, and there it was, as solid as solid could be, though it had now moved a little away to her left and just out of reach. A moment later it was close to her again, so again she tried to pat it, but with as little success as ever. This startled her a little and she turned her head so as to look at it fully, but as she did so it moved forward and continued walking just a few feet ahead of her in the middle of the road for another fifty yards or more when it stopped, turned its head to the left, and vanished into thin air as she was looking at it. Let there be no doubt about it whatever; it did not run off but actually vanished from where it stood in the centre of the road. Besides, at that place there was a ditch, and bank with no gap where a dog could have gone.

Margo then realized vividly that the great dog stood much higher than her hand and it was not possible for her to miss it. Her hand *must* have gone through it as if it were air.

After this, her nervousness turned to positive fear, and she hurried home as quickly as she could without spilling the buttermilk. Her family received the story of her adventure with interest and all sympathy, for they are well aware of the reality of these things.[36]

On one occasion, a motorist actually ran over – or rather, through – a ghostly *white* dog which was in the habit of rushing across the road between Little Snoring and Great Snoring in Norfolk, just before World War II. Not surprisingly unnerved by this, the unfortunate driver left his car by the roadside.[37]

The dogs which people attempted to stroke must have looked friendly, but this action is rare in witnesses of black dogs. The reaction has more often been to hit out at the beast – but with an equal lack of success. A man who struck out with his walking stick at a black dog on the road between Cromer and Overstrand in Norfolk saw the stick pass right through it and the animal disappear.[38] A Lincolnshire lady nearly fainted when she had a similar experience on the road by Blyborough fishpond. A black dog was following her, to her annoyance, so '"Quick as lightning I upped wi' the umbrella I was a-carryin' an' lammed 'im one as 'ard as I could."' But the umbrella '"went clean *thruff* 'im"' and the dog trotted on beside her.[39] There are a number of similar accounts on record, including some from Missouri (USA). Near Bunker in Reynolds County, a ghost dog jumped up behind a horse rider, Dr Gordon. He shot at it, and struck it with his fist, but could feel nothing, nor did he dislodge the dog. In Peniscot County, some hunters saw an 8-foot-long black dog and one man threw an axe at it, but it passed through the dog and stuck in a tree. In Taney County about 1900 a rider struck out at a black dog with his quirt, but it slashed right through it.[40] A native of Gunthorpe, Lincolnshire, once tried to shoot a black dog, but '"'is gunbarrel busted an' 'e caame 'oame white as a sheat!"'[41] Compare this with the comment quoted in Chapter 1, concerning the possible shooting of a water monster: 'Perhaps your Lordship's gun would misfire.'

So much for the reactions of witnesses. The accounts we have just quoted indicate that the witness is rarely in control of the situation, rather it is the dog who is master. The following descriptions of dogs' behaviour will tend to confirm this. The black dog haunting the lane near the church at Geldeston, Norfolk, walks behind people, growling, snarling and becoming vicious if they try to turn back.[42] A black dog from the Vale of Glamorgan also behaves in the same way.[43] The white Gally-trot (North Country and Suffolk) chases people who try to run away from it,[44] while Trash/Skriker often walks backwards ahead of the witness.[45] There are several descriptions of dogs which swell up; and we also have one of a dog which shrank. That happened just before World War II, when the witness went out one night to post a letter in a Suffolk village. Seeing a large black dog, she thought it was her neighbour's dog and went to catch him, at which the creature shrank to cat-size and disappeared.[46] The black dog of Uplyme, Devon, 'grew bigger and bigger as he went along, till he was as high as the trees by the roadside, and then seeming to swell into a large cloud, he vanished in the air'.[47] A first-hand account of a swelling dog comes from Somerset, where a black dog guided an old man through a sea mist. He thought it was his own dog, until he got home and heard his dog barking. He turned to the black dog, and saw it grow larger and then fade away.[48] An American folklorist, N. N. Puckett, wrote: 'One Mississippi slave tells me of seeing a little white pug dog that became bigger and bigger, until it was as large as a calf.' The Negroes he talked with also told of large black dogs with 'big red eyes glowing like chunks of fire', and headless black dogs – and all this across the other side of the world from Britain, traditional home of black dogs.[49]

Having described some of the stranger characteristics of the black dog which are not found in a 'normal' dog, such as glowing eyes as big as saucers, invisibility, impalpability, swelling or shrinking, let us now examine some reports with even stranger features. These can be considered traditional tales, unless actual dates are given. The 'Shag Dog' of Birstall, Leicestershire, had 'luminous open jaws, like dying coals in a dark room',[50] while a pack of white dogs near Wellington, Somerset, 'rushed along with mouths wide open, and flame issuing from between their jaws'.[51] The black dog of Creag an Ordain, Sutherland, spat sparks and belched fire.[52] Two-headed dogs are occasionally mentioned,[53] and two dogs appearing together.[54] Chains are reported more often than one would expect. Fictional ghosts are often accompanied by the clanking of chains, but for a ghostly *dog* to have chains seems ludicrous. The presence of Black Shuck (East Anglia) was traditionally heralded by the rattling of chains, and some time in the nineteenth century a man who met him at Gorleston in Norfolk remarked that the dog was heavily laden with rattling chains.[55] More recently, in May 1945, a Norfolk man had a strange experience at Hilgay which he describes as follows:

I was aware of a faint baying as of a hound . . . after a few minutes the baying seemed to come from the right hand side of the road and was even louder, in fact quite ear-splitting . . . it was accompanied by the noise of a chain or something being dragged along the road . . . I broke into a run, but after a few minutes I had to slow down . . . the noise was much fainter and I realized that this was the first time in my life that I had been afraid of a dog, my hair was literally standing on end, but why I could not understand . . . I love dogs and have never been afraid of the fiercest in all my life.[56]

The Barguest of Grassington, described earlier, was also accompanied by the sound of chains.

Even stranger, some black dogs are not all dog. In a traditional story from Lincolnshire, the site of a former cottage at Knaith was haunted by a black dog with a woman's face,[57] while a dog with a monk's head haunts the area around Clopton Hall, near Great Bealings, Suffolk.[58] These seem to have been permanent characteristics. There are more reports describing dogs which changed their form before the witness. Sometimes the new form was that of another animal, as happened in 1905 at Hoe Benham near Newbury, Berkshire, when on a moonlit night the witness saw a large black dog turn into a black donkey which vanished after rearing up on its hind legs.[59] More often, though, the new form was human. A tale from Lowestoft, Suffolk, tells of a black dog which turned into an evil Italian while swimming with a boy in the sea.[60] Another black dog seen on nine successive evenings by a ploughboy at Lower Quinton, Warwickshire, appeared in the form of a headless woman dressed in a silk gown on the last occasion.[61] In Nova Scotia, a black dog was often seen at Rous' Brook. Sometimes only a bright light was seen, and on one occasion a man who had been drinking, and so felt brave, turned to ask why the thing was following him. It pounced on him and nearly choked him to death. Afterwards he said that 'it looked like a black dog but when it got him by the throat it seemed more like a person'.[62] Witches sometimes used to change into black dogs, and we return to the art of shape-shifting in Chapter 6. The Devil was also thought to change himself into a black dog, in fact some people thought that black dogs were manifestations of the

Devil and their descriptions reflect this belief. The black dog of Creag an Ordain in Sutherland, though at first appearing as a dog, later on seemed to have acquired 'a hideous face, human in form, with horns sticking out of its head',[63] and there are many other instances in the lore where identification of black dog with Devil is even more explicit than this.[64]

We seem to have come a long way from tales of large black dogs with glowing eyes accompanying travellers along lonely roads. Let us now return to factual first-hand accounts as we describe the ways in which black dogs disappear from view. The insubstantial nature of the beast is indicated in those instances where it is seen to walk through some solid object. A black dog which stood as high as the witness's shoulder, seen by her earlier this century near Ballaghadereen in County Roscommon, Ireland, walked straight through a closed gate,[65] as did a black dog seen in Cornwall.[66] In 1930 a black dog 'merged through' a criss-cross wire mesh fence in the Peak District of Derbyshire,[67] while just before World War I, a black dog seen at Barham, Suffolk, vanished through a brick wall.[68]

The inability of witnesses to touch black dogs or to land a blow on them also reinforces their insubstantiality, as does their method of concluding the interview. Both in traditional and modern accounts, the majority of black dogs are reported to vanish or fade from sight. This happened when Coastguard Graham Grant saw what might have been Black Shuck early one morning in 1972. He was on duty at the Gorleston rescue headquarters in Norfolk when:

Looking to the north, at about 04.45, at daybreak, on Wednesday last, April 19th, I saw a large, black hound-type dog on the beach, about a quarter of a mile north of the look-out. What made me look was that the dog was running, then stopping, as if looking for someone. I watched it for one to two minutes and then it vanished before my eyes. I kept on looking for a time, but it did not reappear.

This not unnaturally gave Mr Grant 'quite a shock', for there was nowhere the dog could have gone to – 'One moment it was there, the next it had gone.' It is interesting that Mr Grant had never heard of Black Shuck, as he was a newcomer to the district.[69] This was an instantaneous disappearance. The dog Barbara Myatt saw on the island of Hoy in the Orkneys in 1970 faded gradually from sight. She was spending a holiday in a cottage on the island, and one evening she saw a large black collie rushing along a corridor towards her.

Before she could speak to it, it faded away and none of the family
saw it again. However, on the morning they were to return home, a
loud crash awakened them (a typical poltergeist occurrence), and
some weeks later Mrs Myatt's mother died suddenly.[70] There are
variations in the vanishing. For example, Trash/Skriker tends to
vanish on the witness's inattention,[71] and sometimes a black dog
will vanish if touched.[72]

There are two other occasional methods of vanishing which we
have noted. In the first of these, the dog appears to sink into the
earth. Trash/Skriker is said to sink 'at the feet of the persons to
whom he appears with a loud splashing noise, as if a heavy stone
were thrown into the miry road',[73] and a black dog seen in
Hertfordshire by a village schoolmaster at the beginning of this
century disappeared after a few minutes, 'seeming to vanish like a
shadow or sink into the earth, and we drove over the spot where he
had lain'.[74] Connected with this mode of disappearance is the
sometimes-held belief that black dogs live in the ground. The
Birstall, Leicestershire, black dog was believed to live in a pit known
locally as Shag Dog Pit (now filled in),[75] and a Lincolnshire black
dog was said to live in a hole in a bank of a stream at Belle Hole
Farm near Kirton.[76]

Occasionally a dog disappears in a rather more dramatic fashion.
Near Budleigh Hill in Somerset a black dog 'went up in the air like a
flash of fire' on reaching a stream,[77] while a nineteenth-century
walker on Dartmoor in Devon, who was accompanied by a large
black dog, fell unconscious following an explosion and a flash like
lightning. What happened to the dog is not stated, but it seems to
have disappeared.[78] The dog seen in Pembrokeshire (Dyfed) near
the stones called the Devil's Nags was surrounded by fire,[79] and also
in Wales a 'great mastiff dog' seen near Risca, Gwent, 'transformed
itself into a great fire, as large as a small field, and resembled the
noise which a fire makes in burning gorse.'[80] The possible significance of these fires and explosions will become clearer in Chapter
6. It might be significant to mention at this point the disappearance
of a BHM (big hairy monster)-type creature seen near Uniontown,
Pennsylvania, USA on 6 February 1974. This creature was seen at
very close quarters (6 feet away), and the witness fired a gun at it,
thinking it was going to attack her. To her great surprise, it 'just
disappeared in a flash of light'.[81] (This incident is described in
greater detail in Chapter 5.)

Occasionally a black dog leaves behind traces of its presence. Black Shuck has been reported as leaving a mark on the ground as if gunpowder had exploded there, or as if a fire had been lit.[82] The only visible traces which we know can still be seen today are the burn marks on a door in Blythburgh church, Suffolk. These were said to have been the direct result of the unusual events which took place at both Blythburgh and nearby Bungay churches on Sunday, 4 August 1577. During the morning, when people were at church, a terrible storm arose, and in Bungay church a black dog suddenly appeared. His presence was fatal, for he passed between two members of the congregation and 'as they were kneeling uppon their knees, and occupied in prayer as it seemed, wrung the necks of them bothe at one instant clene backward, insomuch that even at a moment where they kneeled, they strangely dyed.' Another man was injured when the black dog 'gave him such a gripe on the back, that therewith all he was presently drawen togither and shrunk up, as it were a piece of lether scorched in a hot fire; or as the mouth of a purse or bag drawen togither with a string. The man, albeit hee was in so straunge a taking, dyed not, but as it is thought is yet alive.' Abraham Fleming, who reported this event in 'A Straunge and Terrible Wunder', also told what happened at Blythburgh:

On the self-same day, in like manner, into the parish church of another towne called Blibery, not above seven miles distant from Bongay above said, the like thing Entred, in the same shape and similitude, where placing himself uppon a maine balke or beam, whereon some ye Rood did stand, sodainely he gave a swinge downe through ye church, and there also, as before, slew two men and a lad, and burned the hand of another person that was there among the rest of the company, of whom divers were blasted.

This mischief thus wrought, he flew with wonderful force to no little feare of the assembly, out of the church in a hideous and hellish likeness.[83]

The marks on the church door are supposed to have been made by the black dog as he quitted the church.

This is apparently not the only occasion when a large dog has been seen inside a church in frightening circumstances. Bertin, a twelfth-century French historian who compiled the *Annales Francorum Regum*, wrote that in the year 856 a storm arose at Trier during a service, and the church was 'filled with such dense darkness that one and another could hardly see or recognize his or her neighbour. On a sudden, there was seen a dog of immense size in a sudden opening

of the floor or earth, and it ran to and fro around the altar.' Again at
Trier, a large dog was seen in the pontifical chair of the great church
in 867, according to the *Chronicon Saxonicus*; and in 1171 at Andover,
Hampshire, 'a certain priest, at midnight, in the presence of the whole
congregation, was cast down by lightning, with no other injuries . . .
but what looked like a pig was seen to run to and fro between his feet.'
A Tudor historian, John Stowe, wrote of a visitation suffered by St
Michael's church, Cornhill, London, when 'there arose a tempest of
thunder and lightning, and a thing of an ugly shape and sight was
seen to come in at the south window.' This creature left deep claw
marks on stones in one of the church windows, an echo of the events at
Blythburgh.[84] We shall return later in this chapter to the possible
links between black dogs and churches.

The foregoing characteristics (many taken from first-hand reports)
should have given an idea of the behaviour of the black dog; here now
are some interesting cases to give the atmosphere of a black dog
encounter. All three experiences took place this century. The earliest
of the three happened in 1928, in County Londonderry, Northern
Ireland. The witness was no country yokel, but a student at Trinity
College, Dublin, who later became a civil servant. He was a personal
friend of D. A. MacManus, from whose book *The Middle Kingdom* this
account is taken. It was Easter-time, and the witness, at home for a
holiday, decided to go fishing in the river close by.

As he was standing on the dry, gravelly edge of the bed, casting into a small
pool, he suddenly felt constrained to look to his right along the river. He could
not see far, as there was a bend less than a hundred yards away, and there the
hedge of the next field ran down to the bank. But as he looked he saw a huge
black animal come into sight, padding along in the shallow water. He could
not at first make out what it was, whether dog, panther, or what, but he felt it
to be intensely menacing, so without wasting a moment he dropped his rod
and jumped for the nearest tree on the bank, a youngish ash, and climbed till
it bent dangerously with his weight.

Meanwhile, the animal continued padding steadily along, and as it passed
it looked up at him with almost human intelligence and bared its teeth with a
mixture of snarl and jeering grin. His flesh crept as he stared back into its
fearsome, blazing red eyes, which seemed like live coals inside the monstrous
head. Even so, he could only think of it as a wild, savage animal which had,
presumably, escaped from some travelling circus.

It passed on and was soon lost to view round the next bend, and once he felt
it was well on its way, he slid down from his precarious perch, grabbed his
rod, and raced back to his house. His father was out, but he got his shotgun,
loaded it with the heaviest shot he could find, and went off in search of the

animal, feeling that no one in the neighbourhood would be safe while it was still at large. However, he drew a blank. Everyone he met, including those who must have been in its path, denied all knowledge of the animal.[85]

This witness knew nothing about black dogs at the time, and in view of this it is interesting to note the familiar features of his account: 1. dog-like creature, huge and black; 2. closely associated with water (as are many black dogs, and other alien animals); 3. looks up at witness (more discussion of this later); 4. snarls/grins at witness; 5. blazing red eyes.

Our next account is of a sighting which took place on the Suffolk/Norfolk border in the autumn of 1938, and the details were given to Alasdair Alpin MacGregor (who quoted them in his book *The Ghost Book*) by the witness Ernest Whiteland. Mr Whiteland was walking home one evening from Bungay to Ditchingham.

... about halfway between the foreman's house at the Maltings and Ditchingham Station ... I saw a black object roughly 75 yards away, coming towards me. I was on the left-hand side of the road, close to the hedge. As it came close, I could see it was a large black dog, trotting along the same side of the road as I was on. It was a lovely evening – no wind, and everything so quiet and still. As it came to about nine or ten yards away, I could see that it had a long, black, shaggy coat, and was about 28 or 30 inches tall. I moved into the middle of the road to let it pass. When it got level with me, it vanished. I looked round to see if I had made a mistake – to see if it was still running along, but could not see it. I then went and looked over the hedge, expecting to see it on the meadow, or hear it, but could do neither. I stopped, it seemed to me, for some minutes. Then a sudden fear came over me, and it did not take me long to cover the distance to my home.[86]

Mr Whiteland never saw the dog again, though he often passed the same spot; and he was another witness who did not seem to be aware of the black dog tradition at the time of his sighting. Here again we find the familiar features of 1. large black dog; 2. silence; 3. vanishes.

Our third account is taken from a letter to us, written by the witness 30 years after the event. Although she was only four years old when she saw the black dog, during World War II, she has a vivid memory of what happened.

At the time, because of the war, my mother and I usually stayed with an elderly gentleman, who had kindly taken us in as 'refugees' from London. We only went back to the capital when the bombing ceased. The cottage where we lived is still in existence, in Bredon, Worcestershire. My encounter took place one late afternoon in summer, when I had been sent to bed, but was far from sleepy. I was sitting at the end of the big brass bedstead, playing with the ornamental knobs, and looking out of the window, when I was aware of a scratching noise, and an enormous black dog had walked from the direction of the fireplace to my left. It passed round the end of the bed, towards the door. As the dog passed between me and the window, it swung its head round to stare at me – it had very large, very red eyes, which glowed from inside as if lit up, and as it looked at me I was quite terrified, and very much aware of the creature's breath, which was warm and as strong as a gust of wind. The animal must have been very tall, as I was sitting on the old-fashioned bedstead, which was quite high, and our eyes were level. Funnily enough, by the time it reached the door, it had vanished. I assure you that I was wide awake at the time, and sat on for quite some long while wondering about what I had seen, and to be truthful, too scared to get into bed, under the clothes and go to sleep. I clearly remember my mother and our host, sitting in the garden in the late sun, talking, and hearing the ringing of the bell on the weekly fried-fish van from Birmingham, as it went through the village! I am sure I was not dreaming, and have never forgotten the experience, remembering to the last detail how I felt, what the dog looked like, etc.[87]

Again the witness knew nothing about black dogs, yet several features of the encounter are familiar: 1. large black dog; 2. stares at witness; 3. large red glowing eyes; 4. strong breath; 5. vanishes.

We gave details earlier of one aspect of interaction between dog and witness – where the witness has tried to stroke or hit the dog. But there are other examples of interaction, and these are sometimes bound up with another important factor: the significance which the encounter has for the percipient. The black dog interacts with the witness when it causes him injury, and although not all black dogs are potentially dangerous, there are enough cases of injury on record to indicate that, until its intentions are clear, a black dog is best avoided! In some areas, black dogs are traditionally feared and known to be liable to attack. This certainly applies to Black Shuck of East Anglia. In one old book he is described as 'a mischievous goblin, in the shape of a great dog, or of a calf, haunting highways and footpaths in the dark. Those who are so foolhardy as to encounter him, are sure to be at least thrown down and severely bruised, and it is well if they do not get their ankles sprained or broken; of which instances are recorded and believed.'[88] There are some dramatic reports from East Anglia showing what could happen to those who had the misfortune to encounter Black Shuck, and although none are recent enough to assure us of their veracity, we will quote some and let the reader decide their value. Two men driving along a lane at Rockland, Norfolk, in 1893 suddenly encountered a huge dog. 'The driver pushed on in spite of his companion's warning . . . but as the cart touched the Thing the air was alive with waving flame and a hideous, sulphurous stench loaded the atmosphere. Within a short time the over-bold driver died and Shuck has not been seen since in those parts . . .'[89] Also in Norfolk, at Gorleston, a countryman who met Black Shuck and told him to clear off was thrown over a hedge.[90] At Hatfield Peverell, Essex, a man who struck at a black dog was burnt to ashes along with his horse, cart and its load.[91] Our final account of injury comes from Buckinghamshire. A farmer near Aylesbury found that every day when he went to milk his cows, a hedge gap on his route was always blocked by a large black dog with fiery eyes. This happened so often he finally abandoned the short-cut, until one day, when he had a friend with him, he decided to drive the dog away. Accordingly, when he reached its haunt, he raised his yoke in both hands and brought it down heavily on the dog, which promptly vanished. The farmer fell unconscious, and was paralysed for the rest of his life.[92]

Working on the basis of first-hand accounts, there is rather more evidence that black dogs are friendly (or at least harmless) than that they are dangerous. Indeed the dogs are often positively helpful. A Somerset man was led home through the sea mist by a black dog; and also in Somerset it was believed in the Quantocks that the black dog would take care of small children playing in the hills. Even in the 1930s the local women would say of their offspring: 'They'll be all right, the Gurt Dog up over, he'll take care of they.'[93] Surprisingly often, the black dog has filled a role as night-time protector of lonely women travellers, and there are a number of first-hand accounts to support this statement. In Lincolnshire in the 1930s, a school-mistress who often cycled at night along a lonely lane near Manton would be accompanied by a very large dog trotting along the grass verge. She liked to know he was there. Earlier in the century, a woman walking home from Scunthorpe to Crosby (Lincolnshire) found herself accompanied by a strange dog as she passed a group of Irish labourers, who were saying what they would have done to her if the dog wasn't with her. On arriving home she called to her husband, but when he came the creature had vanished. Again in Lincolnshire and at the beginning of this century, a woman walked to a farm near Willoughton one evening to visit a sick friend and was accompanied part of the way by a large black shaggy dog with a long tail. When she returned later in the evening, nervous at having to walk home alone, the dog rejoined her at the spot where he had left her earlier, and walked along with her until they reached the hole in the hedge where he had first appeared. She felt that he was there to protect her.[94] A Somerset woman living in Canada at the end of the nineteenth century was accompanied for several miles through a wood by a large black dog, who also reappeared and saw her home again later, finally vanishing.[95] The black dog in its guardian role protects men as well as women and children. We have already cited the case of the Somerset man who was led home through the mist, and there are tales of black dogs protecting lonely travellers against robbers, of black dogs guiding night-time travellers (for example on Birdlip Hill, Gloucestershire), and on the Isle of Man there was a black dog which prevented a fishing crew sailing to their possible deaths when a gale was imminent.[96]

This last case may indicate that the black dog has an awareness of future death. Indeed its significance for many people is that it appears as an omen of death or disaster. In many counties the black dog is a portent of death, or at least ominous – Cambridgeshire, Essex, Suffolk, Norfolk, Cumbria, Lancashire, West Yorkshire, Derbyshire, Somerset, Wiltshire – though this does not mean that a sighting in any of those counties will automatically be followed by a death. The expected death is sometimes of the witness, but not always. There are a number of first-hand reports of encounters with black dogs which have coincided with or shortly preceded a death. One will suffice to illustrate the point. On the Isle of Man in 1927 a friend of Walter Gill (author on Manx subjects) met a black dog near Ramsey. It had long shaggy hair and eyes like coals of fire and would not let him pass. They looked at each other, until finally the dog moved so that the witness could proceed. His father died soon afterwards.[97] One significant feature of this case is that the dog looked at the witness. It often seems that the dog is definitely aware of the witness, and makes a point of looking at him, as a number of the accounts we have already quoted show. In fact the dog not only looks at the witness, he stares at him, or turns his head so that he can look at him. This acts as a strong link between the two, and may mean that the dog's appearance in front of that particular witness is intentional and has some personal significance for the witness. A

Cambridgeshire man who had seen the black dog described how he would 'glare like an owd bull at yew',[98] and a Cornish witness Samuel Drew said that the dog he saw 'went close by me, and as it passed, it turned upon me and my companions huge fiery eyes that struck terror to all our hearts.'[99] Two cases from Ireland show even more clearly that the animal's looking at the witness is intentional and that the dog may be trying to convey a meaning. A girl who saw a black dog earlier this century near Ballaghadereen in County Roscommon described how it turned its head to look at her, its eyes 'almost human in their intelligence'. In 1913 a school-master staying in Ballygar, County Galway, was followed along a road at dusk as he cycled back to town. The black dog looked up at him 'in a way that made him feel uneasy', though he could not tell why.[100]

In traditional lore the black dog also appears as a forecaster of bad weather. The appearance of Le Tchan de Bouôlé (the dog of Bouley) usually presaged a storm in Jersey,[101] and when Black Shuck was seen on the road between Aldeburgh and Cromer on the East Anglian coast it was nearly always before bad weather.[102] It is interesting to note in this connection that the black dog which wreaked such havoc in Bungay and Blythburgh churches in 1577 did so during a terrible thunderstorm, and that the other appearances of strange animals in churches also took place during storms. The black dog is also widely known as a treasure guardian throughout northern Europe,[103] but as we have no first-hand accounts to support this belief, we cannot enlarge upon it here.

So far there have been few clues to the true nature of the beast. The questions asked by all those who have investigated the data still remain to be answered: *Why* do black dogs appear? *How* do they appear? What do they *mean*? Before we give some tentative answers and present some other researchers' theories, let us consider one last aspect of black dog sightings which may have a bearing on the unanswered questions. This concerns the places where they are seen.

Sometimes black dogs are seen inside houses, but this happens rarely by comparison with the number of sightings in lonely rural situations. Often the black dog is seen, or known, to patrol a set route, appearing and disappearing always at the same places. The black dog seen often between Stewkley and Soulbury, Buckinghamshire, always disappeared just before Soulbury.[104] Early this century, a young man cycling home from Leverton to Wrangle,

Lincolnshire, 'often saw the Black Dog rush out of a drove-end behind him and lope along to another lane which it turned down.' Also in Lincolnshire, a black dog seen regularly in Bourne Wood 'always left them at a certain handgate at a corner of the wood'. The dog of Moortown Hall, Lincolnshire, 'always appeared in the hedge at the same place'.[105] From many accounts it is clear that the black dog usually haunts a certain stretch of road, and knowledge of this fact is part of traditional black dog lore, as is exemplified by this quotation concerning Skeff (Black Shuck) at Garveston in Norfolk: 'He has a lane, and a place out of which he come, and he vanish when he hev gone far enough.'[106]

There are certain features of the landscape which have been noted as being the type of place where the black dog appears, disappears, or haunts. As well as stretches of road, these include: boundaries,[107] fields,[108] hedges (especially gaps),[109] green lanes,[110] crossroads,[111] wayside burials (Staffordshire),[112] graves and gallows,[113] and wells.[114] Trees are often chosen spots. At Algarkirk, Lincolnshire, a black dog was seen near three trees growing close to the church. Near South Kelsey, Lincolnshire, a dog walks along the road beside a small plantation, and the dog which frequented the stretch of road beside the fishpond near Willoughton used to disappear by a certain ash tree. One witness said he actually vanished 'up the tree, or into the tree.'[115] In the Trellech (Gwent) area, a black dog was seen going nine times round a tree,[116] and the Witch Tree near Stogursey, Somerset, was said to be haunted by Harriet the Witch in the form of a black dog.[117] On the other side of the world, a headless phantom dog was thought to live in a hollow elm tree just outside Braggadocio, Missouri, USA.[118]

Water is another prominent feature of black dog accounts, either as the place of origin (the black dog of Creag an Ordain, Sutherland, came splashing out of a loch)[119] or, more often, simply as being near to where a black dog was encountered. The black dog seen between Leverton and Wrangle, Lincolnshire, 'usually appeared near a long, deep pond surrounded by trees', and the often-seen dog near Willoughton, Lincolnshire, used to emerge on to the road where it passed by the fishpond.[120] A bullock-sized white dog reputedly haunted Bath Slough, a boggy pool near Burgh, Suffolk,[121] and the favourite haunt of the demon dog of Hergest Court, Herefordshire, was a pond on the road from Kington.[122] Trash/Skriker of Lancashire was said to plunge occasionally into a pool of water.[123] Also often mentioned are bridges crossing streams or rivers. For example, a black dog is said to haunt a culvert where a stream passes under the Wrawby road just outside Brigg, Lincoln-shire; a bridge crossing a stream on a green lane from Manton to Scotter, Lincolnshire; a bridge crossing the River Till at Willingham, Lincolnshire;[124] a bridge dividing two loughs at Pontoon, County Mayo, Eire;[125] and the place where the old Hundred Stream flows under the road at Barnby, Suffolk.[126] A Somerset black dog near Budleigh Hill vanished on reaching a bridge (as the witness said, 'they things, of course, never can abide running water'),[127] as did a black dog seen near Ballygar in County Galway in 1913. As the cyclist witness 'crossed a small culvert, the dog stopped and left him to go on alone'.[128]

The frequency with which water features in black dog accounts has been noted by several researchers, and reasons put forward to explain it. Ethel H. Rudkin, who did valuable work in collecting first-hand reports in Lincolnshire, felt that 'the Black Dog has to do with an invasion by water, up the main rivers then up the tributary streams to the springline', and she finds links between the places where the black dog was reported, and the sites of Anglian settlements.[129] Ivan Bunn, who is researching into the black dogs of East Anglia, has also noted that the great majority of encounters, in his area at least, take place near water, and he has analysed 62 stories and legends on this basis, finding that 15 dogs were seen on or very near a main river, 15 were seen on or very near the sea/coast, 16 were seen within a mile of the river/sea. The remaining 16 cases were in four categories, covering the distances 2–5 miles away, but as we do not consider that over 1 mile is 'near', we need not detail these categories.[130] Lest we seem to be accepting the black dog/water link too easily, we should also note that there are very few places in Britain where one is very far away from water (except in times of drought!), and that to be valid, Ivan Bunn's analysis should not have concentrated solely on *main* rivers and the sea, but should also have considered minor streams, ponds and pools. It is unlikely that the size of the water source is important, rather its presence. If black dog sightings were analysed in relation to *any* water source, we believe it would be found that a high proportion are very close to water at some stage in the encounter. Steve Moore is another researcher who has touched on the relationship between black dogs and water, and his theory involves the Eastern universal balancing principles of yin and yang.[131]

As some readers may know, we are advocates of the ley theory, and as we delved more deeply into black dog lore we found a number of features which linked up with our ley research. Before we discuss these, we will briefly outline the ley theory for those readers who have not met it before. In the early 1920s a Hereford man, Alfred Watkins, realized that all manner of ancient sites to be found in the British countryside, when accurately plotted on a map, could be aligned. The types of sites which seemed most valid were: stone circles, standing stones, old crosses, barrows, tumuli, mottes and baileys, moats, hillforts and camps, earthworks, holy wells, old churches and cathedrals, abbeys and other old religious buildings. Other features which could later help confirm a line were: straight pieces of road, crossroads, mark stones, old buildings, solitary and prominent hills, skyline notches, hollow or green lanes or other traces of disused road. He called these alignments 'leys', and spent much time on fieldwork which confirmed his theory. In the late 1960s his work was brought to light again, largely by John Michell who wrote a book which has proved exceptionally popular and has introduced the concept of leys to a much wider public. He also introduced a new dimension to the subject, the possibility that leys are not merely old trackways, as Watkins wrote, but have a more esoteric significance. Now a number of people are researching into leys and their meaning, and our own contribution has been to find evidence in the folklore of ancient sites which suggests that some form of energy or 'earth current' used to (and maybe still does) flow along the leys.[132]

It was the type of places where black dogs are often seen which reminded us of our ley researches. Their tendency to patrol set routes made us wonder if these routes might be on leys. Their frequent disappearance at certain points – a particular tree or gate, for example – might indicate that these are ley points, or the places where one ley crosses another. Leys sometimes pass through hedge gaps (old gaps, which have always been there to accommodate a footpath), and black dogs are sometimes seen at such points. The Buckinghamshire black dog which severely injured the farmer who attacked him was guarding a hedge gap, and one of the Willoughton (Lincolnshire) black dogs came out of and went back into a certain hole in the hedge (both cases noted earlier).

Black dogs also appear at other places which can be ley points: churchyards, prehistoric sites, and ancient trackways. Churches, especially pre-Reformation churches because they were often built on ancient sites, are frequently found on alignments. In a great many cases there is evidence which shows that before a church was built there, the site was considered sacred and there may have been a stone circle, standing stone, burial mound or other prehistoric structure located there. If, as we believe may have been the case, the energy which flowed along the leys was tapped at the various points along them, then these sites are potential power centres and this may explain why black dogs are attracted to them, or are able to materialize there. There are many accounts of black dogs appearing at or haunting churches and prehistoric remains. There was a widespread belief that churchyards were guarded by the 'church grim' in the form of a black dog.[133] The Lancashire Trash/Skriker was said to be frequently seen in churchyards,[134] as was the Black Shuck of East Anglia.[135] A friend of black dog researcher Theo Brown saw a knight in armour with a black dog in a Wiltshire church near Chippenham.[136] We have already mentioned the black dog seen beside Algarkirk church, Lincolnshire, and in the same county the churchyard at Northorpe is haunted by a black dog.[137] The Moddey Dhoo of Peel Castle in the Isle of Man frequented a passage in a church.[138] The 1577 black dog visitation took place in the churches at Bungay and Blythburgh; and also in Suffolk, a black dog was seen in Leiston churchyard.[139] In Norfolk a black dog was seen in 1930 on a road near Buxton Lamas church, a black dog haunts the lane near Geldeston church, and another the churchyard at Overstrand.[140] A black dog was seen more than once in the ruins of an old priory at Woodcutts near Sixpenny Handley, Dorset.[141]

Whereas all the churches mentioned above are in England, the prehistoric sites with black dog associations are to be found in England, Wales and Scotland. In England the sites are: the Long Stone, Minchinhampton, Gloucestershire;[142] Wambarrows, Winsford, Somerset (the dog may be guarding treasure);[143] Whiteborough, a tumulus near Launceston, Cornwall, where he appeared to a group of wrestlers;[144] Six Hills at Stevenage, Hertfordshire, haunted by several black dogs.[145] In Wiltshire, Doghill barrow near Stonehenge has a ghostly dog, while West Kennet long barrow and the Devil's Den, Fyfield, are visited by ghostly *white* dogs.[146] The dog seen at the Devil's Nags on Cot Moor in Pembrokeshire (Dyfed), Wales, has already been mentioned; another haunted a circle between Amlwch village and St Elian church, Anglesey.[147] An

Carn Mor, a cairn near Loch Tay (Tayside) in Scotland, was the place where a huge grey dog appeared.[148] Also in Scotland, black dogs were seen at Dun Borbe, Barvas, in the Outer Hebrides; at Caisteal a Choin Dubh (castle of the black dog), Craignish, Argyll; and at Dun a Choin Dubh (fort of the black dog), Knapdale, Argyll.[149] Carnac, the famous prehistoric site in Brittany, France, is also said to be haunted by black dogs.[150]

Ancient trackways and green lanes are sometimes the haunt of black dogs, and this may indicate the one-time presence of a ley along the same route. In Lincolnshire, a black dog was seen near a bridge along the green lane between Manton and Scotter; and near Willoughton Ethel Rudkin discovered that the place where a black dog was seen had once been an old trackway.[151] Peddar's Way, a Roman road which was possibly a prehistoric trackway before that, which crosses the Norfolk Breckland, has its black dog,[152] and in north Devon black dogs have been noted along the route of an ancient track from Copplestone to Great Torrington.[153]

Apart from the places where it is seen, there are also several other features of some black dog stories which are reminiscent of ley lore. In *The Secret Country* we discussed the possibility that traditions of buried treasure refer not to physical wealth but are symbolic of the energy associated with leys. As the black dog has been described as a treasure guardian in a number of traditions, as at the prehistoric sites of Wambarrows in Somerset, might this not also indicate that he has an affinity with earth currents? Also in some accounts he appears at a certain time. A white dog visited the West Kennet burial mound, Wiltshire, at sunrise on the longest day; a white dog also visits the Devil's Den, Wiltshire, at midnight;[154] the Dog o' Mause (near Blairgowrie, Perthshire, Tayside, Scotland) appeared at a certain time of the year;[155] the road between Alfriston and Seaford, East Sussex, was haunted by a white dog on Midsummer Eve every seven years;[156] and travellers on Guernsey saw black dogs between Christmas and Epiphany.[157] We noted this same time feature during our research into the folklore of ancient sites for *The Secret Country*, and there we surmised that the current passing along leys may vary in intensity according to factors not yet determined, and that only when the current is at its strongest can the effects created by it manifest themselves – in this case, black dog apparitions.[158] Similarly some black dogs appear during bad weather (in Bungay and Blythburgh churches, for example), and it may be that during electrical storms the conditions facilitate the dogs' appearances.

Finally, one intriguing tale from Norfolk which may have an important bearing on the black dog's ley associations. At Blickling Hall during the nineteenth century Lord and Lady Lothian demolished some partitions to make a morning-room.

'I wish these young people would not pull down the partitions,' said an old woman in the village to the clergyman. 'Why so?' 'Oh, because of the dog. Don't you know that when A. was fishing in the lake, he caught an enormous fish, and that, when it was landed, a great black dog came out of its mouth? They never could get rid of that dog, who kept going round and round in circles inside the house, till they sent for a wise man from London, who opposed the straight lines of the partitions to the lines of the circles, and so quieted the dog. But if these young people pull down the partitions, they will let the dog loose again, and there's not a wise man in all London could lay that dog now.'[159]

According to *feng-shui** the correct inter-relationship of straight and curved lines was vital if the favourable influences were to be maintained, and the same feature is predominant in this tale. The 'wise man from London' sounds for all the world like the equivalent of a Chinese geomancer. This story is a clear example of the ancient beliefs in the importance of balancing the earth's energies within the landscape.

We have written much about leys and our conjecture that black dogs may be associated with them. To support our beliefs we should provide details of actual leys passing through black dog sites, and this we will now try to do. The problem in trying to find leys in any specific area, based on predetermined sites, is that so many prehistoric remains have been swept away over the centuries, as industrial development has encroached on the countryside. The result is often sketchy, half-formed leys rather than conclusively authenticated ones. Ley hunters today are understandably strict in their definition of a ley, and usually at least 5 points within 10 miles are called for. Not all our black dog leys meet this criterion, but some easily fulfil it. We decided to work solely with Lincolnshire data, because another problem is that black dog sites are rarely closely defined, and accuracy is essential to ley hunting since leys are thought to be very

---

* The Chinese art of *feng-shui* was the means used by the ancient geomancers to determine the most favourable sites for buildings and other features of the landscape.

narrow. The less accurate the work is, the more the results are likely to be attributable to chance. Ethel Rudkin's valuable work on Lincolnshire black dogs has resulted in a number of clearly defined locations being available for study, so we set to work with Ordnance Survey maps and straight-edge to see if any alignments could be found. Our results are as follows:

Algarkirk church black dog[160] (OS sheet 131, 1:50000).

Surfleet church (TF 251283) – Algarkirk church (TF 291353) – moat near Strugg's Hill (TF 299367) – moat at Tytton Hall (TF 328418) (4 points in 10 miles). The ley passes through the trees beside Algarkirk church where the black dog was seen.

Northorpe churchyard black dog[161] (OS sheet 112, 1:50000).

1. Scotter church (SE 887008) – Scotton church (SK 891991) – Northorpe church (SK 894971) – moat (SK 898952) (4 points in 3½ miles).
2. Northorpe church (SK 894971) – moat near Kirton (SK 932984) – Kirton church (SK 934986) – Redbourne church (SK 973000) – edge of Castle Hills, Redbourne (SK 975000 (5 points in 5 miles).
3. Northorpe church (SK 894971) – Hemswell church (SK 931909) – Harpswell church (SK 936900) – Glentworth church (SK 946881) (4 points in 6½ miles).

North Kelsey black dog at end of road from South Kelsey[162] (OS sheet 112, 1:50000).

Newstead priory ruins (TA 000045) – Cadney church (TA 017033) – North Kelsey church (TA 044015) – black dog site (TA 046014) – black dog site near Moortown Hall (TA 065001) (5 points in 5 miles).

Blyborough fishpond black dog[163] (OS sheet 112, 1:50000).

Grayingham church (SK 935962) – black dog fishpond (SK 934946) – chapel (SK 934946) – moat at Willoughton (SK 933932) – moat at Harpswell (SK 931897) – moat at Glentworth (SK 929872) (6 points in 5½ miles).

The 'Jenny Hurn' ley, described in Chapter 6, is also in Lincolnshire, not far from the area of the black dog leys.

We stress that these leys are as yet tentative and await confirmation by fieldwork. But since it is not necessarily easy to find possible leys passing through predetermined points, and we suggest we have found seven of them (including Jenny Hurn), it would seem that the ley theory needs careful consideration. So it should be considered along with the other theories which have been put forward in an attempt to penetrate to the heart of the black dog mystery. Now we can compare other theories which have been suggested, and perhaps this will help clarify things.

Since we have tried to use as many first-hand reports of black dog sightings as possible, many of them originating during this century, one fact that we can be absolutely certain about is that people *do actually see* black dogs. They are more than folk tales, spun round firesides in past centuries. A further proof of their 'reality' is the number of cases on record where living animals accompanying the witness have reacted strongly to the presence of a black dog, showing that they too saw something unusual. A few first-hand reports will illustrate the point. The Moortown Hall, Lincolnshire, black dog was perceived by the horse pulling the baker's van and as a result the baker could not get his horse to go anywhere near the dog, so he had to leave it and walk to the house. Also in Lincolnshire, near Willoughton, a man who was alarmed when an invisible dog jumped up at him one day in 1933 also noted that his small but spirited cairn terrier 'began barking and growling at something in the hedge, backing away from it and showing signs of fright'. He had to drag the dog past the spot by its lead, and later when released it ran home.[164] In the 1930s near Pontoon, County Mayo, Ireland, a lady taking her dog for a walk encountered a black dog. When her setter, again usually a plucky animal, saw the strange creature it 'ran to its mistress with every sign of fear, its tail between its legs as it trembled close to her heels'. Strangely, when the black dog vanished a few moments later, the setter recommenced its roadside sniffing as if nothing had happened![165] Even more dramatic was the effect a French black dog had. Author Pierre van Paassen regularly saw a large black dog (which seemed quite friendly, as it was seen to wag its tail) in his house, and decided to confront it with his two 'police dogs'. The story continues in his own words.

This led to a horrible scene. The dogs pricked up their ears at the first noise on the floor above and leaped for the door. The sound of pattering feet was

coming downstairs as usual, but I saw nothing. W[...]
know, but their hair stood on end and they retreate[...]
room, baring their fangs and snarling. Presently they[...]
in excruciating pain and were snapping and biting [...]
they were fighting some fierce enemy. I had never seen[...]
panic. I could not come to their aid, for I saw nothing[...]
cudgel I held in my hand. The battle with the invisible [...] than
two minutes. Then one of my dogs yelled as if he were in [...] eath-throes,
fell on the floor and died.[166]

Having established in this chapter, we hope, that black dogs
really do 'appear' and are not figments of the witnesses' imagina-
tions, let us see how they have been regarded over the ages.
Sometimes they have been interpreted solely as ghosts, for example
in Somerset,[167] or the ghosts of dead people taking animal form,[168]
and many people have seen them as manifestations of the Devil and
as witches' familiars, as we have already stated. Dogs, sometimes
black, have been seen during poltergeist outbreaks. Woodstock
Manor House, Oxfordshire, experienced poltergeist phenomena in
1649, including the appearance of a dog-like creature (which went
under the beds and seemed to gnaw at the bed cords!),[169] and more
recently, in Canada, a big black dog was seen during poltergeist
eruptions on a farm near Shawville, Province of Quebec, in 1889.[170]
Some black dogs have had connections (at least in the minds of the
witnesses) with religion. Patricia Dale-Green gives examples of
black dogs in the Tyrol, Bavaria, and Pomerania which were
exorcized by the use of religious artefacts;[171] the famous exorcist the
Revd Dr Donald Omand exorcized the black dog of Kettleness,
North Yorkshire, in the 1950s;[172] and in Wales a man who was
regretting having broken the Sabbath was assailed by a variety of
animal ghosts including a large greyhound which vanished as he
watched it.[173]

The tendency of most people to see the black dog as a denizen of
the nether worlds, strongly connected with death and evil, is
perhaps understandable in view of the complete absence of explanation from any intelligent source. But even people who have delved
deeply into black dog lore are at a loss to know exactly which label to
pin on him. His story is so complex. Folklorists naturally tend to
concentrate on the folklore aspects, which leads them to make
statements such as Theo Brown's tentative conclusion: 'It begins to
look as though our creatures are faintly echoing some half-forgotten

...gy of vast antiquity.'[174] We do wonder, though, if the ...orists remember that black dogs have really been seen and *still are seen today*. We feel it is probably misleading to try to base black dogs on myths and archetypes; the people who see them know nothing of these things, indeed usually they have not even heard of the black dog tradition! And if the black dog were an archetype, would it continually reappear in the same place? That it haunts certain locations reveals that it is intimately connected to the earth. People who have not known of earlier sightings have reported seeing the black dog exactly where it was seen before. Equally unlikely, for the same reasons, is the theory that black dog sightings are some faint memory of ancient raiders, as Ethel Rudkin tried to show.[175] Whatever the black dog stimulus is, it is still alive today.

Having come right up to date, we ought finally to consider those instances where a black dog or something closely resembling one has been sighted in circumstances rather different from its traditional role, as demonstrated so far in this chapter. If that black dog and the ones we are about to describe have the same origin, it would seem that the black dog changes its habits to suit the times. When people were preoccupied with the Devil, it was seen as a devilish creature. Today we are experiencing such unusual phenomena as UFOs, cattle mutilations and sightings of big 'cats', and black dogs, or at least large dog-like animals (which is really how we should describe them), have been reported in connection with all these phenomena recently. In Burnley, Lancashire, a woman who had previously sighted a UFO, and whose husband had seen a shadowy figure in their home, was awoken at 2.25 A.M. on 23 August 1977 (*exactly* a year after her UFO sighting, even to the minute) by a knocking on the door. She went and opened it, but there was only a big white dog staring in at her. She went away and the knocking started again, but this time when she opened the door there was nothing there. Going upstairs, she put out the lights and waited with the window open. When the knocking began again she looked out, but there was no one there. The next day a UFO was reported as having been seen over the town during the previous night.[176] In South Africa and the United States there have been reported incidents linking black dogs even more closely with UFOs; more details are given in Chapter 6.

Cattle mutilation sounds like a gruesome subject, and indeed it is. Recently in America, hundreds of cattle have been found dead in mysterious circumstances, over a period of years and over a wide area. Fortunately there are no known cases of this in Britain yet, but we do have information on an equally distressing outbreak, that of pet murders and mutilations. This has happened in several parts of Britain, with no clues as to the culprit and the circumstances often mysterious. The relevance to the black dog phenomenon is that on two occasions black dogs were observed at the scene of the crime, in Coventry in May 1977 (when a man saw a large black dog with three rabbits on his lawn. He trapped the dog in his garden shed but it escaped through a second door which had been forced, as had the rabbit hutch doors – not the work of a dog, one would have thought), and in Pembroke Dock near Haverfordwest, South Wales, in August 1976 (where a woman saw a large black labrador-type dog running off with her rabbit in its mouth. The dog dropped the rabbit when the house-dog began to bark; and it had apparently torn wire-netting to get at the rabbit).[177] Admittedly these black dogs could be ordinary physical dogs of a particularly cruel nature, but there are facets of their behaviour (and in the other cases where no dogs were seen) which do not sound like typical dog behaviour, but have similarities to the behaviour of some of the creatures described in Chapter 2. The connection between these 'big cats' and black dogs is that it has been suggested that the cats are a modern manifestation having the same origin as the black dogs. This may be so, and indeed an Irish black dog witness who saw the creature padding along a shallow river in 1928 (already quoted in detail earlier) did say that at first he could not make out what the creature was, 'whether dog, panther, or what'.[178] This strengthens our suspicions that although 'black dogs' often *look* like dogs, they would not in fact pass the close scrutiny of a Crufts judge. Could it be possible that the pumas, lions and other members of the cat family we have described are in fact really 'black dogs', or vice versa? Sometimes black 'big cats' have been reported, though such coloration is in fact rare in 'normal' big cats.

Let us finally reiterate our own impressions of the black dog, acquired after having read much about him. Although he is a highly complex creature, with his traditional lore overlaid by exaggeration and superstition, his 'reality' shines through, a conclusion confirmed by the number of first-hand reports of him from reliable witnesses. If he sometimes has a close personal link to the witnesses, shown by his tendency to look or stare at them, and apparently with the ability to predict or be aware of present or future family deaths, he also shows an even stronger link to the place he haunts. The black dog is an alien animal in the eyes of twentieth-century man, who cannot understand and rarely comes into contact with forces operating below the surface of his life, but the black dog is not alien to the landscape. He is an often-invisible part of it, brought to sight from time to time by energies we do not comprehend and for reasons which we have not yet grasped.

4

Giant birds and birdmen

We have found monstrous creatures inhabiting the earth's waters and elusive cats and dogs on the land; are there then equally weird creatures in the sky? Although we have fewer reports of alien 'winged things' than of the other creatures, they compensate for their lack of numbers by their variety of appearance. There are four basic types of 'winged thing' in this chronological account of them: enormous birds, usually of unknown species; weird unidentifiable creatures with wings; weird creatures with some human features and wings; and apparently human figures with wings. Not included are those accounts which describe men with wings obviously strapped to them; the foremost criterion is that, as far as can be known, the wings are part of the body.

Our earliest account dates from 1838 and the incident took place in the Valais, Switzerland.

A little girl, five years old, called Marie Delex, was playing with one of her companions on a mossy slope of the mountain, when all at once an eagle swooped down upon her and carried her away in spite of the cries and presence of her young friend. Some peasants, hearing the screams, hastened to the spot, but sought in vain for the child, for they found nothing but one of her shoes on the edge of a precipice. The child, however, was not carried to the eagle's nest, where only two eaglets were seen, surrounded by heaps of goat and sheep bones. It was not till two months after this that a shepherd discovered the corpse of Marie Delex, frightfully mutilated, and lying upon a rock half a league from where she had been borne off.[1]

Nothing too strange about that, one might think, just a tragic 'act of nature'. But zoologist Dr Bernard Heuvelmans says: 'the most powerful eagle cannot lift more than a rabbit or a small lamb';[2] though the American Bald Eagle has been known to take spotted fawns. Later we quote reports of other birds that have attempted to carry off bigger children, as old as ten years, and the experts invariably say, 'There is no known bird that can lift a child.' Their claws are apparently too weak. So, are the experts wrong, or are we dealing with an *unknown* bird? In 1868 an 8-year-old American child was taken, again by an 'eagle', in Tippah County, Missouri. His teacher tells the tale:

A sad casualty occurred at my school a few days ago. The eagles have been very troublesome in the neighbourhood for some time past, carrying off pigs, lambs, &c. No one thought that they would attempt to prey upon children; but on Thursday, at recess, the little boys were out some distance from the house, playing marbles, when their sport was interrupted by a large eagle sweeping down and picking up little Jemmie Kenney, a boy of eight years, and flying away with him. The children cried out, and when I got out of the house the eagle was so high that I could just hear the child screaming. The alarm was given, and from screaming and shouting in the air, &c., the eagle was induced to drop his victim; but his talons had been buried in him so deeply, and the fall was so great, that he was killed – or either would have been fatal.[3]

In the same year, 1868, during April, workmen in Chile reportedly saw a strange sight at Copiapo:

Yesterday, at about five o'clock in the afternoon, when the daily labours in this mine were over, and all the workmen were together awaiting their supper, we saw coming through the air, from the side of the ternera, a gigantic bird, which at first we took for one of the clouds then partially darkening the atmosphere, supposing it to have been separated from the rest by the wind. Its course was from north-west to south-east; its flight rapid and in a straight line. As it was passing a short distance above our heads we could mark the strange formation of its body. Its immense wings were clothed with a grayish plumage, its monstrous head was like that of a locust, its eyes were wide open and shone like burning coals; it seemed to be covered with something resembling the thick and stout bristles of a boar, while on its body, elongated like that of a serpent, we could only see brilliant scales, which clashed together with a metallic sound as the strange animal turned its body in its flight.[4]

The description sounds incredible – feathered wings, body covered with bristles *and* scales? But this account should not be rejected out of hand. The eyes which 'shone like burning coals' are becoming a familiar feature in these alien animal reports and will become even more familiar as we continue; and later in the present chapter and closer to the present day we shall describe some 'birds' which are equally as weird as the Copiapo specimen.

A winged human form was seen in the skies near Brooklyn, New York, on 18 September 1877,[5] and in September 1880, not far away at Coney Island, a similar figure was seen.

One day last week a marvellous apparition was seen near Coney Island. At the height of at least 1,000 feet in the air a strange object was in the act of flying toward the New Jersey coast. It was apparently a man with bat's wings and improved frog's legs. The face of the man could be distinctly seen [1,000 feet away?] and it wore a cruel and determined expression. The movements made by the object closely resembled those of a frog in the act of swimming with his hind legs and flying with his front legs . . . When we add that this monster waved his wings in answer to the whistle of a locomotive and was of a deep black color, the alarming nature of the apparition can be imagined. The object was seen by many reputable persons and they all agree that it was a man engaged in flying toward New Jersey.[6]

A flock of birds resembling giant buzzards but with a wingspan of over 16 feet was seen by Fred Murray in Dent's Run, Cameron County, Pennsylvania, in 1882;[7] but whether the Tombstone, Arizona, 'Thunderbird' of 1886/1890 was seen, let alone killed as was claimed, is a question difficult to answer. In the early 1970s the staff of the Society for the Investigation of the Unexplained were beside themselves, all because of a missing photograph. This is said to have shown the Tombstone thunderbird 'strung up with outstretched wings against a barn, with six men with outstretched arms fingertip to fingertip, to show its size.' Although the picture and the story were said to have been published in the Tombstone *Epitaph*, no trace of them could be found in the paper's files. But many people claimed to have *seen* the picture, though no one could track it down. Despite repeated requests for help in their journal *Pursuit*, SITU do not seem to have located it.[8] If this photograph really shows a giant bird, then it is vital evidence towards proving that such creatures do exist. The disappearance of the photograph is but another variation on the problems (as described in Chapter 1) that occur when photography is used as evidence for the existence of alien animals. The whole Tombstone saga is further complicated by an article from the Tombstone *Epitaph* for 26 April 1890:[9]

A winged monster, resembling a huge alligator with an extremely elongated tail and an immense pair of wings, was found on the desert between Whetstone and Huachuca mountains last Sunday by two ranchers who were returning home from the Huachucas. The creature was evidently greatly exhausted by a long flight and when discovered was able to fly but a short distance at a time. After the first shock of amazement had passed the two men, who were on horseback and armed with Winchester rifles, regained sufficient courage to pursue the monster and after an exciting chase of several miles succeeded in getting near enough to open fire with their rifles and wounding it. The creature then turned on the men, but owing to its exhausted condition they were able to keep out of its way and after a few well directed shots the monster partly rolled over and remained motionless. The men cautiously approached, their horses snorting in terror, and found that the creature was dead. They then proceeded to make an examination and found that it measured about 92 feet in length and the greatest diameter was about 50 inches. The monster had only two feet, these being situated a short distance in front of where the wings were joined to the body. The head, as near as they could judge, was about 8 feet long, the jaws being thickly set with strong, sharp teeth. Its eyes were as large as a dinner plate and protruding about half way from the head. They had some difficulty in measuring the wings as they were partly folded under the body, but finally got one straightened out sufficiently to get a measurement of 78 feet, making the total length from tip to tip about 160 feet. The wings were composed of a thick and nearly transparent membrane and were devoid of feathers and hair, as was the entire body. The skin of the body was comparatively smooth and easily penetrated by a bullet. The men cut off a portion of the tip of one wing and took it home with them. Late last night one of them arrived in this city for supplies and to make the necessary preparations to skin the creature, when the hide will be sent east for examination by the eminent scientists of the day. The finder returned early this morning accompanied by several prominent men who will endeavour to bring the strange creature to this city before it is mutilated.

This apparently is *not* the same incident as the 1886 killing. Researcher Mr X comments: 'No mention of this creature is made in the following issues of the *Epitaph*, and it appears to be an entertaining hoax.' Can the same be said for the 1886 'killing'? If only that elusive photograph could be found!

The final reports of the nineteenth century come from Webster County, West Virginia, where several sightings of a giant bird were made in 1895. On 7 February, Deputy Sheriff Rube Nihiser and his son, who were hunting near Owl Head Mountain, heard screams and saw a 'giant eagle' carry off a fawn. Five days later, bear-hunter Peter Swadley was attacked without warning by a giant bird and badly hurt. His dog was carried off. The same bird was also thought to be responsible for the disappearance of 10-year-old Landy Junkins on 1 February. Her tracks were traced in the snow until they left the path and turned around several times. It seemed that she had vanished into thin air. Also early in February, a sheep was taken from several kept in a shed, through a hole the thief had made in the shed roof. A truly phenomenal eagle! The bird, having a wingspread of 15–18 feet, a body as large as a man's, and big eyes, was also seen several times in the distance; and it was recalled that two large birds had caused trouble in the area many years previously.[10]

Our first report from the twentieth century comes from the Sikhote-Alin mountains near Vladivostok, eastern USSR, just across the sea from northern Japan. The event, an apparent sighting of a winged man, took place on 11 July 1908 near the mouth of the River Gobilli.

The rain stopped, the temperature of the air remained low and the mist appeared over the water. It was then that I saw the mark on the path that was very similar to a man's footprint. My dog Alpa bristled up, snarled, and then something rushed about nearby trampling among the bushes. However, it didn't go away, but stopped nearby, standing stock-still. We had been standing like that for some minutes . . . then I stooped, picked up a stone and threw it towards the unknown animal. Then something happened that was quite unexpected: I heard the beating of wings. Something large and dark emerged from the fog and flew over the river. A moment later it disappeared in the dense mist. My dog, badly frightened, pressed itself to my feet.

After supper I told the Udehe-men about this incident. They broke into a vivid story about a man who could fly in the air. Hunters often saw his tracks, tracks that appeared suddenly and vanished suddenly, in such a way that they could only be possible if the 'man' alighted on the ground, then took off again into the air.[11]

Only six months later, in January 1909, the state of New Jersey, USA, was visited by perhaps the weirdest 'winged thing' described so far. The creature became known as the Jersey Devil, a name which has been used to describe several different kinds of alien animal phenomena in the state over the years.[12] The week of 16–23 January was an active one for Jersey Devil spotters: many people saw the creature, and we can quote only a few of the most spectacular sightings here. E. W. Minster, the Postmaster of Bristol, Pennsylvania (just over the border from New Jersey), was an early witness, seeing it on 17 January.

I awoke about two o'clock in the morning . . . and finding myself unable to sleep, I arose and wet my head with cold water as a cure for insomnia. [!]

As I got up I heard an eerie, almost supernatural sound from the direction of the river . . . I looked out upon the Delaware and saw flying diagonally across what appeared to be a large crane, but which was emitting a glow like a fire-fly.

Its head resembled that of a ram, with curled horns, and its long thick neck was thrust forward in flight. It had long thin wings and short legs, the front legs shorter than the hind. Again, it uttered its mournful and awful call – a combination of a squawk and a whistle, the beginning very high and piercing and ending very low and hoarse.

In Gloucester City, New Jersey, Mr and Mrs Nelson Evans watched the monster for ten minutes on their shed roof at 2 A.M. on 19 January and described it as

about three feet and a half high, with a head like a collie dog and a face like a horse. It had a long neck, wings about two feet long, and its back legs were like those of a crane, and it had horse's hooves. It walked on its back legs and held up two short front legs with paws on them. It didn't use the front legs at all while we were watching. My wife and I were scared, I tell you, but I managed to open the window and say, 'Shoo!', and it turned around, barked at me, and flew away.

The drawing made at the time and based on that description shows how incredible a beast it must have been! (We do not know if Nelson Evans approved of the newspaper artist's sketch.) Evans' description was not unique, however. Others noted tracks as if made by horseshoes; and most reports mentioned its long thick neck and long thin legs. Its facial features were apparently more difficult to describe. Trolley conductor Lewis Boeger saw the Jersey Devil at Haddon Heights, New Jersey, *again* about 2 A.M., on 21 January and described its features as 'hideous'. He also commented that it generally 'resembled a kangaroo'. In Trenton on the same morning, theatre doorkeeper William Cromley saw a beast with the face of a German Shepherd dog, with large sparkling eyes; and also on the 21st it seemed that the Jersey Devil had at last reached the end of the line. William Wasso, track-walker on the electric railway between Clayton and Newfield, watched the beast sniff the rail, and saw its long tail touch it. An explosion melted 20 feet of track and the Jersey Devil was no longer there. But the sigh of relief in New Jersey was premature, for that same afternoon he was seen again in Philadelphia (just over the border in Pennsylvania)! He stood in a house yard and spewed flames from his mouth as Mrs J. H. White went to fetch in her washing. And at 7 P.M. that evening he was back in New Jersey, at Camden, where he seized a pet dog. He was seen again the next day, Friday, but then disappeared as suddenly as he had arrived.

An interesting account from the *Philadelphia Record* describes an event that took place some time during that same incredible week.

Theodore D. Hackett tells how he rescued a fellow telephone company lineman from the Jersey Devil.

In an isolated spot in the Jersey Pines, about five miles from Pleasantville, at a place known as Beaver Pond, one of the linemen, Howard Campbell, was detailed on a piece of work a little distance from the rest of the men on duty. After walking a little way into the woods, his attention was attracted by something coming down the path toward him. He became so frightened by the unusual appearance of the thing that he straightway made for the nearest telegraph pole. Letting out several yells for help and losing his wits entirely by the time he reached the top of the pole, Campbell threw himself out on the mass of wires between the two poles and was lying there helpless by the time the rest of the gang, including myself, had arrived.

Seeing the 'Terror' on the pole, I raised my gun and fired. One shot broke a wing and it fell to the ground, uttering hideous screams; but before anyone could collect his wits the thing was up and off with long strides and a sort of hop, dragging one wing, and then disappearing into the pine thicket.

We got ropes and other tackle and helped Campbell down from his precarious position. As nearly as I can describe the terror, it had the head of a horse, the wings of a bat and a tail like a rat's, only longer.

Neither shooting nor electrocution seems to have deterred the Jersey Devil. Its vanishing trick when electrocuted and its sudden arrival and departure in the area suggest that it may not have been an entirely physical creature. As we have already seen, many apparently substantial alien animals seem on occasion to be insubstantial.

There is a time lapse of 17 years before the next case we have on record, and that is a brief account of two young boys being attacked by a very large and very aggressive 'feathered thing' between Mount Hawke (!) and Porthtowan in Cornwall. The bird was killed, after a struggle, but could not be identified.[13] Around 1930 the Jersey Devil may have put in a brief reappearance, for two Erial, New Jersey, men saw a creature with the 'body of a man, head of a cow, large bat wings, big feet' which 'flew up in the air, and cut off the tops of trees'. Two girls, one a daughter of an Erial witness, saw the same thing at the same place a while later, and in 1935 Philip Smith saw what may have been the Jersey Devil in Woodstown, New Jersey.[14]

In the 1940s huge birds again stole the scene. An early sighting took place around 1940 when author and local historian Robert Lyman claims to have seen a thunderbird in the Pennsylvania Black Forest.

It was on the ground in the center of the Sheldon Road, about 2 miles north of Coudersport. It was brownish in color. Legs and neck were short. It was between 3 and 4 feet tall and stood upright like a very large vulture. When I was about 150 feet away it raised to fly. It was plain to see its wingspread was equal to the width of the roadbed, which I measured and found to be 25 feet. I will concede it may have been 20 feet but no less. The wings were very narrow, not over one foot wide.

How could such a bird fly through the woods? The bird I saw could have gone straight up the road and missed the trees but it did no such thing. It flew off at right angles to the road, through dense second-growth timber and had no trouble.[15]

As Fortean researcher Curt Sutherly remarks in relation to this sighting: 'Most people fail to realize the vastness of our remaining American wilderness, the presence of literally hundreds of thousands of square miles of forest and unpenetrated swamplands occupying huge areas from coast to coast. *Something* lives in these areas. Why not Bigfoot or the thunderbird?'[16] Why not, indeed.

Having mentioned the thunderbird several times, some explanation of the origins of the term might be helpful. It comes from American Indian mythology in which thunder is associated with birds. Whether this happened because the Indians needed some explanation for the phenomenon of thunder and a huge bird seemed an obvious choice, or whether they actually saw huge birds which made a sound like thunder with their wings, is not known. But since we have reliable recent accounts of sightings of huge birds, there is no reason to doubt that American Indians across the continent have been seeing similar birds for centuries, and incorporated them in their folklore. They still see them, too. James Red Sky, an Ojibway Indian from the Thunder Bay, Ontario, Canada, region, said: 'We saw a thunderbird a few summers ago. A huge bird it was; a lot bigger than planes you see go by today. It didn't flap its wings. Not even once. It was white on the underside, black on top.' The folklorist who collected this account heard other similar ones from the Ojibway Indians.[17]

The piasa ('bird which devours men') was also a part of American Indian lore and petroglyphs illustrating the creature were painted on rock near the present-day city of Alton, Illinois, some centuries ago. The first account of the petroglyphs was given by missionary explorer Jacques Marquette in 1675. He said that the creatures are as large As a calf; They have Horns on their heads Like those of a deer, a horrible look, red eyes, a beárd like a tiger's, a face somewhat like a man's, a body covered with scales, and so Long A tail that it winds all around the body, passing above the head and going back between the legs, ending in a fish's tail.

Interesting similarities to note are that at least one witness of the Jersey Devil has described horns on its head; red eyes are a regular feature of alien animals; manlike faces will reappear later in this chapter; the Chilean 'bird' had a scaly body; and the Jersey Devil had a long thin tail. Others saw and described the petroglyphs in later years and the mention by P. A. Armstrong in 1827, that the wings were batlike but in the shape of an eagle, is, we think, significant. Batlike wings will be mentioned again in this chapter. The Indians dreaded the image of the piasa and used to fire at the painting as they passed by on the river. The original Piasa Rock no longer exists, but in the 1970s a traditional version of the piasa design was repainted on a bluff in Norman Park.[18]

Later in the 1940s reports of 'big bird' sightings began to accumulate. The first case we have on record dates from April 1947 and tells how farmers around Ramore, Ontario, Canada, saw a giant black bird with yellow eyes 'the size of silver dollars', huge talons, and a hooked beak which was preying on livestock.[19] Nine months later 12-year-old James Trares was the first to see the big bird which soon became a frequent visitor to the Illinois skies. One evening in January 1948 he rushed indoors to tell his mother: 'There's a bird outside as big as a B-29!' It was a grey-green colour and flapped its wings as it flew. Not until 4 April was it seen again in the state, this time by former army colonel Walter Siegmund. He did not draw his companions' attention to the sight, a gigantic bird flying at about 4,000 feet, because, he said, 'It looked too incredible.' He commented: 'I thought there was something wrong with my eyesight, but it was definitely a bird and not a glider or jet plane. It appeared to be flying northeast. Two army planes had just flown over in the same direction and I thought it was a pursuit craft following them. But from the movements of the object and its size, I figured it could only be a bird of some tremendous size.' A few days later, on 9 April, Mr and Mrs Robert Price saw the 'monster' bird from their farm near Caledonia, Illinois. It was bigger than a plane, had a long neck and big powerful wings, and behind it trailed what they supposed were its feet. On the same day truck driver Veryl Babb of Freeport, Illinois, also saw the bird. The next day, 10 April, it was seen by Mr and Mrs Clyde C. Smith and Les Bacon of Overland, Illinois. Mr Smith was the first to see it, in the morning. 'I thought it was a type of plane I had never seen before. It was circling and banking in a way I had never seen a plane perform and I kept waiting for it to fall.' Later in the morning all three saw it, and thought it was a plane until it began to flap its wings.

'An enormous, incredible thing with a body that looked like a naval torpedo' was seen over Alton, Illinois, on 24 April by E. M. Coleman and his son. They estimated its height at 500 feet, and said that it 'cast a shadow the same size as that of a Piper Cub at the same height.' On the same day two St Louis, Missouri, policemen saw the bird, 'as big as a small airplane', flying at night and silhouetted against the moon. Patrolman Francis Hennelly commented: 'Its wings were flapping and it was headed southwest, flying at altitude of several hundred feet. I thought it was a large eagle but I've never seen one that big before.' On 26 April St Louis chiropractor Dr Kristine Dolezal saw the 'big bird' from her apartment window. It nearly crashed into a plane, but flapped its huge wings and flew off into the clouds. The bird appeared greyish-black and had an unusual tail 'like a rectangular box which had been sawed or divided down the center.' She could also see ridges across its wings when outspread. Instructors at the Mississippi School of Aeronautics at Lambert-St Louis Field saw an 'awfully big bird' at about 1,200 feet on 27 April. At the end of April, just as official interest in 'big bird' was being aroused, the sightings suddenly ended. The last seems to have been on 30 April, when Mary and Charles Dunn and Clifford Warden saw it over St Louis, Missouri, about 10 P.M. Dunn commented:

I thought people who reported seeing the thing were 'bugs' until I looked into the sky last night. It was flapping its wings and moving quite fast at about 3,000 feet altitude and appeared to be illuminated by a dull glow. It looked about the size of a Piper Cub plane but there was no engine sound and it was not a plane. I could hardly believe my eyes.[20]

Data is scanty for the 1950s and some of those cases we do have on record involve UFOs, a new development in our 'winged things' lore. Early in the decade, two winged men were seen at Pelotas in the state of Rio Grande do Sul, southern Brazil. Luiz do Rosário

Real and his wife Lucy Gerlach Real took a walk one night in a wood beside the sea. Suddenly two fast-moving shadows crossed their path, which was lit by the full moon. Looking up, they saw two gigantic 'birds' (as they thought) flying at treetop level. When the 'birds' descended vertically and landed near the witnesses, they saw that the figures looked human and were about 6 feet tall. The 'birdmen' then crouched down on the ground. The witnesses felt they were being observed, and Luiz, being curious, wished to get nearer, but his wife prevailed upon him to leave, and they did so.[21]

A strange sighting, again of a winged man, was made in Houston, Texas, on 18 June 1953. It was 2.30 A.M. on a hot night, and three people sat talking on a front porch. Suddenly, about 25 feet away, Hilda Walker saw 'a huge shadow across the lawn. I thought at first it was the magnified reflection of a big moth caught in a nearby street light. Then the shadow seemed to bounce upward into a pecan tree.' She told her companions and they all saw 'the figure of a man with wings like a bat. He was dressed in grey or black tight-fitting clothes. He stood there for about thirty seconds, swaying on the branch of the old pecan tree. Suddenly the light began to fade out slowly.' They had time to see the man in detail and describe him as about 6½ feet tall, wearing a black cape, skin-tight pants, and quarter-length boots. 'He was dressed in a uniform like a paratrooper wears. He was encased in a halo of light,' said one witness. Mrs Walker added: 'I could see him plain and could see he had big wings folded at his shoulders. There was a dim light all around him.' Immediately after the sighting, they heard 'a loud swoosh over the housetops across the street. It was like the white flash of a torpedo-shaped object.'[22]

Three years later, on 5 April 1956, employees at the Tennessee Coal and Iron Division of US Steel at Birmingham, Alabama, reported seeing a silver-coloured 'angel' flying north over the plant, flapping its wings.[23] A 'big bird' was seen in 1957 over Renovo, Pennsylvania. On 27 March H. M. Cranmer and a friend saw it at a height of about 500 feet. 'Its wing motion,' said Cranmer,

reminded me of a blue heron, except the bird was lighter and grayer in color. I called the American Legion and inquired if anyone had seen a big bird half an hour before. A man who had just come in said it had flown over Westport, come down Fishdam Run and then flown up Two-Mile Run. He said its wingspread was 25 or 30 feet. A week later another flew the same course. Two weeks later another flew a different course . . . Each time there were several witnesses.[24]

If the 1950s was a quiet decade for sightings of 'winged things', the 1960s more than made up for it. The first sighting of the decade which we have on record was made in West Virginia, where in 1960–1 a lady driving with her father along Route 2 by the Ohio River saw a tall manlike figure on the road in the Chief Cornstalk Hunting Grounds.

I slowed down and as we got closer we could see that it was much larger than a man. A big gray figure. It stood in the middle of the road. Then a pair of wings unfolded from its back and they practically filled the whole road. It almost looked like a small airplane. Then it took off straight up . . . disappearing out of sight in seconds. We were both terrified. I stepped on the gas and raced out of there. We talked it over and decided not to tell anybody about it. Who would believe us anyway?[25]

It was in this same area that the incredible 'Mothman' appeared a few years later, in 1966.

In May 1961 a 'big bird' was seen over the Hudson River Valley by a businessman flying a small plane. It buzzed him 'like a fighter plane making a pass', and he saw with amazement that it was huge, drifting 'with scarcely a movement of its wings'. He added the information that it was 'a damned big bird, bigger than an eagle. For a moment I doubted my sanity because it looked more like a pterodactyl out of the prehistoric ages.'[26] This comment casts a new light on the 'big bird' sightings. Are these creatures really birds, or prehistoric winged reptiles? Some features of the witnesses' descriptions may suggest a pterosaur (a group of extinct gliding reptiles, for which 'pterodactyl' is another name) rather than a bird – batlike wings, enormous wingspan, weird facial features, long neck – so we certainly ought to keep an open mind about this possibility, incredible though it may seem. The skeleton of a pterosaur was discovered in Big Bend National Park, Texas, in 1975 by Douglas Lawson, a graduate student at the University of California.[27] It had a wingspan of 51 feet, and it would not seem possible for such a creature to take off from the ground. It is thought that it jumped off cliffs and glided on air currents. It is also thought that the chest bone could not support muscles capable of flapping the huge wings, and so they were used for manoeuvring in the air currents. The main visible features of the pterosaur are: long, thin hind legs; neck held upright in flight with head at right angles pointing forward; long slender beak; large eyes; hair-covered body; batlike, leathery wings.

Some of the sighting reports described so far do sound similar to this, especially the reports of the Jersey Devil. But can we really claim that the Jersey Devil was a pterosaur? The problem is, of course, that all pterosaurs became extinct by the end of the Cretaceous period, that is, 65 million years ago. But just suppose that a form of pterosaur had survived until the present day. After all, the coelacanth did. But the nature of his environment meant that he could remain hidden relatively easily. If pterosaurs lived today, especially gigantic kinds, then far more sightings would be expected than is the case. Unless, to add another weird dimension to the whole enigma, the creature is not wholly physical but materializes from time to time when the conditions are right. While discussing pterosaurs we should also mention the *Archaeopteryx*, an early form of bird, because some of the recent sightings might possibly be identified as this large feathered creature. As well as feathered wings he had a long feathered tail and hooked claws on his wing ends. His jaws were long and contained small sharp teeth. He is thought to have been a glider, as was the pterosaur, and it is interesting that some reports of 'big bird' include the information that it was never seen to flap its wings.

If an article in an 1856 issue of the *Illustrated London News*[28] is to be believed, at least one pterosaur survived until the last century in France.

A discovery of great scientific importance has just been made at Culmont (Haute Marne). Some men employed in cutting a tunnel which is to unite the St Dizier and Nancy railways, had just thrown down an enormous block of stone by means of gunpowder, and were in the act of breaking it to pieces, when from a cavity in it they suddenly saw emerge a living being of monstrous form. This creature, which belongs to the class of animals hitherto considered to be extinct, has a very long neck, and a mouth filled with sharp teeth. It stands on four long legs, which are united together by two membranes, doubtless intended to support the animal in the air, and are armed with four claws terminated by long and crooked talons. Its general form resembles that of a bat, differing only in its size, which is that of a large goose. Its membranous wings, when spread out, measure from tip to tip 3 metres 22 centimetres (nearly 10 feet 17 inches). Its colour is a livid black; its skin is naked, thick, and oily; its intestines only contained a colourless liquid like clear water. On reaching the light this monster gave some signs of life, by shaking its wings, but soon after expired, uttering a hoarse cry. This strange creature, to which may be given the name of living fossil, has been brought to Gray, where a naturalist, well versed in the study of paleontology, immediately recognized it as belonging to the genus

Pterodactylus anas, many fossil remains of which have been found among the strata which geologists have designated by the name lias. The rock in which the monster was discovered belongs precisely to that formation the deposit of which is so old that geologists date it more than a million years back. The cavity in which the animal was lodged forms an exact hollow mould of its body, which indicates that it was completely enveloped with the sedimentary deposit.

Since no reference has been found to any examination being made of this creature's body, which surely would have been done as it is not every day a recently dead pterosaur is handed over to the scientists, we must have grave doubts as to the validity of this story. The publication of totally spurious news stories as if they were factual is reprehensible, which surely those responsible for such publications realize, and we find it hard to believe that many such stories are or have been published. Surely most must have some basis in fact, even if the reporter has got the details wrong and therefore does not realize he is publishing a misleading story. If such is the case, what were the facts on which the 'living pterodactyl' story was based?

Before concluding this speculation on pterosaurs let us note that, in 1976 three school-teachers driving near San Antonio, Texas (the same state where the fossil pterosaur was found) saw a huge flying creature they later identified as a pteranodon (a kind of pterosaur). (More details of this sighting are given later in this chapter.)

Now back to the 1960s, and to Sandling Park near Hythe, Kent. During the evening of 16 November 1963 four teenagers were walking along a country road when they saw a 'reddish yellow light coming out of the sky at an angle of 60 degrees.' It went behind a clump of trees and a bright golden light 15–20 feet across was then seen in a field close to the witnesses. It floated 10 feet above the ground and seemed to be watching the fearful four. It went behind trees and 'a few seconds later a dark figure shambled out. It was all black, about the size of a human but without a head. It seemed to have wings like a bat on either side and came stumbling towards us. We didn't wait to investigate.' Another of the witnesses added that the figure seemed to have webbed feet. Other strange lights were seen in the area on succeeding nights.[29]

Three years later 'big bird' put in a few brief appearances again in the USA. In mid-July 1966 a huge bird 'about as big as a Piper Cub airplane' was seen circling over Deseret, Utah;[30] and in late

November 1966 a 6-foot tall bird with a 10-foot wingspan pursued a car at speeds up to 70 mph at Point Pleasant, West Virginia. Thomas Ury was the terrified driver, and he described how the bird 'came up like a helicopter and then veered over my car. It began going around in circles about two or three telephone poles high. I zoomed up to 70, but it kept up with me easily.' The newspaper report added that the authorities believed it to be a sandhill crane.[31] Four giant brown and grey birds with reddish heads, standing 5 feet tall and with 10-foot wingspans, were seen at Lowell, Ohio, on 26 November 1966; and five pilots at Gallipolis Airport, Ohio, saw a giant bird moving at 70 mph which they at first thought to be a plane. This was on 4 December 1966. Two days later a postman in Maysville, Kentucky, saw a giant birdlike creature.[32]

This was a time of intense 'winged things' activity in a small area of the USA, especially near the disused TNT Area, a World War II ammunition dump near Point Pleasant, West Virginia. The creature responsible for all the panic and publicity was dubbed 'Mothman', and it may be that some of the 'big birds' we have just described were in fact sightings of Mothman. John Keel investigated the Mothman epidemic and published his findings in several articles and a book, *The Mothman Prophecies*,[33] and we recommend this to readers who wish to know the full story. A weird one it is, too. All we have space for here is a brief résumé of some of the most dramatic confrontations with the creature. One of the earliest took place around midnight on 15 November 1966 outside an abandoned power plant on the TNT Area. Mr and Mrs Roger Scarberry and Mr and Mrs Steve Mallette, driving along a dirt road by the plant, saw a grey figure, as tall as a man, with glowing red eyes and wings, shuffling towards the door of the plant. As they drove quickly away, at times reaching 100 mph, the creature appeared overhead and kept up with them without flapping its wings. Soon afterwards a poltergeist attack broke out at the Scarberrys' home. The figure they saw is the model for all the other Mothman sightings: 5–7 feet tall, broader than a man, no arms, manlike legs (feet never seen), luminous bright red eyes 2–3 inches in diameter and apparently set in the shoulders, no head, wingspread about 10 feet and wings folded against back when not in use. (John Keel notes that such a wingspread would not support a creature of this size, but a spread of at least 35 feet would be needed in order to glide.) Other features: wings do not flap, makes a mouselike squeaking noise, grey (though some witnesses said brown) in colour, whether clothed or covered with skin not known, fast in flight (over 100 mph). On the day after the Scarberry/Mallette sighting, Mothman showed himself to Marcella Bennett of Point Pleasant, who at 9 P.M. on 16 November was visiting a friend living in the TNT Area. As she got out of the car, a grey figure with red eyes seemed to rise from the ground behind it. He was staring at her, and she stood as if transfixed while her companions ran for the house. Somehow she picked up her young daughter, whom she had dropped in fear, and got into the house. A number of sightings of Mothman were made, most of them in November and December 1966, though four men hunting in Chief Cornstalk Park, West Virginia (the same location as the encounter on page 120), saw a giant grey figure with red eyes in November 1967, a year after the main epidemic. UFOs were also seen in West Virginia while Mothman was around.[34]

An extraordinary 'bird woman' was seen near Da Nang, Vietnam, in July or August 1969. The main witness was Earl Morrison, at that time serving with the US 1st Division Marine Corps. At 1–1.30 A.M. on a still night he was on guard duty with two other men and they were sitting on top of a bunker, talking and looking around. Suddenly they saw a figure in the sky, coming slowly towards them. Earl Morrison tells the story.

... we saw what looked like wings, like a bat's, only it was gigantic compared to what a regular bat would be. After it got close enough so we could see what it was, it looked like a woman. A naked woman. She was black. Her skin was black, her body was black, the wings were black, everything was black. But it glowed. It glowed in the night – kind of a greenish cast to it ... She started going over us, and we still didn't hear anything. She was right above us, and when she got over the top of our heads she was maybe 6 or 7 feet up ... we watched her go straight over the top of us, and still she didn't make any noise flapping her wings. She blotted out the moon once – that's how close she was to us. And dark – looked like pitch black then, but we could still define her because she just glowed. Real bright like. And she started going past us straight towards our encampment. As we watched her – she had got about 10 feet or so away from us – we started hearing her wings flap. And it sounded, you know, like regular wings flapping. And she just started flying off and we watched her for quite a while.

Questioning by researcher Don Worley elicited further details: that she had fur ('I guess it had to be fur because it didn't look like feathers'); that her head hair was black and straight; that 'the skin of her wings looked like it was moulded on to her hands'; that her wings 'rippled' and their movement suggested she didn't have any bones in her arms; that her body, the front of which the men saw from below, seemed to be that of a normal, well-developed woman.[35]

Usually our reports of winged human figures describe them as 'men', but without any indication whether features are seen which tell the witness definitely that it is a man. In view of this we suspect that so-called 'birdmen' should strictly be termed 'bird people' or 'bird persons', and that no sex attribution can honestly be made. However the Da Nang sighting definitely does not come into that category. The only other female winged figure we have on record is a creature from Welsh folklore, the Gwrach-y-rhibyn. She resembled the Irish banshee, moaning and wailing to foretell death in a family, and one folklorist described her as

having long black hair, black eyes, and a swarthy countenance. Sometimes one of her eyes is grey and the other black. Both are deeply sunken and piercing. Her back was crooked, her figure was very thin and spare, and her pigeon-breasted bust was concealed by a sombre scarf. Her trailing robes were black. She was sometimes seen with long flapping wings that fell heavily at her sides, and occasionally she went flying low down along watercourses, or around hoary mansions. Frequently the flapping of her leathern bat-like wings could be heard against the window-panes.[36]

The Gwrach-y-rhibyn is not the only folklore example of a winged being. There are in many parts of the world folklore traditions which suggest that giant birds and birdmen/women are not solely a twentieth-century phenomenon but may have been around for many centuries. We have already described the American Indian traditions of the thunderbird and the piasa. In New Zealand the *poua-kai* of Maori tradition was a man-eating bird which used to fly down from its mountain nest and seize men, women and children; while in Fiji the giant bird known as Ngani-vatu or Ngutu-lei lived in a cave.[37] The roc or rukh is a more familiar name, and comes from Eastern tradition. This bird gave its name to the chess rook. It ate young elephants, and lived in Madagascar, so it was probably based on tales of the *Aepyornis*, a giant bird.[38] In Welsh lore, three giant eagles with fiery red eyes were said to guard a treasure chest in an underground vault at Castell Coch, South Glamorgan.[39] Further north, the lochs of Argyll in Scotland are said to be the home of a giant water bird, the Boobrie, which has 'a loud harsh voice and webbed feet and gobbles up sheep and cattle.' A man who saw it said it was black with a 3-foot neck, a hooked 17-inch bill, short legs, and webbed feet with huge claws.[40]

Further 'bird persons' in traditional lore include the Harpy, who is part bird, part woman – she has an eagle's body and claws, but a woman's head and breasts.[41] One assumes that her wings and body were feathered, and she sounds very like the Da Nang bird woman. But we cannot assume that the three guards in Vietnam had been reading classical literature and had somehow hallucinated a Harpy!

The Garuda was the sacred bird of India, sometimes depicted with partly human features such as having arms and legs, feathered wings and body, and a face half-man half-bird.[42] There are also part-human, part-bird-like creatures in Japanese lore, the Tengus. They haunt the mountains and especially the woodlands and forests, and have a man's body, arms and legs, but with a large beak, long wings and glittering eyes. They have a close affinity with trees, and act as guardians of the larger ones. (The Owlman, who is to be described later in this chapter and whose description is somewhat similar to that of the Tengu, usually appears in a wood.) There are stories of the Tengu, disguised as a golden eagle, kidnapping children and carrying them away, later returning them to the normal world with supernatural powers. As a result they become famed ascetics, or are treated as halfwits. (Remember that we have noted several cases of 'eagles' carrying off children.)[43]

About the same time that Earl Morrison was goggling at the Da Nang 'birdwoman', people living at Buckland and Locks Heath, Hampshire, across the other side of the world, were seeing and hearing a large brown bird early in the morning. A 'frightening, eerie screeching with two distinct notes' was heard, sometimes lasting as long as 30 minutes, and a large brown bird with a wingspan of about 4 feet was seen. Not too large a bird by comparison with those reported from America, but we include it here because the reports were unusual enough to be given space in the local newspaper, and the bird could not be immediately identified.[44] In Pennsylvania some time during 1969 a huge bird was watched by three road workers as it flew over a lake in Kettle Creek. They also saw it pick up a live fawn weighing around 15 pounds.[45]

Early in August 1970 the people of Tongham, Surrey (a village in Surrey puma country) were puzzling over a large bird, over 3 feet tall, which was seen around the village. One man said: 'It looked like something between a peacock and a turkey. It had dark wings on the outside, but when it flew away, it had white centres to them. It made a noise very much like a duck when flying.' One suggested identification was the African crowned crane, two of which had escaped from a local aviary some time before. But not all the features of the bird seen fit the description of a crowned crane. That bird is tall with a long neck and long legs, whereas the Tongham bird was described as 'between a peacock and a turkey', which would make it fatter and squatter than the crane. Although the crowned crane is dark on top and light beneath, it also has a distinctive golden 'crown' on its head which anyone describing it would hardly forget to mention. So the identification as a crowned crane is by no means certain.[46] Rather more likely to have been a crowned crane was the bird seen in a field at Harmondsworth, Middlesex, on 28 August 1974. According to a spokesman at the Windsor Safari Park, a bird of this species was apparently living in the Staines reservoir area, and they had been receiving reports of it for 18 months or two years.[47] Synchronistically, a man driving across moorland in north Powys, Wales, saw two crowned cranes feeding about 100 yards from the road near Talerddig, on the very same day as the previous sighting, 28 August 1974.[48] Since these birds could have escaped from private aviaries, we cannot claim them as true 'alien animals'. Nevertheless we record the sightings because it struck us as curious that crowned cranes should be seen on the same day in unexpected locations 200 miles apart.

During the previous year, on 21 May 1973, a huge black bird was seen in woods near Kristianstad, Sweden. When one of the witnesses tried to photograph it with a telephoto lens, the film jammed![49] (This constant 'psychic sabotage' explains why so few photographs of alien animals exist; researchers must consider themselves fortunate that they have any at all.)

The first five years of the 1970s are poor in 'winged things' sightings, and 1975 is little better. But something strange was happening in Puerto Rico that year. Between February and July there were many mysterious animal deaths, with some of the victims appearing to have been mutilated. UFOs were often seen in the areas where the mystery killings were being carried out. (This activity echoes the cattle mutilations in the United States which occurred throughout the 1970s.) Owners of some of the Puerto Rico animals reported hearing loud screeches or the flapping of gigantic wings; and during March several sightings of 'big birds' were made. Pellín Marrero of Rexville, Bayamón, saw 'a whitish-coloured gigantic condor or vulture' flying around on 25 March, and the following day a workman, Juan Muñiz Feliciano of Moca, was attacked at night 'by a terrible greyish creature with lots of feathers, a long thick neck, bigger than a goose', weighing about 50 pounds. A gigantic bird was seen flying around by two other witnesses, also on 26 March.[50]

As a big contrast to 1975, 1976 opened with a bang. On 1 January, a 'horrible-looking' large black bird, more than 5 feet tall, with wings bunched up at its shoulders, a grey 'gorilla-like' face with dark red eyes, and a thick 6-inch beak, was seen by two children, Tracey Lawson (11), and Jackie Davis (14), at Harlingen, Texas. It stood in a ploughed field only 100 yards away and Tracey was able to look at it through binoculars. They told their parents, and three-toed prints were found, 8 inches across and 1½ inches deep in hard ground. One man weighing 170 pounds could not make a footprint anywhere near that depth, though he tried. On the same day as the Harlingen incident, many miles away in New Jersey, Dr Berthold Schwarz saw an enormous long-necked bird near Great Notch. He commented: 'I wouldn't have thought anything of it, except that it was so huge and its wings didn't seem to be flapping much at all. But what disturbed me the most was that it was so white, even as dark as it was. How could it have been so white? Unless – I know this sounds ridiculous – it was luminous.'

Was the Harlingen bird seen again at Brownsville, Texas, a week later, on 7 January? Alvérico Guajardo heard something hit his trailer home and when he went out to see what it was, he had rather a shock. He saw a 4-foot creature with black feathers, batlike wings folded across its shoulders, a long beak and blazing red eyes. It made a horrible noise in its throat (the Harlingen children had described a shrill *eeeee* sound) as it backed off into the darkness.

On 11 January near Poteet, Texas, two men on a ranch saw a 5-foot bird standing in a water tank. It apparently took off into the air without flapping its wings. Armando Grimaldo was actually attacked by a weird bird on 14 January at Raymondville, Texas. Hearing a noise at 10.30 P.M. like the flapping of batlike wings and a strange whistling, he went to investigate and felt something grab at him with big claws. Seeing what it was, he ran for cover, nearly scared to death. What Grimaldo saw was a 5–6 foot 'bird' with a

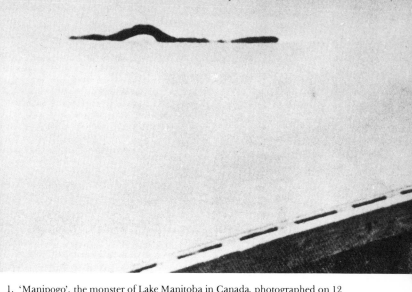

1. 'Manipogo', the monster of Lake Manitoba in Canada, photographed on 12 August 1962 by fishermen Richard Vincent and John Konefell. Mr Vincent described seeing 'a large black snake or eel . . . which was swimming with a ripple action . . . it was about a foot in girth, and about 12 feet of the monster was above water. No head was visible.' They estimated that the monster was 50-75 yards away, but couldn't catch up with it, even though their boat had a 10 horsepower engine

2. N. F. Gladkikh's sketch of the monster he saw in Lake Khaiyr, as it appeared in *Komsomol'skaya Pravda*, 21 November 1964

Загадка озера

С июня по октябрь этого го- | чество рыбы: чир, форель, щу-
мы работали в Янском райо- | ка, бараматка, и только в таин-
Якутском АССР. Мы исследо- | ственном озере, как уверяют,
ли четвертичные отложения | нет рыбы. Не садятся на его
парного хребта и прилежа- | поверхность ни гуси, ни утки

3. Ragnar Björks demonstrates how he hit out at the Storsjö monster with an oar

4 & 5. Doc Shiels' two photographs of the Loch Ness Monster, taken on 21 May 1977 from Urquhart Castle. A was taken first; note that the water is fairly undisturbed. In B, taken immediately afterwards, the creature has turned, moved forward a little and begun to sink, so that the water shows some disturbance.

The difference in appearance between these two photographs is because black and white negatives were made from the original colour slides for different purposes. Picture A was copied directly from the original slide to show maximum detail; Picture B was copied for newspaper reproduction, which means that they wanted a contrasty picture. Unfortunately, before other copies could be made the original colour slide of Picture B disappeared on the way to America, and the only black and white copy negative, in fact a glass plate, was dropped and broken. So another copy negative had to be made from a rare print surviving from the glass negative, with an inevitable loss of quality

A

6 & 7. The two photographs of 'Morgawr' taken by 'Mary F.' during the first half of February 1976 from Rosemullion Head near Falmouth. Unfortunately 'Mary F.' has remained anonymous and no one has been able to trace her, nor the negatives. But despite that, the photographs are thought to be genuine, and to be two of the best pictures ever taken of a water monster. If there were only one photograph, then just possibly it could have been faked. But we see here two photographs, apparently taken in quick succession, in which the monster has not only moved its neck but also its body. (We do not know which photograph was taken first). In her letter to the *Falmouth Packet* 'Mary F.' said that the monster was visible for only a few seconds. Also that the part she could actually see was about 15-18 feet long. Her letter continued: 'It looked like an elephant waving its trunk, but the trunk was a long neck with a small head on the end, like a snake's head. It had humps on the back which moved in a funny way. The colour was black or very dark brown, and the skin seemed to be like a sealion's . . . the animal frightened me. I would not like to see it any closer. I do not like the way it moved when swimming.'

8. Doc Shiels standing on Parson's Beach, Mawnan, from where he and David Clarke saw Morgawr in 1976

9. Colin Palmer's drawing of the Barmouth sea monster, based on eye-witness accounts

10. A comparison between a plaster cast of a zoo puma's paw print (right) and one of the prints of the Munstead Monster, found near Godalming, Surrey on 7 September 1964

11. Hurtwood Common, near Guildford, Surrey, location of many 'puma' sightings

12. Two pumas *(Felis concolor)* safely behind bars in Chessington Zoo, Surrey

13. The 'puma' photographed by two ex-police photographers at Worplesdon, Surrey, from a distance of 35 yards in 1966. They were sure it was not a feral tomcat

14. Armed policemen hunt the Nottinghamshire 'lion' during the summer of 1976

A ſtraunge,

and terrible Wunder wrought
very late in the pariſh Church
of Bongay, a Tovvn of no great di-
ſtance from the citie of Norwich, name-
ly the fourth of this Auguſt, in ẙ yeare of
our Lord 1577. in a great tempeſt of vi-
olent raine, lightning, and thunder, the
like whereof hath béen ſel-
dome ſéene.

With the appæarance of an horrible ſha-
ped thing, ſenſibly perceiued of the
people then and there
aſſembled.

Drawen into a plain method according to the written copye.
by Abraham Fleming.

15. The title page of 'A Straunge Wunder in Bongay' which describes the black dog seen in Bungay, Suffolk, in 1577

16. The marks still to be seen on a door in Blythburgh church, Suffolk (seen here at Harvest Festival time), said to have been made by the black dog which ran through the church in 1577

17. Earlier this century, two ladies in Leiston churchyard, Suffolk, at midnight 'saw a sleek shadow go slinking away among the tombstones' which they recognized as the black dog

18. This green lane at Uplyme in Devon follows the route of the county boundary, and is also haunted by a black dog, after which the adjoining inn has been named

19. Marie Delex carried off by an 'eagle' in the Swiss Alps, 1838.

20. A drawing of the Jersey Devil as seen by Mr and Mrs Nelson Evans in 1909; published in the *Philadelphia Evening Bulletin*

21. An artist's impression of Mothman, based on a sketch by Roger Scarberry, who saw the creature on 15 November 1966

Mawnan "Bird-Man" based on sketch by June Melling, witnessed and drawn 17/4/76.

Birdman monster. Seen on 3rd July, quite late at night but not quite dark. Red eyes. Black mouth. It was very big with great big wings and black claws. Feathers grey.

B. Perry 4th July 1976.

I saw this monster bird last night. It stood like a man then it flew up though the trees. It is as big as a man. Its eyes are red and shine brightly.

Sally Chapman 4/7/76.

22. The Cornish Owlman as depicted by three young witnesses

23. An unidentified footprint measuring 13 inches by 18 inches, photographed by Eric Shipton in 1951 on the Menlung Glacier, Nepal

24. Russian BHM hunter Igor Bourtsev holds a cast of a footprint found in the Gissar Range of the Pamir-Alai Mountains in Tadzhikistan, USSR, on 21 August 1979. The track was 34 cm long and 16 cm wide at the toes

25. Albert Ostman who was kidnapped by a BHM in British Columbia in 1924, here photographed by researcher René Dahinden in 1957

26. Not only North American BHMs have been accused of abducting women. This illustration from the Taymouth Hours, an English 14th-century manuscript, shows a wild man abducting a damsel

27. A BHM photographed on cine film by Roger Patterson on 20 October 1967 near Bluff Creek, northern California. The film has been extensively examined and the figure's movements analysed by many authorities, and although not all have accepted it as authentic, the balance is weighted very much in its favour. It has been estimated that the creature filmed is approximately 6 feet 8 inches tall and weighs about 440 pounds

28. The Tingewick ghost dog. Note how its head fades away above the neck. From its posture, it is apparently watching the activity above it, and could even be wagging its tail, which is also hazy. The dog did not appear on other photographs taken at the same time, of the same scene

29. The Polish medium Franek Kluski was famous for his materializations, and this photograph shows one that looks like a large bird of prey. This appeared at several séances in 1919, as did 'a strange creature intermediate between ape and man' which the sitters called the *Pithecanthropus*. In several respects it resembles some of the BHMs of Chapter 5. It is interesting to speculate whether such materializations were produced in the same way that Madame David-Neel produced her *tulpa;* and whether alien animals are also formed in this way

30. Three skyclad witches invoke Morgawr, the Cornish sea monster, at Midsummer 1976 on Parson's Beach below Mawnan church. They claimed a success

10–12 foot wingspan. It had a bat- or monkey-like face, large red eyes, no beak, and dark leathery skin without feathers. Although the creature managed to tear his clothes, his skin was not scratched.

In mid-January a 'big black bird' with a batlike face was seen by Libby and Deany Ford near Brownsville, Texas. They identified it as a pteranodon after looking through a book on paleontology. A man driving near Olmito, Texas, on 18 January saw a cat- or monkey-faced bird 4–5 feet tall with wings extended 6 feet on either side, and on the same day Homer and Marie Hernandez saw a 4-foot bird with a 4–6 inch beak standing beside an irrigation canal at San Benito, Texas. On 21 January, Francisco Magallanez of Eagle Pass, Texas, claimed to have been attacked by a dark, bat-winged, red-eyed bird, but since there are doubtful features to his story we will spend no more time on it but will move quickly to San Antonio, Texas, where a possible pteranodon was sighted on 24 February. Three elementary school-teachers driving to work near the city saw a huge 'bird' with a 15–20 foot or more wingspan swooping over their cars. Patricia Bryant said: 'I could see the skeleton of this bird through the skin or feathers or whatever, and it stood out black against the background of the gray feathers.' David Rendon added the information that the creature glided rather than flew, and that the huge wings had a bony structure. Later they found their 'bird' illustrated in an encyclopaedia, where it was captioned 'pteranodon'! Fortean researchers Jerome Clark and Loren Coleman went to Texas to investigate the 'big bird' sightings and discovered that, in the San Benito area at least, the creature has been around for more than 30 years. In their book *Creatures of the Outer Edge* they describe some of the pre-1976 sightings they were told about, including an attack on a woman.[51]

Texas did not have the monopoly on weird winged things during 1976. In England, south-west Cornwall was undergoing a three-pronged mystery attack: Morgawr, UFOs and the Owlman. Mawnan, a small village on the south coast, was the Owlman's haunt, and he was first seen on 17 April 1976 by 12-year-old June and 9-year-old Vicky Melling. June described a big feathered birdman they saw hovering over the church tower, and she also drew what they saw.[52] The church stands not far from a cliff edge, the slope of which, down to the stony beach, is covered with trees. The next sighting of the Owlman was made on 3 July 1976, this time among the trees. Sally Chapman and Barbara Perry, both 14, were camping in the wood when around 10 P.M. they heard a strange hissing noise. Looking round, they saw a figure standing among the pine trees only 20 yards away. Sally said:

It was like a big owl with pointed ears, as big as a man. The eyes were red and glowing. At first, I thought it was someone dressed up, playing a joke, trying to scare us. I laughed at it, we both did, then it went up in the air and we both screamed. When it went up, you could see its feet were like pincers.

Barbara added: 'It's true. It was horrible, a nasty owl-face with big ears and big red eyes. It was covered in grey feathers. The claws on its feet were black. It just flew straight up and disappeared in the treetops.'[53] They too both drew what they had seen.

During the very next morning after their experience, Jane Greenwood of Southport, another young girl on holiday in the area, saw the Owlman, and her sister saw him too. In a letter to the local paper she wrote:

It was Sunday morning and the place was in the trees near Mawnan Church, above the rocky beach. It was in the trees standing like a full-grown man, but the legs bent backwards like a bird's. It saw us and quickly jumped up and rose straight up through the trees.

My sister and I saw it very clearly before it rose up. It has red slanting eyes and a very large mouth. The feathers are silvery grey and so are his body and legs. The feet are like big, black crab's claws.

We were frightened at the time. It was so strange, like something in a horror film. After the thing went up there was crackling sounds in the tree tops for ages.

Later that day we spoke to some people at the camp-site, who said they had seen the Morgawr Monster on Saturday, when they were swimming with face masks and snorkels in the river, below where we saw the bird man. They saw it underwater, and said it was enormous and shaped like a lizard. [This means that Morgawr was seen on the same day as the Owlman – the Chapman and Perry sighting – and at locations only yards apart. What is the link between these two monsters so different in physical appearance and environment?]

Our mother thinks we made it all up just because we read about these things, but that is not true. We really saw the bird man, though it could have been somebody playing a trick in very good costume and make-up.

But how could it rise up like that? If we imagined it, then we both imagined the same thing at the same time.[54]

No further sightings of the Owlman were reported during 1976, but he was seen again in 1978 (see page 133). We visited Mawnan church and the woods in April 1978 along with Doc Shiels and on our own, but the Owlman refused to co-operate; Morgawr too stayed hidden. However we did notice one significant feature: that Mawnan church is built in the middle of a prehistoric earthwork. This led us to speculate whether the church was on a ley, and indeed we have found several alignments passing through Mawnan church, as follows:

1. Nare Point (SW 800251) – Mawnan church (SW 788272) – Mabe church (SW 767325) – Stithians church (SW 731371) (4 points in 8½ miles).
2. Mawnan church (SW 788272) – St Anthony church (SW⁻783257) – The Three Brothers of Grugwith (SW 762198) – tumulus on Arrowan common (SW 754176) (4 points in 6½ miles).
3. Mawnan church (SW 788272) – Manaccan church (SW 764250) – earthwork, St Martin-in-Meneage (SW 750238) – tumulus on Goonhilly Downs (SW 725215) (4 points in 5¼ miles).
(All alignments are on Ordnance Survey sheet 203, 1:50000.)

There may well be more alignments than these. However, we are not claiming that these map alignments do definitely constitute leys. To establish that will involve time-consuming fieldwork. But we feel we have established that some research of this kind would be fruitful. The repeated appearances of the Owlman by Mawnan church and the synchronistic sighting of Morgawr in the sea below suggest to us that here is a powerful earth energy centre.

In Texas in December 1976 three interesting 'big bird' sightings were reported. On 8 December John S. Carroll, living on a pig ranch in the Montalba area, spotted an enormous bird standing in a pond. It was about 8 feet tall he reckoned, bluish steel-grey with a golden breast, and a 12-inch bill. It took off and flew around before landing in a tree. Carroll, fearful for the safety of his pigs, shot at it and was surprised to see it fall as he was some distance away. But all he could find was a blood-stained feather.[55] A similar bird was seen at Bethel, Texas, on 17 December, feeding in a field, and the witness said it seemed to have an injured wing. She lived 15 miles north-west of Carroll, the rancher who had shot at the bird.[56] Three miles away at Catfish Creek, the bird was seen again on 22 December.[57]

In 1977 it was the turn of Illinois to have a 'big bird' influx. That was in July. Two months earlier, in May, a 5-pound beagle puppy was stolen by a large bird at Rabbit Hash, Kentucky, and then dropped in a nearby pond.[58] The major report of the Illinois invasion describes an incident at Lawndale on 25 July when 10-year-old Marlon Lowe was lifted off the ground and carried 30 feet by a large bird. He was playing hide-and-seek outdoors and was running when the bird, accompanied by another, snatched him. Marlon was 4 feet tall and weighed around 60 pounds. The birds were about 4½ feet tall, with each wing at least 4 feet wide. When Mrs Lowe screamed, the bird dropped Marlon and both birds flew off.[59] David Fideler comments succinctly: 'Perhaps it should be noted that there are not any birds in North America – or the world for that matter – that can lift a 60-pound boy. Nor are there any birds in the vicinity of Illinois with an 8 to 12 foot wingspan.'[60]

Only a few days after Marlon Lowe's lucky escape, a mail truck driver, James Major, saw a giant bird try to steal a baby pig weighing 50–60 pounds. This was between Armington and Delavan, Illinois, only 10 miles from Lawndale. Again there were two birds together, and Major said they looked like Californian condors with 8-foot wingspans. But Dr James Karr, associate professor of ecology at the University of Illinois, said it was very unlikely to be a Californian condor, which is nearly extinct. And anyway such a bird could not pick up a 60-pound pig or boy. Also they feed on dead animals, not live ones.[61] Other sightings were made in the same area. The bird Stanley Thompson saw near Covellat, Illinois, had a 9-foot wingspan, a 6-foot body, and was brown with white wingtips.[62]

On 28 July the big bird was seen near Lincoln, Illinois, by a group watching radio-controlled model planes. It resembled a condor and flew quietly and gracefully.[63] Two days later, 'Texas John' Huffer, writer and construction worker, filmed two large black birds in a tree by Lake Shelbyville. He said they had 8-foot wingspans and made a 'clacking, screeching noise'. The birds have been tentatively identified as turkey vultures which are not unexpected in that area, but it is unlikely that all the Illinois 'big birds' are turkey vultures, even if the Lake Shelbyville ones are, since they are not unknown in the state and would therefore surely be easily identifiable by Illinois residents. Also, of course, they are not capable of lifting a 10-year-old boy.[64] The last 1977 sighting in Illinois seems to have been made on 11 August near Odin. John and Wanda Chappell saw a giant bird land in a tree near their home. It was so big it had difficulty finding a suitable place to land. The witnesses said it was grey-black with a 6-foot body and 12-foot wingspan.[65]

The big birds faded into obscurity again in 1978. The only US report we have for that year tells how a 6-foot-4-inch, 185-pound man jogging was knocked over and scratched by a huge bird. It had a 5–6-foot wingspan and a white underbelly and tail. On looking at photographs, the jogger said it might have been a young Bald Eagle or a Crooked-Leg Hawk. This incident took place near Kansas City, Missouri, in June.[66]

In the United Kingdom at about the same time a large bird resembling a vulture was seen by an RAC patrolman and air traffic control at Birmingham's Elmdon Airport. But no trace could be found of such a bird, and the curator of a local zoo said: 'It was probably a large British bird. I find it inconceivable that it should be spotted at Elmdon and that there should be no other reports from the public.' He did say, though, that he had heard reports that there are some vultures (two pairs, actually) living in the wild in the UK, but hastily advised us not to panic, since the vulture is 'not really dangerous to human beings'.[67] A black vulture with an 8-foot wingspan had been seen in mid-Wales in February.[68]

During the 1978 holiday season the Cornish Owlman popped up again, the first sighting of the year being made around 4 June. A 16-year-old girl saw 'a monster, like a devil, flying up through the trees near old Mawnan church'. On 2 August three young French girls saw him, again near Mawnan church. They were frightened by something 'very big, like a great big furry bird'. It was white with 'a gaping mouth and big round eyes'. It was 'up in a tree, then went up higher and disappeared'.[69]

The Harlingen area of Texas, where a strange bird was seen early in 1976, hit the headlines again in 1983 with a report from James Thompson that on 14 September, while driving an ambulance from South Padre Island to Harlingen, he saw a strange birdlike creature 8–10 feet long. Its tail caught his attention: 'It had a black or greyish rough texture. It wasn't feathers. I'm quite sure it was a hide-type covering . . . I just watched him fly away.' The creature's wingspan was estimated at 5–6 feet, as wide as the ambulance, and the wings seemed to be about an inch thick, 'like a shark's fin', with indentations top and bottom. The creature had a hump at the back of its head, almost no neck, and a small pouch near its throat. The witness had a clear view of the bird as it flew across the road 150 feet in front of him, but its identity remains unknown.[70]

It may well be that some witnesses of 'big birds' in the United

States are in fact seeing conventional species, either extra-large specimens, or normal-sized ones that are foreign to the area. A number of species have been named as possible solutions to the 'big bird' mystery, including Abyssinian Ground Hornbill, Jabiru Stork, Marabou Stork, Californian Condor, White Pelican, Bald and Golden Eagles, Great Blue Heron, Sandhill and Whooping Cranes, Albatross, and Turkey Vulture (though the first three are not native to the United States). We would add the Black Vulture and the Wood Stork to the list. However, we would be wary of dismissing *all* the 'big birds' as specimens from this list, because many of the descriptions do not fit any of these birds, and because none of them is as huge as the witnesses claim. Even allowing for over-estimates of wingspans by excited witnesses, there is a big difference between the 11-foot wingspan of the Wandering Albatross, which is the largest wingspan of all living birds,[71] and the 20 feet or more claimed by some witnesses. Also, some of the weirder descriptions are very unlikely to refer to known birds, and especially those sightings where the witnesses have identified their 'birds' as pteranodons. But it should not be forgotten that really big birds have lived on earth until recent times. The *Aepyornis* of Madagascar stood up to 10 feet tall and weighed nearly 1,000 pounds. It may have survived until the last century.[72] The largest New Zealand moa was nearly 12 feet tall and some smaller species may even survive today.[73] However, both these birds were wingless, and so by no stretch of the imagination could specimens be flying over the United States in the twentieth century.

Might some of the sightings be ascribed to giant bats? We have not read of any such creatures living in the United States, but Ivan T. Sanderson saw what he considered was a giant microbat while engaged in zoological work in West Africa. One night by a river he suddenly saw 'an apparition, such as I had never imagined existed, about 15 feet away and just above the level of my eyes. It was coming straight at me awfully fast, so I ducked down into the water.' He and his companion estimated it had a 12-foot wingspan; they also noted its monkey-like muzzle, white teeth a good 2 inches long, and coal-black colouring. Sanderson also reports on the tradition of the Ahool in Indonesia, again probably a giant microbat.[74]

The main problem with the 'birds' seen periodically over the United States is their size. 'Real' birds so huge would surely continue to be seen and their progress traced across country. That this does not happen suggests they may be apparitional, haunting an area for a brief period, then suddenly seen no more. There are some traditions describing large phantom birds. One relates that in the eighteenth century West Drayton church, Middlesex, was haunted by a great black bird which vanished when about to be seized;[75] while more recently a man making hurdles at Eastcombe in Cranborne Chase, Dorset, saw a dark bird, larger than an eagle, flying towards him. It landed close by, but then seemed to disappear into a heap of brushwood.[76] In the final chapter we shall consider the apparitional nature of these winged creatures in greater detail, but first we will examine reports of what is perhaps the most amazing of all the alien animals.

5

Man or manimal?

It was in the image of a man but it could not have been human. I was never
so benumbed with astonishment before. The creature, whatever it was,
stood fully five feet high, and disproportionately broad and square at the
fore shoulders, with arms of great length. The legs were very short and the
body long. The head was small compared with the rest of the creature, and
appeared to be set upon his shoulders without a neck. The whole was
covered with dark brown and cinnamon coloured hair, quite long in some
parts, that on the head standing in a shock and growing close down to the
eyes, like a Digger Indian's.

The year was 1869, the place was Orestimba Peak, a mountain in
central California, USA. The speaker was a hunter, camping in the
forest, who had returned to his camp several times to find traces of
disturbance. One day he lay in wait, and witnessed an extraordinary
scene. His description of his visitor we have just quoted; here now is
his description of that visitor's behaviour:

As I looked he threw his head back and whistled again, and then stopped
and grabbed a stick from the fire. This he swung round until the fire on the
end had gone out, when he repeated the manoeuvre. I was dumb, almost,
and could only look. Fifteen minutes I sat and watched him as he whistled
and scattered my fire about. I could easily have put a bullet through his
head, but why should I kill him? Having amused himself, apparently, as he
desired, with my fire, he started to go, and, having gone a short distance
returned, and was joined by another – a female, unmistakeably – when both
turned and walked past me, within twenty yards of where I sat, and
disappeared in the brush.[1]

This hunter was not sure whether his visitors were men or
animals, and although such creatures have been seen in many parts
of the world many times in the hundred years since this particular
sighting, people are still none the wiser as to their true nature.
Sometimes they seem almost human: 'Although I have called the
creature "it", I felt now that it was a human being, and I knew I
would never forgive myself if I killed it.'[2] Sometimes they seem truly
bestial: 'The head was horrible . . . its ears were large like pigs' and
the nose was also like a pig's. I'm sure the eyes glowed orange, and

the teeth were like fangs.'[3] So in the absence of any authoritative scientific pronouncement on this puzzling question, we shall consider the creatures' claim for human status as yet unproven, and include them in our collection of 'alien animals'. These 'big hairy monsters' or BHMs have been given a variety of names around the world, one book having a nine-page list of them,[4] which illustrates their ubiquity. Many of the names are local, such as Kaptar in the Russian Caucasus, Chuchuna in north-east Siberia, Almas in Mongolia, Kangmi in Tibet, Sasquatch in British Columbia, Canada, and Bigfoot in California, USA. Names like Yeti, Abominable Snowman and Bigfoot have achieved prominence, but for simplicity we will here adopt the purely descriptive title BHM.

A few BHMs now exist only in legend, but most are represented by recent sightings. In areas where there are still great tracts of virtually unexplored land, such as South America and Africa, it is difficult to be sure whether reports of hairy hominids refer to big hairy monsters such as we are concerned with here, or unknown species of ape or monkey, or even unknown native tribes. There are many such tales from Africa, for example, most of them describing small hairy creatures, but in 1978 information on huge manlike beings code-named X by researcher Jacqueline Roumeguere-Eberhardt of the Centre Nationale de la Recherche Scientifique in Paris was published. She has collected 31 accounts of sightings and encounters in 11 Kenyan forests, and there seem to be four types of being. 'X One' is big and hairy, and sounds like the classic North American BHM. He always shows curiosity when he comes across natives. Those he has captured he examines carefully, along with their possessions, but does not harm them, so far as we know. One who was kidnapped and then released was even pointed in the direction home by the BHM.[5] We intend to concentrate on those areas of the world where there is no indigenous ape or monkey population, and therefore no possibility that such creatures are being misidentified.

Many books have been published on the Yeti (who is still the best-known BHM), in which can be found the most interesting sighting reports (see Bibliography). There have been more sightings of possible Yeti footprints than of the elusive creature himself, but footprints are open to many interpretations and rarely provide conclusive proof, especially in such a field as this, where the very existence of the BHM is not generally accepted. Face-to-face confrontations provide the researcher with information of a different kind, but even close encounters do not prove the creature's existence to the unbeliever. Nothing short of a corpse will convince many people – and even then there can be doubt! In December 1968 biologist Ivan T. Sanderson and zoologist Dr Bernard Heuvelmans went to Minnesota to examine the corpse of a hair-covered hominid frozen in a semi-opaque block of ice, and despite the problems of conducting an examination in such circumstances, they agreed that it appeared to be the fresh corpse of a hitherto unknown form of living hominid. However, the owner apparently later substituted a model, and from that point the 'Bozo' affair became a fiasco, with no one but Sanderson and Heuvelmans at all sure that the original 'corpse' had been a real one.[6]

But back to the Yeti. A dramatic report came in 1974 from a 19-year-old Nepalese girl, who claimed that her yak herd had been attacked by a Yeti. Lakpa Sherpani was on a mountain pasture at a height of about 14,000 feet near Mount Everest when a creature covered in thick dark hair killed five of her yaks by twisting their horns around their necks. The Yeti also knocked her unconscious, but she saw him long enough to describe him as 4–5 feet tall, with thick black hair below the waist and brown hair above. He had thick fingers with long nails, and his heel was turned forward. (An incredible feature which nevertheless is reported from time to time in Yeti lore. No one is quite sure what it means, but that is no reason to disregard it.) He walked on two feet, and police found his footprints and handprints.[7]

The sparsely populated lands of China and Russia to the north and north-west of the Himalayas are also rich in BHM lore, including some fairly recent sightings. In late July 1957 Professor V. K. Leontiev was camping in the Caucasus mountains at the head of the Jurmut River. His first inkling of a strange creature in the area was when he found some unusual tracks in the snow. Then at night he heard a strange cry; and the following day he saw a tall creature crossing a nearby snowfield. 'It was sufficient to have only one glance of him to know that this was a Kaptar . . . He was walking on his feet, not touching the ground with his hands. His shoulders were unusually wide. His body was covered with long dark hair. He was about 2.2 metres [about 7 feet] tall.' Leontiev took a shot at the Kaptar's feet, but must have missed for the creature ran quickly out of sight among rocks. However he did see its face, and thought it too was hair-covered. He concluded his description: 'His general appearance was human-like. If you want to compare the Kaptar with some living creature the best comparison would be to think of him as a tall, massively built, wide shouldered man, with a heavy growth on his face and the rest of his body.' If he did not catch the Kaptar, Leontiev did get an opportunity to examine its footprint, and said of it: 'This footprint has no resemblance to the footprints of any of the animals that I know. It doesn't look like a footprint of a bear, and, of course, is entirely different from a footprint of a human heel.' This is not an isolated sighting. The Kaptar has been seen many times by local people.[8]

Leontiev's description of the Kaptar is very similar to descriptions given by witnesses of BHMs in places far distant from the Caucasus. Is there worldwide hoaxing? Are people reading reports such as Leontiev's and making up their own sightings? Such an explanation for the thousands of BHM reports is hardly credible, for many of the witnesses are poorly educated or with little time for or no interest in reading. And in case our mention of 'thousands' of BHM reports may itself sound wildly exaggerated, researcher Rex Gilroy of New South Wales, Australia, has a collection of over 3,000 sightings on the Australian continent alone. The sightings are of a giant hairy creature who seems to be well known to the aboriginals, for they have many names for him, among them Yahoo and Duligahl (and similar-sounding names). The popular name for Australia's BHM is the Yowie, and that is what we shall call him. The earliest recorded sighting by a European seems to have taken place in 1795 near Sydney Cove, New South Wales; further sightings were made in the same area in 1800 and 1822. Since then, sightings have occurred frequently right up to the present day, and in every part of Australia. However, the majority of reports come from the east, particularly New South Wales (especially the Blue Mountains) and Queensland (especially the Gold Coast). A few first-hand reports will help set the Australian BHM scene.

In 1894 a 'wild man or gorilla' was seen between Snowball and the Jinden P.O. in New South Wales by a boy, Johnnie McWilliams, who said that

a wild man suddenly appeared from behind a tree, about thirty yards from the road, stood looking at him for a few seconds, and then turned and ran for the wooded hills a mile or so from the road. The animal ran on for two hundred yards across open country before disappearing over a low hill so that the boy had ample time to observe the beast. The boy states that he appeared to be over six feet in height and heavily built. He describes it 'as a big man covered with long hair'. It did not run very fast and tore up the dust with its nails, and in jumping a log it struck its foot against a limb, when it bellowed like a bullock. When running it kept looking back at the boy, until it disappeared.[9]

A human touch, that the BHM should cry out when it stubbed its toe!

In 1912 a BHM was seen drinking from the creek near Packer's Swamp between Bombala and Bemboka, New South Wales. Its hair was grey and George Summerell, who saw it, at first thought it was a kangaroo, until it stood up, when he realized it was definitely not. About 7 feet tall, it had a face 'like that of an ape or man, minus forehead and chin, with a great trunk all one size from shoulders to hips, and with arms that nearly reached to its ankles.' After finishing its drink, it picked up a stick and walked away among the rocks and timber. The following morning, a friend of the witness rode to the spot and found hand- and footprints. The latter he described as 'resembling an enormously long and ugly human foot in the heel, instep, and ball [with] only four toes – long (nearly 5 inches), cylindrical, and showing evidences of extreme flexibility. Even in the prints which had sunk deepest into the mud there was no trace of the "thumb" of the characteristic ape's "foot".'[10]

1912 also yielded another close and clear sighting, by Charles Harper, a Sydney surveyor, who was in the jungle along the Currickbilly mountain range in New South Wales. Hearing noises one night, Mr Harper and his companions threw dry kindling on their fire, and in the firelight they saw that they had a visitor whose description is best given in Mr Harper's own words:

A huge man-like animal stood erect not twenty yards from the fire, growling, grimacing, and thumping his breast with his huge hand-like paws. I looked round and saw one of my companions had fainted. He remained unconscious for some hours. The creature stood in one position for some time, sufficiently long to enable me to photograph him on my brain.

I should say its height when standing erect would be 5 ft 8 in to 5 ft 10 in. Its body, legs, and arms were covered with long, brownish-red hair, which shook with every quivering movement of its body. The hair on its shoulder and back parts appeared in the subdued light of the fire to be jet black, and long; but what struck me as most extraordinary was the apparently human shape, but still so very different.

I will commence its detailed description with the feet, which only occasionally I could get a glimpse of. I saw that the metatarsal bones were very short, much shorter than in the genus homo, but the phalanges were extremely long, indicating great grasping power by the feet. The fibula bone of the leg was much shorter than in man. The femur bone of the thigh was very long, out of all proportion to the rest of the leg. The body frame was enormous, indicating immense strength and power of endurance. The arms and forepaws were extremely long and large, and very muscular, being covered with shorter hair. The head and face were very small, but very human. The eyes were large, dark and piercing, deeply set. A most horrible mouth was ornamented with two large and long canine teeth. When the jaws were closed they protruded over the lower lip. The stomach seemed like a sack hanging halfway down the thighs, whether natural or a prolapsus, I could not tell. All this observation occupied a few minutes while the creature stood erect, as if the firelight had paralysed him.

After a few more growls, and thumping his breast, he made off, the first few yards erect, then at a faster gait on all fours through the low scrub. Nothing would induce my companions to continue the trip, at which I was rather pleased than otherwise, and returned as quickly as possible out of reach of Australian gorillas, rare as they are.[11]

Further north in New South Wales, to the west of Dubbo, a man on a kangaroo shoot in 1924 saw a Yowie. Suddenly aware he was not alone, David Squires looked around and saw a creature 8 feet tall standing beside a tree, its hand resting on it. It had thick, coarse, curly greyish hair about 3 inches long, and large grey-blue eyes in a face half-human, half-ape-like. After watching Mr Squires for some minutes, while he finished his task of kangaroo skinning, the Yowie reached up and scratched at the tree-trunk before turning and walking slowly away into the undergrowth. When measured later, the scratches were found to reach as high as 13 feet above the ground.[12] The behaviour of this Yowie is typical of BHMs the world over – they show apparent curiosity, but are not afraid of man. They come and watch, but do not interfere. However, not all BHMs behave so passively. In 1968 bushman George Gray was attacked by a Yowie one night at the isolated saw-milling settlement of Kooka-burra, 80 kilometres west of Kempsey in New South Wales. He was woken by the weight of something on top of him and found it was a creature somewhere between an ape and a man. He grabbed its arm, which felt greasy, and struggled with the creature for 10 minutes. During this time he was able to see it clearly, and described it as 'no more than 4 feet tall and [with] a face somewhere between that of an ape and a man, with hair all over its body between 5–6 inches long and grey in colour.' It tried to drag him out of his hut, but he escaped and it fled.[13] A Queensland Yowie also was not afraid to approach human dwellings. On 29 January 1978 a hairy creature looked in at the door of a house at Springbrook on the Gold Coast, apparently curious to see inside. The witness threw a chair at it, and it 'hopped or limped away'. He saw the creature clearly, for a light was on, and he described its head as egg-shaped. The Yowie had deep-set eyes, a small, flat, screwed-up nose, flat ears, and was black in colour. It was about 6 feet tall and smelt like a badly kept public lavatory. 'Its fingers were very long and held in a curled position, and its eyes were very glazy, like porcelain. When it limped away its hands were held just above the ground, it was hunched over and walked to the side.'[14]

Less than two months later, on 5 March 1978, a man cutting timber saw another Yowie in the same area. On hearing what he thought was a pig grunting,

I went into the forest to see if I could find it. I heard the grunting again but couldn't find any tracks. Then something made me look up, and there about 12 ft in front of me, was this big black hairy man-thing. It looked more like a gorilla than anything. It had huge hands and one of them was wrapped around a sapling . . . It had a flat black shiny face, with two big yellow eyes and a hole for a mouth. It just stared at me and I stared back. I was so numb I couldn't even raise the axe I had in my hand.

The 7-foot tall Yowie suddenly gave off a bad smell and moved away sideways.[15]

Whatever the Yowie is, it is obviously something very strange, something which according to man's present knowledge should not be in Australia. This obviously worries the scientists, indeed it worries them so much that they do not seem able to believe that people are reporting exactly what they are seeing. A typical reaction is that of a professor of anthropology who said, when approached following a Yowie sighting, that he regarded sightings of Yowies in Australia as 'highly improbable'. 'There is no reliable recurrable evidence for Yowies, abominable snowmen, yetis, bigfoots or wild men of the woods or whatever they are called. I believe you simply won't find a human primate of this sort in Australia . . . The first and only primates to have lived in Australia were human beings.' He agreed to analyse hairs discovered after a Yowie was seen at Woodenbong, but concluded somewhat sceptically: 'If there is a

Yowie at Woodenbong, I'll be the first down there.'[16] As long as scientists refuse to follow up reported sightings, the Yowie will remain undiscovered. Considering the disaster that civilized man has brought to every simple culture which he has contacted, it is undoubtedly preferable that science continues to remain ignorant of the Yowie.

We only have space for a meagre sampling of the many reported sightings of Yowies in Australia, but they seem to be as active there as they are in America. Before we move to that continent, what is the situation in the UK? So far as we know, there have been no reports of sightings of creatures *exactly* resembling the BHMs we have been describing, but a study of UK folklore has revealed some intriguing legends which may indicate that the BHM did once have a home in Britain. Best known is the woodwose[17] or wild man of the woods, a figure sometimes seen in medieval art and East Anglian church carvings. He is manlike but covered in hair except for his hands and feet, and carries a club (as sometimes the American BHMs are reported as doing).[18] The American BHM is also said to hurl rocks at unwelcome intruders into its territory, and there are legends of stone-throwing giants all over the British Isles. Perhaps such legends originated with living, stone-throwing BHMs. It is not clear whether the occasionally reported wild men, such as the one who was seen at Sproughton in Suffolk in the sixteenth century, and the 'horrible uncouth creature' who lived in woods near Salisbury, Wiltshire, about a hundred years ago and who attempted to abduct a farmer's wife, have any relevance to our story.[19] A legend which does bear more comparison with what we know of the BHM comes from North Wales, where the people of Nanhwynan were troubled by a robber who took food from the houses, milk from the goats and cows, and stole the best sheep. One day a shepherd saw a big man covered all over with reddish hair and, thinking he must be the robber, alerted the villagers who made plans to catch the giant. But he saw them coming and nimbly ran off. They tried again later, setting their dogs on to him, but he was easily able to evade them. The desperate villagers called in a magician, but his suggestion also failed. However one day the giant was outwitted by a farmer's wife who sat up at night hoping to catch him. She caught him climbing in through a window and chopped off his right hand with a hatchet. He escaped, and the next day the men followed a trail of blood to a cave under a waterfall. As the giant was never seen again, he was thought to have died of his wound, and the cave became known as the Cave of Owen Lawgoch, or the Cave of the Hairy Man.[20] Hair-covered giant figures (sometimes with red hair), stealing animals, easily able to escape from pursuers, these are all familiar features in present-day BHM reports; and the American BHMs are also thought by some researchers to live in caves.

The Nanhwynan man was a legend which may have been based on factual events; the following tale from Flintshire in North Wales is an authentic nineteenth-century report, told to his rector by Richard Roberts, the man involved. Roberts, instead of going to church on a Sunday, got into the habit of wandering in the fields, and on one autumn Sunday spent his time gathering nuts. He saw a bush loaded with nuts and stretched out his hand to reach them, when he saw a hairy hand reaching for the same branch. Unfortunately for us he did not look to see whose hand it was, but ran off, convinced it was Satan who had come to him as a punishment for not attending church. In the United States BHMs have been seen picking fruits off bushes . . . Of course there may not have been a BHM attached to the hairy hand Roberts saw, but then again there might have been. We shall never know.[21]

In the past centuries Wales, in which the two previous tales were set, would have been one of the best areas of Britain to harbour BHMs, being partly mountainous and sparsely populated. The same applies to Scotland, and there is at least one tradition from that country that might just possibly relate to BHMs – the Big Grey Man of Ben MacDhui.

Ben MacDhui is a mountain (4,300 feet) in the Cairngorm range in Grampian. Over the years a number of climbers have experienced a strange fear there, as Professor Norman Collie describes. He was speaking in 1925, of events that actually took place in 1891.

I was returning from the cairn on the summit in a mist when I began to think I heard something else than merely the noise of my own footsteps. For every few steps I took I heard a crunch, and then another crunch as if someone was walking after me but taking steps three or four times the length of my own.

I said to myself, 'This is all nonsense'. I listened and heard it again but could see nothing in the mist. As I walked on and the eerie crunch, crunch, sounded behind me I was seized with terror and took to my heels, staggering blindly among the boulders for four or five miles nearly down to Rothiemurchus Forest.

Whatever you make of it I do not know, but there is something very queer about the top of Ben MacDhui and I will not go back there again by myself I know.[22]

Such footsteps have been heard by others, but sightings of the owner of the feet are much more rare. Richard Frere has had strange experiences on the mountain, but it was a friend of his who saw the Big Grey Man (Fear Liath Mór). Frere describes what happened when the man decided to spend a night alone beside the large cairn on the summit.

About 20 yards away . . . a great brown creature was swaggering down the hill. He uses the word 'swaggering' because the creature had an air of insolent strength about it: and because it rolled slightly from side to side, taking huge measured steps. It looked as though it was covered with shortish, brown hair . . . its head was disproportionately large, its neck very thick and powerful. By the extreme width of the shoulders compared to the relative slimness of its hips he concluded its sex to be male. No, it did not resemble an ape: its hairy arms, though long, were not unduly so, its carriage was extremely erect . . . He tells us that the creature was at least twenty feet in height. And he seeks to use elementary trigonometry to prove it.[23]

Equally unexpected on a Scottish mountain is the figure seen by tough, 'mountain wise' climber Tom Crowley in the early 1920s as he descended from Braeraich in Glen Eanaich (near Ben MacDhui).

Suddenly he heard footsteps behind him, and looking over his shoulder he saw a huge grey figure. He turned about and faced it for a moment before he too was seized with terror and fled from the mountain to the glen below. And what he beheld was an undefined, misty figure with pointed ears, long legs, and feet with talons which appeared to be more like fingers than toes.[24]

We should bear these descriptions in mind when we come to the wealth of BHM reports from the United States. There are some strange similarities between them. But first we must briefly mention the Brenin Llwyd (Grey King or Monarch of the Mist), a powerful being of the northern mountains of Wales. He was feared as a stealer of children and adults who ventured too unwarily into the misty heights. Could this be a memory of a Big Grey Man-type figure?[25] The remote Faroe Islands, too, once had their Grýla, a shaggy giant of the mountains.[26]

For sheer quantity of BHM reports we must look to the North American continent. We have in our files reports of sightings in forty of the American states and five Canadian provinces; and we have details of nearly 500 separate locations where sightings have taken place. Often, more than one sighting was made at each location, by a number of witnesses. If we estimate an average of two sightings per location (which is probably a conservative estimate), that makes a total of 1,000 sightings in our files.* One American research group, Vestigia, has suggested that only one in ten sightings is ever reported to anyone, which means that there have been at least 10,000 BHM sightings in North America during the last hundred years. The actual figure is probably far higher, because our files by no means contain all the reported cases. So with all this material to consider, where shall we begin?

The traditional territory of the Bigfoot or Sasquatch (as BHMs are known in these areas) is coastal British Columbia and the north-west United States (northern California, northern Idaho, and the Cascade mountains in Oregon and Washington), areas with literally thousands of square miles of forested mountains where roads are few, the population sparse, and visitors infrequent. BHM researcher Peter Byrne estimates that this area is more than 125,000 square miles in extent,[27] plenty of space for families of BHMs to live private lives isolated from the strange, noisy lifestyle of that other primate which has settled on the same continent – man. Sometimes the two cross each other's paths briefly, as the following memorable encounters show.

American Indian lore contains many references to beings which sound like the same BHMs that are being seen today,[28] which suggests that they have been around for a long time. It was only in the 1800s that reports of sightings by white men began to filter out of the forests, and we began this chapter with one of the most intriguing of the early sightings. Even more fantastic is the story told by Albert Ostman. Indeed it is so fantastic that people unversed in Bigfoot lore may find it hard to believe. However, experienced investigators who have met Mr Ostman believe his story,[29] for it rings true. In brief, the facts are as follows. In 1924 Mr Ostman was camping in the mountains behind Toba Inlet on the British Columbia coast. One night, half asleep in his sleeping bag, he was suddenly picked up and carried off through the forest. He could not move and was very uncomfortable as for what seemed like three hours he was carried uphill and down dale by . . . who or what?

---

* For detailed descriptions of the best of these cases, see our books on Bigfoot, listed in the Bibliography.

Finally he stopped and let me down. Then he dropped my packsack, I could hear the cans rattle. Then I heard chatter – some kind of talk I did not understand. The ground was sloping so when he let go of my sleeping bag, I rolled over head first downhill. I got my head out, and got some air. I tried to straighten my legs and crawl out, but my legs were numb. It was still dark, I could not see what my captors looked like. I tried to massage my legs to get some life in them, and get my shoes on. I could hear now it was at least four of them. They were standing around me, and continuously chattering. I had never heard of Sasquatch before the Indian told me about them. But I knew I was right among them.

There were four BHMs, two big and two small, all hair-covered, apparently a family of parents and two children, a boy and a girl. (Ostman later hinted that he believed he had been kidnapped as a mate for the young female.) He wondered how he could escape. When it got light he could see he was in a small valley or basin of 8–10 acres, with high mountains all around and the 'old man' guarding the only way out. He decided to sit tight, and took stock of his supplies. He had some food, a little ammunition for his rifle, a knife, a few matches, and some snuff. Next day Ostman tried to leave, but the 'old man' pushed him back. He decided not to shoot his way out, but to think of another way to escape. Meanwhile he had a chance to look around, and while exploring he saw the BHMs' sleeping quarters in a sheltered corner. 'The floor was covered with lots of dry moss, and they had some kind of blankets woven of narrow strips of cedar bark, packed with dry moss. They looked very practical and warm – with no need of washing.' He also saw the 'old lady' coming home with food. 'She came home with her arms full of grass and twigs of all kinds from spruce and hemlock as well as some kind of nuts that grow in the ground ... The young fellow ... picked some kind of grass with long sweet roots. He gave me some one day – they tasted very sweet.'

Ostman also wrote detailed descriptions of his captors' physical appearance, and they contain features which constantly recur in BHM sighting reports.

The young fellow might have been between 11–18 years old about 7 feet tall and might weigh about 300 lb. His chest would be 50–55 inches, his waist about 36–38 inches. He had wide jaws, narrow forehead, that slanted upward round at the back about 4 or 5 inches higher than the forehead. The hair on their heads was about 6 inches long. The hair on the rest of their body was short and thick in places. The women's hair was a bit longer on their heads and the hair on the forehead had an upward turn like some women have – they call it bangs, among women's hair-do's. Nowadays the old lady could have been anything between 40–70 years old. She was over 7 feet tall. She would be about 500–600 lb.

She had very wide hips, and a goose-like walk. She was not built for beauty or speed. Some of those Lovable brassieres and uplifts would have been a great improvement on her looks and her figure. The man's eyeteeth were longer than the rest of the teeth, but not long enough to be called tusks. The old man must have been near 8 feet tall. Big barrel chest and big hump on his back – powerful shoulders, his biceps on upper arm were enormous and tapered down to his elbows. His forearms were longer than common people have, but well proportioned. His hands were wide, the palm was long and broad, and hollow like a scoop. His fingers were short in proportion to the rest of his hand. His finger-nails were like chisels. The only place they had no hair was inside their hands and the soles of their feet and upper part of the nose and eyelids. I never did see their ears, they were covered with hair hanging over them.

If the old man were to wear a collar it would have to be at least 30 inches. I have no idea what size shoes they would need. I was watching the young fellow's foot one day when he was sitting down. The soles of his feet seemed to be padded like a dog's foot, and the big toe was longer than the rest and very strong. In mountain climbing all he needed was footing for his big toe. They were very agile.

After several days in captivity, Ostman did manage to escape, and this happened because of a lucky chance. During the previous days the young male BHM had tasted some of Ostman's supply of snuff and apparently liked it. Ostman hoped he might somehow be able to use the snuff to escape, perhaps by giving the 'old man' a large dose which would incapacitate him, or by blinding him with it. One morning the 'old man' came for some snuff and grabbed the whole box before Ostman could stop him. Having swallowed it, he was soon in trouble.

After a few minutes his eyes began to roll over in his head, he was looking straight up. I could see he was sick. Then he grabbed my coffee can that was quite cold by this time, he emptied that in his mouth, grounds and all. That did no good. He stuck his head between his legs and rolled forwards a few times away from me. Then he began to squeal like a stuck pig. I grabbed my rifle. I said to myself, 'This is it. If he comes for me I will shoot him plumb between his eyes.' But he started for the spring, he wanted water. I packed my sleeping bag in my packsack with the few cans I had left. The young fellow ran over to his mother. Then she began to squeal. I started for the opening in the wall – and I just made it. The old lady was right behind me. I fired one shot at the rock over her head.

This frightened the 'old lady' and Ostman was able to escape, which he did at speed. 'Must have made three miles in some world record time.' Eventually he found a logging camp and got a lift down to the beach and so back to Vancouver.[30]

BHMs are not in the habit of abducting people, but there are several other accounts of kidnap on record. Only four years after Ostman's ordeal, and also in British Columbia, an Indian called Muchalat Harry claimed he was kidnapped one night from his camp near the Conuma River and carried several miles dressed only in his woollen underwear. At daybreak he found himself surrounded by about twenty BHMs, who were curious about him, and especially his 'loose skin' (the underwear), which they pulled at. Later in the day, when his captors' attention was distracted, Muchalat Harry ran for it. He ran 12 miles to his canoe and paddled 45 miles on a winter's night, still dressed only in his underwear, until he reached his home in an exhausted state.[31] There are also Indian tales of women being captured,[32] and details of one such ordeal suffered by an Amerindian woman in 1871 were obtained by J. W. Burns from the lady concerned. (She died in 1940 aged 86.) She was kept by the BHM for a year, after being kidnapped at the age of 17 and forced to swim the Harrison River (British Columbia), before being carried by the BHM to his rock shelter where he lived with his old parents. He treated her kindly, she said.[33] In Guatemala, El Sisemite (as the BHM is called there) allegedly kidnapped a young girl in the 1940s;[34] and a Chinese family living in Tibet 'lost' one of their women, who returned a year later and told them that

she was taken, while gathering wood, by what she called a *Kish-Kiik*, or wild man. He was comparatively little different from an [ordinary] man but was covered with hair and could not speak. She also said that she was expecting a child by him. Hearing that, her husband killed her; and he was taken by the police. The woman also told where the wild man's den was. They went up there and actually saw wild men and women all covered with hair.[35]

We also have on file details of five apparent kidnap attempts made by BHMs in the United States during the period 1942–76, and have already described the Kenya BHMs' taking of tribesmen and George Gray's tussle with a Yowie in Australia, which may have been an attempted kidnap. So unless there are a great many kidnap victims who have never returned to tell their stories, it does not seem that the BHMs' main concern is the abduction of humans. With their strength they could have abducted far more people had they wanted to.

Their behaviour is usually cautious when suddenly confronted with humans, as William Roe found in 1955 when he was exploring Mica Mountain near the town of Tete Jaune Cache in British Columbia.

I had just come out of a patch of low brush into a clearing, when I saw what I thought was a grizzly bear in the brush on the other side. I had shot a grizzly near that spot the year before. This one was only about 75 yards away, but I didn't want to shoot it, for I had no way of getting it out. So I sat down on a small rock and watched, with my rifle in my hand.

I could just see part of the animal's head and the top of one shoulder. A moment later it raised up and stepped out into the opening. Then I saw it wasn't a bear.

This to the best of my recollection is what the creature looked like and how it acted as it came across the clearing directly towards me. My first impression was of a huge man about 6 feet tall, almost 3 feet wide, and probably weighing near 300 pounds. It was covered from head to foot with dark brown, silver-tipped hair. But as it came closer I saw by its breasts that it was female.

And yet, its torso was not curved like a female's. Its broad frame was straight from shoulder to hip. Its arms were much thicker than a man's arms and longer, reaching almost to its knees. Its feet were broader proportionately than a man's, about 5 inches wide in the front and tapering to much thinner heels. When it walked it placed the heel of its foot down first, and I could see the grey-brown skin or hide on the soles of its feet.

It came to the edge of the bush I was hiding in, within 20 feet of me, and squatted down on its haunches. Reaching out its hands it pulled the branches of bushes towards it and stripped the leaves with its teeth. Its lips curled flexibly around the leaves as it ate. I was close enough to see that its teeth were white and even. The head was higher at the back than at the front. The nose was broad and flat. The lips and chin protruded farther than its nose. But the hair that covered it, leaving bare only the parts of its face around the mouth, nose and ears, made it resemble an animal as much as a human. None of this hair, even on the back of its head, was longer than an inch, and that on its face much shorter. Its ears were shaped like a human's ears. But its eyes were small and black like a bear's. And its neck also was unhuman, thicker and shorter than any man's I have ever seen.

As I watched this creature I wondered if some movie company was making a film in this place and that what I saw was an actor made up to look partly human, partly animal. But as I observed it more I decided it would be impossible to fake such a specimen. Anyway, I learned later there was no such company near that area. Nor, in fact, did anyone live up Mica Mountain, according to the people who lived in Tete Jaune Cache.

Finally, the wild thing must have got my scent, for it looked directly at me through an opening in the brush. A look of amazement crossed its face. It looked so comical at that moment I had to grin. Still in a crouched position, it backed up three or four short steps, then straightened up to its full height and started to walk rapidly back the way it had come. For a moment it watched me over its shoulder as it went, not exactly afraid, but as though it wanted no contact with anything strange.

The thought came to me that if I shot it I would possibly have a specimen of great interest to scientists the world over. I had heard stories about the Sasquatch . . . Maybe this was a Sasquatch, I told myself.

I levelled my rifle. The creature was still walking rapidly away, again turning its head to look in my direction. I lowered the rifle. Although I have called the creature 'it', I felt now that it was a human being, and I knew I would never forgive myself if I killed it.

Just as it came to the other patch of brush it threw its head back and made a peculiar noise that seemed to be half laugh and half language, and which I could only describe as a kind of whinny. Then it walked from the small brush into a stand of lodge-pole pines.

I stepped out into the opening and looked across a small ridge just beyond the pine to see if I could see it again. It came out on the ridge a couple of hundred yards away from me, tipped its head back again, and again emitted the only sound I had heard it make, but what this half laugh, half language was meant to convey I do not know. It disappeared then, and I never saw it again.[36]

It was the publication of Roe's story by newspaper editor and BHM researcher John Green that led Albert Ostman to tell the story of his abduction.

The sightings we have described so far have been made from close quarters, but a great number of witnesses only see a fleeting glimpse of Bigfoot. He is elusive, wary, and chooses to keep away from man, it seems. Sightings are often made as the BHM quickly crosses a country road under the cover of darkness, as happened to Verlin Herrington, deputy sheriff of Gray's Harbor County, Washington, on 27 July 1969. At 2.35 A.M. he was driving home along Deekay Road near Copalis Beach and rounding a bend he saw a large hairy creature standing in the road. He had to brake to avoid hitting it; and as he got out of the car with a spotlight he had a chance to study the beast. As he cocked his pistol, intending to shoot at it, it went out of his spotlight and into the woods. As he later described it to researcher René Dahinden:

I would estimate its height at 7 to 8 feet and its weight at something over 300 pounds. It had hair all over it of a dark brown colour, but the hair on its head was longer than that on the rest of its body – between 5 and 7 inches long. The first thing that startled me was that it had breasts on it like those of a woman; they had hair on them also, except for the nipples which were black, like the thing's face. While it was standing I could see the back of one hand and the palm of another and I could distinguish fingers. It had legs like a human and buttocks like a human.[37]

(It is coincidental that we have described several obviously female BHMs in this chapter, when in fact most of the creatures seen do not have obvious breasts and it is not easy to tell what sex they are.) Next day Herrington and colleagues returned to the area and found several footprints measuring 18 by 7 inches.[38]

Judging by his reactions, the BHM does not welcome industrial man's intrusion into his habitat. Men at work in the desolate forests have had their camps attacked (Ape Canyon, Washington, 1924, where miners were driven out after an attack lasting several days[39]); hunters and other 'intruders' have had rocks thrown at them (an Amerindian, Frank Dan, canoeing along Morris Creek in British Columbia in 1936, had rocks hurled down at him from the mountain[40]); and new installations using mechanical equipment have been inspected (many huge footprints were found in soft soil in Bluff Creek Valley, northern California, where new logging roads were being built in 1958, as if the BHM were fascinated by the work[41]) and destroyed (a 'hairy giant' 'picked up a 20-foot section of sluiceway and smashed it to bits against a tree' near Mount Shasta, California, in the 1850s[42]).

Despite the number of sightings made of BHMs in the north-west United States and British Columbia over the years (and these are the areas where the creatures are most often seen), the existence of the BHM is not officially accepted. Scientists will only believe something exists if they can study it in their laboratories, and this has not been possible for one important reason: the BHMs are notoriously difficult to kill or capture. They usually keep out of man's way. (There is of course an ethical question – does man's curiosity justify the killing or capture of a BHM? We feel it definitely does not, and that there is no justification for the suffering any captured BHM would be subjected to, just so that scientists can classify it. Let it suffice us to know it exists, and let us allow it to live in peace.) There are, in fact, on record some vague stories of BHMs being killed or captured, the most famous being that of Jacko, the young BHM supposedly captured near Yale, British Columbia, in 1884.[43] However there is some suspicion that this story was a hoax.[44] John Green reports that five or more Sasquatch have been reported killed on the North American continent, all vague reports;[45] an 8½-foot tall BHM was reportedly shot by a Washington hunter recently;[46] one was said to have been captured in Saline County, Arkansas, in the nineteenth century;[47] and in Kentucky a so-called 'Wild Man of the Woods' was put on exhibition in 1878.[48] There are also various reports of killed or captured BHMs from Tibet, the USSR and Panama, but none is more recent than 1941, when a Soviet army lieutenant-colonel, V. S. Karapetyan, was able to examine a hair-covered man captured in the mountains near Buinaksk, in Dagestan.

I can still see the creature as it stood before me, a male, naked and bare-footed. And it was doubtlessly a man, because its entire shape was human. The chest, back, and shoulders, however, were covered with shaggy hair of a dark brown colour . . . The fur was thinner and softer below the chest . . . his height was above the average – about 180 cm. He stood before me like a giant, his mighty chest thrust forward. His fingers were thick, strong, and exceptionally large. On the whole, he was considerably bigger than any of the local inhabitants. His eyes told me nothing. They were dull and empty – the eyes of an animal. And he seemed to me like an animal and nothing more.

As I learned, he had accepted no food or drink since he was caught. He had asked for nothing and said nothing. When kept in a warm room he sweated profusely. While I was there, some water and then some food was brought up to his mouth; and someone offered him a hand, but there was no reaction. I gave the verbal conclusion that this was no disguised person, but a wild man of some kind. Then I returned to my unit and never heard of him again.[49]

Why are the bones of dead BHMs never found? ask the unbe-lievers. There are several possible explanations, apart from the sceptical 'Because they do not exist'[50]: 1. They bury their dead. 2. They conceal themselves before death, and the remains are therefore hidden. 3. They eat the remains of their own dead (this suggestion comes from Professor Porshnev of the USSR who made a long study of BHM behaviour).[51] 4. Scavengers eat the remains. 5. The soil conditions cause the bones to dissolve. The bones of other wild creatures, apart from the very recently dead, are rarely found, so why should things be any different in the case of the BHM?

Other questions asked by sceptics include: Where do the BHMs go in winter? How can such huge creatures find enough food to live on? Both can easily be answered, we feel. As far as their winter behaviour is concerned, they may: 1. Stay where they are, for they are far better equipped than man would be to live through a harsh winter in the wild. Giant footprints have been found in snow-covered regions. 2. Migrate to warmer areas for the duration of the winter, such as to the coast from the mountains in British Columbia. 3. Hibernate, as do a number of other animals, including bears. BHMs are thought often to live in caves anyway, which could easily be made cosy for the winter. Food supplies would not appear to be a problem for any creature that knows what is edible and is prepared to eat anything that is available. The evidence suggests that the BHM is omnivorous; we have details of it being seen eating or collecting roots, clams, huckleberries, spruce and hemlock tips, grasses, ferns, leaves, fish, mussels, minnows, deer, rodents, berries and shoots, water plants, cultivated corn, turnips and tomatoes, rabbits, and geese, and they are not above rummaging around dustbins if they wander near to human settlements. BHMs do not appear to be vegetarian, as some people have suggested, but even that would not be impossible, because it is only non-vegetarians who believe that vast quantities of greenstuff are necessary to support life if no meat is eaten. Vegetarians know otherwise; few people today understand that far less food is necessary for life than is generally eaten in civilized countries, and that a more frugal diet makes for a healthier individual. So we are sure that the BHM has no food problem, for at his speed of travel his food-gathering territory is surely large.

If we consider evidence only from the north-west United States and British Columbia, it seems fairly incontestible that some large, unidentified primate is living (and presumably breeding) in the forests and mountains. Roger Patterson and Bob Gimlin even got some movie film of one near Bluff Creek, California, in 1967.[52] But the story becomes far more complex when we cast our net further afield and consider the evidence emanating from the other American states. For although the volume of reports from any individual state is not as great as from any of the areas we have considered so far, many of the reports outdo the north-west reports in terms of strangeness. Consider this, for example.

During the evening of 6 February 1974, a lady living near Uniontown, Pennsylvania, was sitting at home watching television. She heard a noise in her porch and went to investigate, thinking that dogs were to blame. She took a loaded shotgun with her, to scare the intruders. She turned on the porch light, opened the door and stepped into the doorway and was horrified to see a 7-foot-tall hairy ape-like creature standing only 6 feet away. Thinking it was about to attack, for it had raised its arms above its head, she fired into its middle. But amazingly, the BHM 'just disappeared in a flash of light'. That was not the end of the affair, for when her son-in-law, who lived nearby and heard the shot, came to help, he saw four or five shadowy forms at the edge of the nearby woods. As they approached he saw they were hairy, 7 feet tall and ape-like, with very long arms. They also had 'fire red eyes that glowed in total darkness'. At the same time, a bright red flashing light was seen hovering over the woods.[53]

It is at this point that many convinced believers in the existence of the Bigfoot or Sasquatch of the north-west switch off. And who can blame them for finding it hard to accept the bizarre tales that are being reported, regularly and even increasingly, by apparently sane United States citizens? However, the reports do exist, investigators have questioned the witnesses and come away convinced of their truthfulness, and so we have really no option but to accept what they say, and to keep an open mind on the matter while searching for an explanation. Before we examine all the possibilities, let us describe some more of these bizarre cases and the features that set them apart from 'conventional' BHM reports. There are similarities, too, just to further confuse the situation.

One night in August 1972 a member of the Rogers family who lived in a trailer home at Roachdale, Indiana, saw a luminous object in the sky over a nearby cornfield. Afterwards noises were heard in the yard at night, and when one of the men went out, he caught a glimpse of a large, broad-shouldered creature going into the cornfield. As it always came at night, the Rogers could not see it too clearly, but they did see that it was covered in black hair, and they could certainly smell its rotten odour, 'like dead animals or garbage'. It once looked in through the window, and Mrs Rogers told how it stood like a man but ran on all fours. In that position it was about 5 feet 9 inches tall. The strangest thing about the beast was its apparent insubstantiality. 'What was weird was that we could never find tracks, even when it ran over mud. It would run and jump but it was like somehow it wasn't touching anything. When it ran through weeds, you couldn't hear anything. And sometimes when you looked at it, it looked like you could see *through* it.' Other people in the area saw the creature, including farmers who had nearly 200 chickens taken by it. The BHM did not appear to have eaten the birds, just killed them, and their remains lay scattered around. Carter and Junior Burdine found other traces of the creature on their farm, including a broken fence and trampled grass. The BHM had also taken tomatoes and cucumbers from a pig food bucket. Later they saw the creature in the doorway of the chicken house, and Junior described it thus:

This thing completely blocked out the lights inside the chickenhouse. The door is 6′ × 8′. Its shoulders came up to the top of the door, up to where the neck should have been. But this thing didn't have a neck. To me it looked like an orang-utan or a gorilla. It had long hair, with kind of a brownish cast to it. Sort of rust-lookin' colour. I never saw its eyes or its face. It was making a groaning racket.

The men chased it and shot at it, but although they were close and surely unable to miss, the BHM seemed unaffected by the firing. More dead chickens were found, but this was the end of the BHM's depredations at Roachdale, for it was not seen there again. It seems to have moved north to the Parke-Fountain County line, where a '10-foot-tall monster . . . covered with fur . . . feet 21 inches long' was being seen.[54]

There are many features of this case which are rarely, if ever, found in reports of the north-west Bigfoot – UFO sighting, attraction to houses, bad smell, running on all fours, apparent insubstantiality (but it was substantial enough when it left traces at the Burdine farm), apparent immunity to gunfire. Such features are not uncommon in BHM reports elsewhere in the United States, and we have on file many other examples of each feature. There are others, too, which frequently occur, such as the 'big red eyes that glow in the dark' of the Tabor City, North Carolina, BHM seen in 1973.[55] The size of the eyes is often remarked upon – 'as big as light bulbs' said a witness to the Marshall, Michigan, BHM in 1956.[56] Other physical peculiarities which have been reported include clawed hands (as seen, for example, by Mike Lofton of South Crossett, Arkansas, in June 1978 – the BHM 'was approximately 7½ feet tall and covered with hair. Its arms were extended overhead . . . and from the ends of what appeared to be its fingers, long beak-like claws protruded.'[57]). Also seen: webbed feet (the Conser Lake, Albany, Oregon, monster of 1960);[58] and fangs (the Beech Hills, near

Jeannette, Pennsylvania, BHM seen on 27 August 1973 had prominent fangs).[59] Usually BHMs vary between 5 and 9 feet tall, with the average height being about 7 feet, but occasionally extra tall specimens are reported, like the 15-foot creature which charged three campers at Monarch, Montana, on 20 August 1977.[60]

Not all BHMs are smelly, but some are, and the witnesses usually strive to express the revolting nature of the odour: 'It was a stink like a dead person, long dead. It stayed in the air for maybe 10 to 15 minutes afterwards' (Little Eagle, South Dakota, 1977);[61] 'Like strong BO. You could really smell it . . . like somebody who hadn't taken a bath for a year' (Ingalic Creek, Washington, 1977);[62] 'It smells like burning rubbish and the sweat of a hundred high school football teams' (Louisiana, Missouri, 1972).[63] BHM calls are often heard, too, and are described in a number of ways, such as like a child crying, like a woman in distress, screaming, whistling, grunting, growling, whining, roaring, laughing, and a 'beller which sounded something like a young bull would make' (Cashton, Wisconsin, 1976).[64]

Much attention has been paid to BHM footprints, because these are found more frequently than the creatures are seen. (Though there have been suggestions that the BHM sometimes takes care not to leave tracks if possible, and will even make efforts to confuse his trail.)[65] Many of the prints found, though far larger than a big man's footprint, look basically similar to human prints, but recently, and increasingly, unexpected prints have been found. If only one had been found it could be considered an isolated aberration (a poor print, perhaps), but there are many cases on record of each type, especially three-toed prints. Of those cases we have noted, most date from the mid- and later 1970s, and none before 1969. Less frequent but also recorded are two toes, four toes, and six toes. John Napier, an anthropologist, writes extensively in his book *Bigfoot* on 'The Evidence of the Footprints', and remarks that some of the tracks 'appear distinctly static'.[66] This may strike the sceptic as evidence of fakery, and in a few instances this may indeed be so, but in most cases the odds are against fakery, for the following reasons: the detail in the prints, which would be difficult and time-consuming to incorporate in any mould; the fact that they often show peculiarities which an anthropologist would expect to see in the print of a creature like the BHM, but which would be unknown to the average faker;[67] the stride is too long for a human to have reached; the prints are usually deeply impressed, indicating a heavy creature, and something difficult for the relatively lightweight human faker to achieve; and the prints are usually found in very isolated parts, and often by chance. If these are faked, it means that the faker wanders around uninhabited forested mountain areas, often in winter, wearing cumbersome fake feet or soles, without any certainty of the tracks ever being discovered. Obviously a madman! If, as Napier suggests, some prints are static, then we must look elsewhere than to a joker for an explanation. Maybe the prints are not made by a BHM but are 'evidence' planted in the same way that the BHM himself is planted. But we are anticipating our speculations at the end of this chapter and in the final chapter; first we should consider the behaviour of these beasts.

The BHMs away from the north-west United States seem to be interested in people and their dwellings; there is more interaction between BHM and witness (albeit unwillingly on the part of the latter). BHMs are often seen standing in yards and gardens (for example at Whitney, Pennsylvania, in 1973, where a man heard a banging noise and looked outside, to see a tall, hairy, manlike creature standing motionless, its back towards him and facing a home where young children were sleeping).[68] Sometimes they look in through windows; a particularly scary occurrence of this kind took place near Derry, Pennsylvania, on 21 August 1973. A woman in bed with the curtains drawn but the window open had been sleeping, but awoke with the feeling that someone was watching her. She turned over and saw, about 3 feet away, a horrible face staring in at the window. (The creature must have drawn back the curtains.) It had upright oval eyes, dark with no whites, and no eyelids or eyelashes. The nose was 'pushed in'. When the woman moved, the creature moved back awkwardly from the window (which was over 9 feet above the ground), though no sound was heard as it moved.[69] BHMs even try to get inside dwellings on occasion – they scratch at doors and pry at windows, and also put their hands through windows. They have also been known to rummage through outhouses (Ruby Creek, British Columbia, 1941);[70] eat scraps by the back door (Albany, Kentucky, 1973);[71] drink at a water-tank hose (Hoopa Valley, California, 1975);[72] rip open an electric power box (Derry, Pennsylvania, 1973);[73] and go inside a shed and tear at bags of salt (Mason, Michigan, 1978).[74]

Cars also seem to attract BHMs. Sometimes they are accidentally hit by moving cars; sometimes they attack cars and their occupants. When the former happens, the car driver does not step out to find a dead or injured BHM lying in the road. More often the creature limps or runs off into the trees, leaving the driver with a dented car, but in Pennsylvania during the big BHM scare of 1973 a driver who hit a large, ape-like creature which ran out in front of his car reported that upon impact the creature disappeared.[75] BHMs seem to dislike cars, for attacks upon them are not rare. Or maybe they are trying to get at the occupants? In 1967 near Elfers, Florida, a thing looking 'like a big chimp' but greenish in colour 'with glowing green eyes' jumped on a parked car's bonnet,[76] while near Morristown, New Jersey, in 1965 a huge 'monster' thumped on the back of a parked car.[77] In a third parked car incident (all three cars contained young people, and this circumstance may be significant) near Chittyville, Illinois, on 11 August 1968 a 10-foot-tall figure 'with a head as large as a steering wheel and a round, hairy face' suddenly emerged from bushes and threw dirt in at the young couple through the car window.[78] Three years earlier 17-year-old Christine van Acker had had a rather more damaging encounter with a BHM near Monroe, Michigan. In August 1965, while she and her mother were driving through the area, a 7-foot, 400-pound ape-like creature covered in black hair reached through the car window and touched Christine's head, giving her a black eye![79]

This last injury may have been an accident, but apparently intentional attacks on people are not unknown. As early as 1902 an 8-foot hairy monster brandishing a club attacked skaters near Chesterfield, Idaho. Tracks later found were 22 inches long and 7 inches broad, with only four toes.[80] A forestry worker cutting grass near Kinchafoonee Creek, Georgia, on 1 August 1955 had a nasty scare when attacked by a hairy, gorilla-like creature at least 6 feet tall, with 'tusk-like teeth and pointed ears'. As it approached, Joseph Whaley swung out with his scythe, but the BHM kept coming and Whaley fled for his jeep. Before he could drive off, the creature managed to rip his shirt and scratch his arm and shoulder.[81] Reports of BHMs actually killing anyone are rare, though Ivan Sanderson does have two such early reports in his valuable book *Abominable Snowmen: Legend Come to Life*. He quotes an account from *Wilderness Hunter*, an 1892 book by Theodore Roosevelt, in which the death of a hunter at the hands of a BHM near the Wisdom River in Idaho in the early 1800s is described. Fellow hunter Bauman lived to tell the tale, which he did to Roosevelt, who was impressed and here describes what happened when Bauman returned to their camp.

At first Bauman could see nobody; nor did he receive an answer to his call. Stepping forward he again shouted, and as he did so his eye fell on the body of his friend, stretched beside the trunk of a great fallen spruce. Rushing towards it the horrified trapper found that the body was still warm, but that the neck was broken, while there were four great fang marks in the throat.

The footprints of the unknown beast-creature, printed deep in the soft soil, told the whole story.[82]

Sanderson also reports another killing, in 1890 on the Chetco River on the border between California and Oregon. After BHM activity in the area, two men were found smashed by having been repeatedly slammed to the ground. They had apparently shot at their killer, who perhaps therefore killed in self-defence.[83]

The BHM seems to have a particular dislike of dogs, judging by the number of times dogs are attacked and/or killed by them. Often, when a BHM is in the vicinity, even brave dogs hide in fear, but sometimes dogs have attacked BHMs. When the two fight, it is not always clear which side initiated the tussle. In June 1962 a 6-foot hairy black monster attacked and mauled two dogs in Trimble County, Kentucky, [84] and in June 1969 a Sasquatch was seen fighting with several dogs in Shasta-Trinity National Forest, California. Covered in dark brown hair (except for its face) and 6 feet tall, it threw some of the dogs into the air.[85] On occasions dogs are found horribly slaughtered in an area where a BHM has been seen, with the obvious suspicion that it was to blame. In 1926 two hunters saw the 'Manbeast' near the Mountain Fork River in Oklahoma and sent their dog to chase it. An hour later they found the dog, which had 'been just almost tore in two'.[86]

But in contrast to all this violence and bloodshed, a gentler side to the BHM has been reported, though very rarely, it must be admitted. John Green mentions several reports of 'Sasquatch taking food and leaving things in exchange, and two accounts of injured men being carried back to camp by them.'[87] An American Indian, recalling in 1968 his or her grandfather's encounters with the Matah Kagmi (Sasquatch), tells how he first met one in 1897 near his cabin home in the mountains near Tulelake, California. At dusk he was walking along a trail and realized that what he thought was a bush was in fact a tall, hair-covered ('thick coarse hair, much like horsehair') creature.

Although it was growing darker, Grandfather was able to see quite clearly two soft brown eyes through the hairy head part, then the creature moved slightly, and Grandfather made a motion of friendship and laid down the string of fish that he had been carrying. The creature evidently understood this, as it quickly snatched up the fish and struck out through the timber nearby.

A few weeks later Grandfather heard strange noises outside his cabin early in the morning, and when he looked out he found fresh deerskins ready for tanning. He heard in the distance a call he had heard the Sasquatch make before. At other times, wood for fuel, wild berries and fruits were left.

Several years later (which would make it early in the twentieth century) Grandfather acted as guide for treasure-hunting white men in the Mount Shasta area. While exploring alone, he was attacked by a rattlesnake.

Grandfather killed the snake and started to come back down to a more comfortable spot, but soon found it difficult to go on, and as best as he can remember he became sick at his stomach and fainted. When he came round again, he thought he was dreaming, for he was surrounded by three large Sasquatch about 8 to 10 feet tall. He noted that they had made a small cut on the snakebite and had somehow removed some of the venom, and placed cool moss on the bite. Then one of the Matah Kagmi made a kind of grunting sound and the other two lifted him up and took him down a trail that he did not know. Finally after some little descent down the mountain side, they placed him under a low brushy tree and left.[88]

Finally, before airing some theories, we will describe one of the best authenticated BHM sightings of the weirder kind. This took place in May 1977 near Wantage, in a remote rural part of northern New Jersey, and the case was fully investigated by a team from the Society for the Investigation of the Unexplained. On 12 May 1977 Mrs Sites found that several pet rabbits had been killed, and whatever was to blame had ripped away a wooden door to get at them. The bodies were there, apparently squeezed to death. More ripped and clawed boards were found, where the beast had first tried to get at the rabbits. That night the family saw a creature standing under the bright light in the yard (was it perhaps waiting to be seen?). 'It was big and hairy; it was brown; it looked like a human with a beard and moustache; it had no neck; it looked like its head was just sitting on its shoulders; it had big red glowing eyes,' said Mrs Sites. When a dog went for it, it brushed it off with an arm and sent it flying 20 feet. The next night (Friday the 13th) four adults waited with loaded guns, and at late dusk it again came under the lamp. The men opened fire and the BHM ran into a shed, then out through a window and stood under a tree. Mr Sites: 'I shot at it three or four times with deer slugs in my .410 gauge shotgun, and I know I hit it.' It merely growled and so Mr Sites ran to join the others who had gone back to the house, out of ammunition. The BHM made for an orchard up the road and Mr Sites followed in his truck, but it ran off into fields. Although a thorough search was made next day, no blood could be found. The SITU team were impressed by the sincerity of the family, and were able to examine the barn damage done only five days before, as well as the rabbit corpses. They were not lucky enough to see the unwanted visitor, but did hear a scream coming from the nearby swamp which Mrs Sites identified as the creature. The BHM appeared shortly after their departure, and was again chased by Mr Sites in his truck. The children saw him again too, when out picking berries. He was crawling in the grass, hand extended, as if injured and seeking help. The children ran home screaming. Mrs Sites also thought she saw the creature lying in a field near a cow on another occasion.[89] The most striking feature of this strange but true story is the creature's obvious invulnerability when shot at by four men with shotguns and rifles. We have many other similar cases on file, and this apparently inexplicable phenomenon presents us with the opportunity for a much-needed discussion of what the BHM really is.

If we were to discount the weirder cases entirely, to put them down to hallucination, malicious hoaxing or misreporting, then the BHM scene would appear relatively uncomplicated. John Napier, basing his discussion solely on the Yeti and the north-west North American Sasquatch, has a useful summing-up of the evidence in his concluding chapter of *Bigfoot*, and, a good paragraph coming from a scientist, says:

I am convinced that the Sasquatch exists, but whether it is all that it is cracked up to be is another matter altogether. There must be *something* in north-west America that needs explaining, and that something leaves man-like footprints. The evidence I have adduced in favour of the reality of the Sasquatch is not hard evidence; few physicists, biologists or chemists would accept it, but nevertheless it *is* evidence and cannot be ignored.[90]

There has been much speculation that the BHM is a survival of some kind of prehistoric man, but we will not go into the pros and cons of that here, for it has already been done by people more knowledgeable on the subject than we are.[91] Our feeling on this is that some of the world's BHMs may well be prehistoric survivals, an early form of ape called *Gigantopithecus* or men who have developed along a different branch of the evolutionary tree than did *Homo sapiens*. That does not mean such men would be 'inferior' to us; indeed they may be in some ways superior for they have retained the ability to survive in a natural environment. The least likely candidates for the 'prehistoric survival' explanation are the Yowie of eastern Australia, the 'Big Grey Man' of Ben MacDhui in Scotland, and the North American BHMs from all states except the north-west and British Columbia. This is a very sweeping classification. We realize that if we are correct in describing a large number of the world's BHMs as prehistoric survivals, there is likely to be more than one kind. There would have to be to explain the physical differences. Also, there are probably reports of the *other* kind of BHM emanating from the areas where prehistoric survivals are living, which confuses the issue even more. Our decision to classify the BHMs of British Columbia and the north-western United States as prehistoric survivals is a tentative one only, based on our belief that such creatures could live in that terrain, and on the fact that far fewer 'weird' reports originate in those areas. But some do, which suggests either that both kinds of BHM appear there, or that they are all the weird type, but a more cautious breed.

Every researcher who has tackled the BHM enigma has his favourite theory, and we have ours. It is an easier task for those who choose to disregard the weird reports, but researchers who ignore reports which do not support their own preconceptions cannot claim to be unprejudiced, and their ideas are to that extent of less value. However unpalatable and inexplicable the weird reports may seem, they must be faced. Some theories that have been advanced are not solidly based on the existing evidence, and these we will briefly describe first of all, leaving till later those which seem to us to be more closely in accord with the facts.

An unusual theory originates in Japan, where Hibagon, as their BHM is known, has been seen in the Hiba Heights district of Hiroshima Prefecture.

A dreadful, real-life 'monster' that looks like an ape and smells like decaying flesh has been observed by several reliable witnesses in the mountains of Japan, near Hiroshima. The creature may be the product of a mutation from the deadly atomic radiation unleashed when the first A-bomb was dropped on that city more than a quarter-century ago, according to some investigators ... Eyewitness reports indicate that the monster lurks amid the low shrubbery clinging to the foothills of Mt Hiba. The area, one of the few wildernesses that teeming nation has preserved, includes Hibayama National Park.

A typical sighting of the creature is reported by one Mr Sazawa, the owner of a drygoods store near the town of Saijo. Mr Sazawa was scrambling through the foothills digging wild sweet potatoes when he saw the thing. 'It is about 5 feet tall, with a face shaped like an inverted triangle, covered with bristles, having a snub nose and large, deep, glaring eyes,' he reported ... Mr Sazawa is certain what he saw is not a monkey, for monkeys in Japan grow no taller than 3 feet at the most. The accumulation of these and other bits of data has led to increasingly intense speculation. Is this a gorilla? A wild man? A deserter from the Japanese army, hiding in fear? Or is it the offspring of some unfortunate peasant, grossly deformed by the ravages of atomic radiation?

The report also tells how Boy Scouts, searching for Hibagon, found large footprints about 10 inches long and 6 inches wide, and concludes with another sighting report dating from the autumn of 1972:

Mrs Reiko Harada, 46, a seamstress from the town of Hiwa, was the witness. Walking home with her small son, Mrs Harada was alerted by the sound of rustling in the underbrush. Then she saw something that looked like a gorilla standing at the roadside. It raised its arms, she said, as though begging her to stop. Its face was chocolate brown, she remembers, and its body was covered with dark hair. 'When I saw that monster ... I suddenly went numb and couldn't walk. I started shaking with fear, but then, somehow, I got the nerve to pick up my little boy and run.' ... That evening, four residents armed themselves heavily and went hunting for the beast. They saw nothing but trampled shrubbery. But, one reported, 'the place smelled like a dead body after it starts decomposing.'[92]

So many features of this report repeat those in United States reports that it is hard to believe that this report originated in Japan. The increased level of background radiation could possibly be a factor in some appearances of alien animals, but as few places have received the level of radiation to which the first atomic bomb targets were exposed, this can neither wholly account for all the BHM reports around the world, nor the reports which were made before experiments with atomic energy were started.

We have already noted UFO sightings occurring at the same time as BHM sightings and in the same area, and we have a number of such 'coincidences' on file, though very rarely occurring earlier than 1966. (This may be because earlier than ten years ago a UFO sighting may simply not have been reported; only recently has public awareness extended to encompass and accept the UFO.) But interestingly, there is only one case in which BHMs were actually seen emerging from a landed UFO, and that is suspect because reported anonymously.[93] One of the best documented UFO/BHM cases took place near Uniontown, Pennsylvania, on 25 October 1973, when at about 9 p.m. a 'bright white' object was seen in pastureland, following the sighting of a large red ball in the sky, slowly descending. The people who went to look saw two 'very tall, ape-like creatures with glowing green eyes' moving around near the woods; experienced investigators were soon on the scene and although the UFO and creatures were gone (apparently), farm animals and a dog were disturbed. The main witness to the incident suddenly began to growl like an animal, attacked two men, and ran around the field before collapsing. The investigators began to suffer physical distress, light-headedness and difficulty in breathing, and a smell of sulphur filled the air.[94] This is a well-attested case, and seems to indicate strongly that *sometimes* UFOs and certain types of BHM are somehow linked. However, this case, and the others where a UFO has been seen, are only a small proportion of the total number of BHM cases, and from the evidence so far available it cannot be claimed that BHMs have a direct connection with UFOs. But some may do. By now it must be apparent that there are so many threads in the complex web of BHM data that no one explanation is likely to cover all the cases.

The UFO/BHM connection may be strongly suggested by some of the data; the theory that BHMs are part of a biological experiment by aliens certainly is not well founded, we feel. Basing her theory on 1. a personal vision (of a female BHM holding a thin infant BHM, and apparently asking for help); 2. a witness's mental image of a BHM saying 'What is to become of my people?'; 3. another witness's 'feeling' that 'it wished it could be me'; 4. a girl researcher's receipt of a telepathic message from a BHM: 'They are taking our children!'; and 5. another researcher's mental conversation with BHMs in which they told him that they were here first and we are ruining their planet, B. Ann Slate wonders:

Are the aliens physically removing the offspring of the tiny population of Bigfoot for genetic experimentation and colonization on some other distant planet? It would appear that is the message ... they are telepathically appealing to us as their biological half-brothers to aid them against outsiders who continue to kidnap, experiment with, and monitor them.[95]

We do not reject this explanation completely, for as long-time UFO researchers ourselves we are fully aware that the UFO presents one of the most multifarious enigmas that mankind has ever had to face, and has far-reaching implications. But we cannot readily accept an explanation for which the evidence is so weak.

It is clear enough that the 'weird' reports are very weird indeed, especially those which suggest that the BHMs may not always be completely physical in the generally accepted sense. There are the cases which suggest that BHMs can be impervious to bullets. (Surely not *all* the gun-toting witnesses were bad shots!) BHMs have also been seen to walk through fences (Point Isabel, Ohio, in 1964),[96] and 'In a couple of cases [Pennsylvania, 1973/4], only a part of the animal was seen running about: either the head and torso or the lower appendages with nothing else visible.'[97] As described earlier, one of the Uniontown, Pennsylvania, BHMs vanished in a flash of light when shot at, and this has happened on other occasions too. Also mentioned earlier was the case where a BHM vanished as it was hit by a car, again not an isolated incident; equally strange are the reports of giant footprints which, quite inexplicably, suddenly end. The reported ability to disappear also features in Indian beliefs: a Coast Salish, British Columbia, Indian informed anthropologist Wayne Suttles that the Sasquatch can disappear 'like a spirit'.[98] Even transmogrification has been reported: a Point Isabel, Ohio, BHM (1964) 'changed into another form right before our very eyes', reported the witness. 'This thing just crouched down; its hands became paws and it went on all fours, and it all happened like a slow-motion movie. Then it was gone. It vanished into thin air!'[99] The foregoing would suggest that the creatures which exhibit this inexplicable behaviour have a fluid composition rather than being solidly physical. This could explain the multiplicity of forms in which they appear. But it still does not answer the questions: Where are they from? Why are they here? How do they originate?

Some aspects of the evidence suggest that BHMs are attracted to certain types of people, and places, and are most active during certain weather conditions. It was noted by Stan Gordon during the 1973–4 Pennsylvania scare that they were most active at the time of the full moon and on humid, foggy nights.[100] Also, at Sharpsville, Indiana, during a period of BHM sightings in 1971–2, it was remarked by one witness that: 'The only time it seemed to come around was when it was fair weather. I never saw it after a major frost or before a good summer yet. It didn't appear in cold weather.'[101] As far as we know, no research has been done into this aspect of the phenomenon.

BHMs seem often to take a particular interest in women (the Nowata, Oklahoma, BHM of July 1974 'bypassed houses where only men resided' and showed 'a certain peculiar interest in women'),[102] especially menstruating women;[103] babies and young children;[104] and courting couples.[105] May these attractions perhaps have something to do with the person's hormone output? In the instances cited (except perhaps for babies and young children), the people would be likely to be giving off strong hormone 'signals'. The BHM's other main attractions seem to be to trailer homes (especially those made of aluminium), electricity meters on the houses, and chemical or fuel spills (trailer homes often have fuel storage tanks nearby).[106] R. Martin Wolf reminds us that UFOs, BHMs and other paranormal phenomena occur near to 'microwave towers, high-tension power lines, nuclear power installations, hydro-electric dams, bodies of water, missile silos, railroad tracks, and even mobile homes'; most of these having some association with electro-magnetic energy. Wolf continues:

Combine the frequencies produced by an air conditioning unit with those from a television set. Add fluorescent lighting. Although we cannot visually observe the resulting electrical interference patterns, we can consider the fact that patterns produced by microwaves would undoubtedly behave very differently inside an aluminium structure (such as a mobile home, for example) than they would in the open air. If we had the capability to measure and record our results, and if we could find a mind suitable to receive, register and transmit the resulting energy interference pattern, then we may very well have the formula necessary to create monsters.[107]

So it is possible that when the atmospheric and electro-magnetic forces combine to form a certain pattern, a BHM or other form of alien animal appears, roams an area for a few hours or days, terrorizing the inhabitants, and then, as the flux of the natural and manmade energies changes, just fades away. This conjecture, hardly to be called an explanation for the incredibly weird BHM confrontations that so many ordinary citizens are reporting, still leaves many questions unanswered. Why does the manifestation take the form of a BHM? Is there any motive when they terrify the witnesses? Why are UFOs sometimes seen close to BHMs? These, and other questions, can also be asked about all of the alien animals discussed so far, and in the next chapter we will attempt to answer them.

Animals that aren't: following where the evidence leads

The answers to the many questions raised in the preceding chapters are as elusive as the creatures themselves. But the evidence is rich in clues towards possible explanations, and in this chapter we shall pick out these clues and see what they suggest. It is unwise to try to force an all-encompassing explanation on to any problem as complex and diverse as this; it is possible that there may be several interlinking explanations. We intend instead to present many possible explanations which have been put forward by various researchers, leaving readers to choose for themselves those which they feel to be the most likely (or least unlikely) answers to the major questions: What are alien animals? Where are they from? Why are they here?

Those who are still unable to accept that ordinary folk all over the world have seen, and continue to see, alien animals, are unlikely to be able to accept the theories outlined in this chapter. The problem is that the subject we are dealing with has no place in our materialistic twentieth-century existence. It has no connection with wars, with politics, with the state of the economy, with industry, with TV programmes, with fashion, with the consumer society or any of the other trivia with which so many people occupy themselves. Man is now so conditioned to see the world as those in authority want him to see it that it comes as a shock to learn of a hidden undercurrent of activity which includes creatures that are completely alien to us, so alien in fact that we don't know who or what they are, where they come from, or why they are here. (We are not speaking here solely of alien animals, but of all anomalous phenomena termed Forteana, which includes UFOs.) The natural reaction is to deny that alien creatures exist, to accuse people who see them of hallucination, misidentification, or even fabrication. But if thousands of people of all races are independently hallucinating, misidentifying or lying, then this in itself is a phenomenon which should be closely examined. It is more reasonable to accept that most people are describing what to them was a real event. The experienced investigators of their reports are convinced, as we are, that normal, sane people are seeing and reporting creatures which are both inexplicable and terrifying.

An extremely puzzling feature of the alien animal reports is the variety of forms in which the creatures appear. We could treat each form as a separate phenomenon, but they possess features in common, which fact suggests that each creature is but one manifestation of a single phenomenon. Having described lake monsters, cat-like animals, calf-size black dogs, big birds and other winged monstrosities, and hairy monsters of basic human form, we have no space to give detailed accounts of all the other 'out-of-place' animals we have on record – some, such as crocodiles and alligators in the United States, could be escaped or abandoned pets, but others, such as the many sightings of kangaroos in urban areas of the United States since the turn of the century, are unlikely to be so easily dismissed.[1]

These recognized species seen 'in the wrong place' will not receive too much attention here, since conceivably some could sometimes have escaped from captivity. But this could not be said of creatures which are definitely insubstantial and are therefore classed in the literature as apparitions. They could not even be the ghosts of dead animals, for the species described by the witnesses are unknown on this earth. Such a creature was seen on a spring night in 1966, when 21-year-old Margaret Johnston was driving with her boyfriend near Drogheda in County Louth, Eire. They saw 'a huge horse with a man's face and horrible bulging eyes'. Margaret described the encounter as follows:

Suddenly, John was forced to brake hard as a horse loomed up before us. I was thrown back on the seat. When I looked out the window I saw this monster or ghost or whatever it was. I could see by John's face that he saw it too. I think I screamed, but both of us were so frightened that we were paralysed. The thing had a horse's body. But it was the face, leering and hairy and huge which shocked. The animal stretched right across the road and completely blocked the car. It stayed there for nearly two minutes. We were petrified. Then it vanished. John quickly swung the car around and drove to my home, about a mile away. We were so frightened that we drove through the gate and knocked it off the hinges.

Interestingly, there is a story connected with Rath House, outside which the monster was seen, which says that when a priest was ordered off the lands, his horse reared up and crashed a hoof on the step, leaving a mark behind.[2] Although we have not visited the site of this report, it may be significant that the name of the house, 'Rath', is also an Irish word for a prehistoric earthwork, so this could be another case where an apparition has materialized at an ancient site.

Something nicknamed the 'Man-Monkey' used to terrify people at a bridge over the Birmingham and Liverpool Canal near Woodseaves, Staffordshire. On the night of 21 January 1879 a man was taking a load from Ranton to Woodcote when, about 10 P.M., he reached the bridge. 'A strange black creature with great white eyes' jumped out of the bushes and on to the horse's back, and when the witness tried to push it off with his whip, he found to his horror that the whip only went through the creature, which stayed where it was for a while as the horse broke into a canter and rushed along the road. When the man reported his experience he was told that others had seen the Man-Monkey at the bridge ever since a man was drowned in the canal there.[3]

These are both relatively recent first-hand accounts, and more follow. Abbey House in Cambridge had a strange animal ghost which was seen by the children and parents living there between 1904 and 1910. It was 'a furry animal which walked on its hind legs and had flipper-like front paws and a long beak'. It was later seen elsewhere in Cambridge.[4] Author D. A. MacManus' grandfather saw a large animal 'the shape of a fox with a large bushy tail, but of enormous size . . . he clapped his hands and called. "Shoo!", whereat it stopped at once, stood up on its hind legs, and turned to face him.' Shocked, he saw that the creature, his own height, was headless, but he could tell it was looking at him, and 'pouring out hate, bestiality, and evil'. He made the sign of the cross and the creature dropped on all fours and ran off, disappearing in the darkness. This happened in the late 1860s in Ireland.[5] Another fox, but this time with a head, was seen in Scotland by Richard Curle when a boy. One night he awoke to hear footsteps approaching his room, and in walked, on its hind legs, 'a creature with the face of a fox'. It wore a top hat (!), but was foxlike and had a fox's bushy tail, though the creature was larger than an ordinary fox. It gazed at him fixedly, until he shouted 'Go away!', which it did. Curle states that he was wide awake at the time.[6] This tale has certain similarities to the preceding one, from Ireland.

Another account, again first-hand, comes from Willoughton, Lincolnshire, where a local resident cycling along a lane at night saw something come out of a hedge. It was as big as a hare, but had two horns and only two feet, which clattered on the road. It ran along fast, and the witness could not get past it because it blocked his efforts to do so. Suddenly it hopped up on to the grass verge and seemed to disappear.[7] Finally, a man who later, in Africa, had a reputation as a big-game hunter, described a creature he saw at the Hangley Cleeve barrows in Somerset as the most terrifying thing he had ever seen, and that was long after the sighting. What he saw was a 'crouching form like a rock with matted hair all over it, and pale, flat eyes.'[8]

These abbreviated accounts show that not all non-human apparitions take the form of recognizable or believable creatures, though there are many of those too. We have on record ghost pigs, ducks, colts, horses, donkeys, foals, deer, rabbits, calves, lambs, lions, cats and dogs, and there are probably others. The importance of the accounts just given is that they contain features which our alien animals also exhibit – the 'great white eyes' of the Man-Monkey; the ability to disappear; and, above all, the apparent arbitrariness of the shape taken by the creature. Why a fox wearing a top hat? Such creatures are often obviously insubstantial. They disappear (the Lincolnshire creature) or an object can be passed through them (the Man-Monkey); just as the alien animals often seem to be insubstantial. The American BHM, for example, sometimes does not leave tracks where tracks would be expected, is transparent, disappears as the witnesses watch, and sometimes an incomplete BHM has been seen, such as in Pennsylvania when only its head and body were apparent.[9] It should be noted that the whole of a water monster is rarely seen, but because of the nature of its environment, it is always possible to say that the rest of it was hidden by the water. We cannot know whether this is the case, or whether the beast has only partially materialized. It may be significant that sometimes UFO entities are physically incomplete, a point we shall return to later.

Originally we assumed that headless ghosts were totally fictional, but that was before we began to delve into the accounts. Now we find that apparitions with various extremities missing are regularly rather than rarely seen. A headless ghost dog was photographed at Tingewick, Buckinghamshire, by Arthur Springer, a retired CID inspector from Scotland Yard, some time around 1916. He was actually photographing a tea party in the garden, and no animal was seen during that time. It was only when the plates were developed that the headless dog became apparent. No one recognized the ghost dog, and there was no similar dog living in the village. (There are a number of cases on record where apparitions have been photographically recorded but were not visible at the time the exposure was made.) This and other incomplete ghosts again tend to demonstrate the arbitrary nature of the manifestation. Sometimes it appears as a recognizable species, complete in all details, sometimes it is recognizable but incomplete (ghost dog), while on other occasions it takes fantastic forms that have never been seen on this earth. When seen more than once, such fantastic creatures sometimes agree in details (as do the BHM reports), but sometimes an unexpected feature is seen (as when a BHM with a bushy tail is reported – e.g. Mamquam, British Columbia, 1969).[10]

If more evidence is needed to show that the choice of form is arbitrary, the fact that in some reports ghost creatures change from one shape to another surely provides that evidence. This ability, usually known as shape-shifting, takes several forms. 1. Humans (usually witches) are said to change into animals and back again. 2. Ghost people have been seen to change into ghost animals. 3. Ghost animals have been seen to change from one species to another. British folklore is rich in cases of witches turning into various animals, but especially hares. One occurrence of this, apparently a true happening, took place early this century near Lytchett Matravers in Dorset. Beagles chased a hare for miles and had nearly caught it when it was seen to cross a road and disappear. Immediately a ragged old woman, out of breath, appeared at the point where the hare had disappeared and ran across the road. She could not be found, though the bushes were beaten. A boy who saw all this was questioned by the author of the pamphlet where we read of it.[11] Werewolves are a subdivision of category one, since a werewolf is said to be a human being in changed shape. Is it conceivable that some alien animals are were-animals, that is, humans who have assumed animal form?

Alien animals sometimes change shape too. On page 166 is an account of a BHM changing shape before the witness, and the evidence suggests that the Loch Ness Monster may have the ability to change its shape: its appearance varies from sighting to sighting. Sometimes several humps are seen; and sometimes it resembles an upturned boat. In 1933, Mr W. U. Goodbody, a member of the Ness Fishery Board, saw the monster and tried to count its humps. His daughters tried too, but they could never make their totals agree, or stay the same. As F. W. Holiday comments: 'This was legerdemain of the first order.'[12]

We are suggesting that many apparitional phenomena (among which we feel it is legitimate to include alien animals) arbitrarily adopt a physical form in which to manifest. Where do they take these forms from, and why do they select one form rather than another (assuming they have a choice)? These are difficult questions for which we have no immediate answers, but we have gathered some thoughts which may be relevant. Theo Brown makes an interesting suggestion: that a ghost without form can make use of any suitable image at hand; or that the human witness senses the invisible ghost and 'clothes' it in any image which is available in his or her mind or surroundings. She illustrates this by quoting the case of a woman who saw a ghost dog in her house which she thought was her own, live, dog, but found later it definitely could not have been.[13]

An extension of this possibility is the idea that the human mind is, by its power of 'image making', capable of creating a physical being which can then exist as an independent creature. If this stretches the bounds of credibility too far, we shall soon cite a case which supports this possibility, but first let us suggest three mechanisms by which the human mind could create its own alien animals. They are:

1. Initially someone *thinks* he or she sees an alien animal, others flock to the area to look for it, and their combined mental images, based on the original witness's description, create the creature. This might explain some but not all sightings. It is not a likely explanation when the first report is very detailed, and there are few later sightings, as has occurred with the Owlman of Mawnan in Cornwall.

2. Initially someone sees an alien animal and as the details become generally known the creature's image grows stronger as it is fed by the mental images from the minds of all those who are visualizing it. If the first witness did not publicize or think about his sighting, the image would more likely fade through lack of sustenance. (Later we will enlarge on this concept in our examination of the importance of energy.)

3. Alien animals in some degree correspond to people's expectations and desires: mankind is fascinated by the idea of the 'monster'. So

are they solely hallucinatory, taking shape from the archetypal monster image? They might sometimes originate in this way, but then take on an independent existence, feeding by vampirism on whatever energy source is available.

The idea of creating an independent being by the sole means of human 'mind power' is not so irrational as it may sound. Madame Alexandra David-Neel describes her successful attempt to form a *tulpa*, or illusory creation, in her book *With Mystics and Magicians in Tibet*.[14] She chose to create a monk, and after a few months of isolation and 'the prescribed concentration of thought and other rites', he took form and became lifelike. When she went on a tour, the monk joined the party.

The phantom performed various actions of the kind that are natural to travellers and that I had not commanded. For instance, he walked, stopped, looked around him. The illusion was mostly visual, but sometimes I felt as if a robe was lightly rubbing against me and once a hand seemed to touch my shoulder.

The features which I had imagined, when building my phantom, gradually underwent a change. The fat, chubby-cheeked fellow grew leaner, his face assumed a vaguely mocking, sly, malignant look. He became more troublesome and bold. In brief, he escaped my control.

Once, a herdsman who brought me a present of butter saw the *tulpa* in my tent and took it for a live lama.

I ought to have let the phenomenon follow its course, but the presence of that unwanted companion began to prove trying to my nerves; it turned into a 'day-nightmare'. Moreover, I was beginning to plan my journey to Lhasa and needed a quiet brain devoid of other preoccupations, so I decided to dissolve the phantom. I succeeded, but only after six months of hard struggle. My mind-creature was tenacious of life.

There is nothing strange in the fact that I may have created my own hallucination. The interesting point is that in these cases of materialization, others see the thought-forms that have been created.

Tibetans disagree in their explanations of such phenomena; some think a material form is really brought into being, others consider the apparition as a mere case of suggestion, the creator's thought impressing others and causing them to see what he himself sees.

If it can happen in Tibet, why not elsewhere in the world? Admittedly the people who see alien animals have not subjected themselves to long periods of 'concentration of thought', but there may be circumstances in which the necessary mental state could be spontaneously achieved.[15] During the time when frequent sightings of Morgawr, the Cornish sea monster, were made, 'monster-raising' experiments were carried out with some degree of success, a fact which should certainly be taken into consideration when trying to assess whether alien animals are in any way linked to the minds of their percipients. Witches in Cornwall swam sky-clad on several occasions in 1976 and 1977, and according to Doc Shiels,

It is also a fact that they were pretty successful in raising the monster. I happen to know some of the ladies involved and, on several occasions, I was present when one or more of the witches were out monster-baiting. In the early Spring of 1976, around Easter time, at least *three* young witches . . . took a dip in Falmouth Bay and the Helford River in order to invoke Morgawr. They were successful, too, because various sightings were reported around this time and a young boy from Helston took a rather murky picture of the sea-serpent . . . The naked witches have been regarded either as a jokey press gimmick or as a complete non-event. The truth of the matter is that the witches played a very important role in a whole series of monster invocations. It should also be remembered that the Owlman showed up for the first time during the Easter weekend of 1976, around Mawnan Church, when, in that part of the river below the church . . . , Vivienne and Psyche swam naked and called up the monsters.[16]

After a swim by the witches on May Eve 1976, two London bankers fishing from Parson's Beach below Mawnan church saw *two* monsters (on 4 May). They reported: 'Suddenly, something rose out of the water, about 150 or 200 yards away. It was greeny-grey in colour and appeared to have humps. Another, smaller one also appeared. They were visible for about 10 seconds and looked straight at us.'[17]

Doc Shiels was also involved in two 'Monstermind' experiments in 1977, designed to raise water monsters. The first lasted from 31 January to 2 February and involved psychics in Britain, India, the United States, USSR and Mexico. The water monster in Lake Kolkol was raised by Chandra Rao in Calcutta, several sightings were made of the Loch Ness Monster, a possible sighting of a monster in Loch Shiel was reported, and photographs were taken of the Loch Morar creature and of Morgawr. The second experiment began on 1 May 1977 and was due to last three months, but in view of 'psychic backlash' suffered by several participants in the first experiment, a number of them could not take part, and Doc himself dropped out after two months. He had, however, taken two excellent photographs of the Loch Ness Monster (see Chapter 1) on 21 May.[18] To non-psychic observers such as ourselves, it is not clear exactly by what means the witches and Monstermind teams managed to raise the monsters. Doc says that the techniques of those involved varied somewhat, he himself using 'wizardry' – 'I think I was successful because I had a strong desire for success.'[19] In view of Alexandra David-Neel's experiences with the *tulpa*, could they have been actually *creating* the monsters rather than just raising them?

Lyall Watson seems to think that the human mind is concerned in the formation of all manner of strange phenomena. He writes:

Some special people can do this ['produce physical effects at a distance by purely mental means'] well under almost any conditions, but the research suggests that many otherwise normal people can produce the phenomena in certain circumstances. Perhaps one of the necessary conditions is provided by the magnetic flaws that exist at special places. Perhaps fairies, dwarfs, elves, leprechauns, dragons, monsters, vampires, werewolves, ghosts, poltergeists and flying saucers all exist. And perhaps the cynics who say that it is all in the mind are also right, because all these things exist or are produced at the second or etheric level.

The strange behaviour of all apparitions suggests that they obey laws not quite like those of conventional physics, and that they probably belong to a reality with slightly different space-time references. The fact that those who come closest to these phenomena, usually receive information structured to support their own beliefs or fears, suggests that these apparitions cannot be entirely independent of the minds of those involved. Taken together, these two suggestions provide the basis for a concept that could account for a great many mysteries.[20]

Although alien animals (and UFOs) are elusive and rarely leave traces of their presence, they sometimes do leave marks or debris of some kind, and this too might be explained by an unconscious psychokinetic ability on the part of the witness. But we do not want to give the impression that we are explaining away alien animals as being 'all in the mind'. Madame David-Neel's experience shows very well that if alien animals are originally created by thought power (and this is by no means proven, of course), they can take on an independent life of their own and be harder to kill than a normal physical creature.

We wrote earlier that all the varieties of alien animals have features in common which suggest they are all aspects of a single phenomenon, together with UFOs and other weird apparitions, on all of which there is a huge recorded literature. Before continuing our discussion of the theories which have been formulated to account for the phenomenon, we will give examples to support our statement that alien animals exhibit similarities to one another. One obvious similiarity is the glowing eyes, often red, described by witnesses of many black dogs and BHMs, and sometimes winged monstrosities (e.g. Mothman, Owlman), and big cats. Another link between black dogs and BHMs is that both have often been reported as staring at the witness (for example: the Worcestershire black dog described in Chapter 3 – 'It swung its head round to stare at me'; and the Lemmon Creek, British Columbia, BHM seen in 1960 – 'It just stood there staring at me.'[21]). The Surrey puma, too, sometimes behaves this way. A Bagshot woman who saw it from her bedroom window described how it 'slowly walked up and down, staring at me'. Both black dog and BHM sometimes depart from the witness's view in an unconventional manner: by disappearing in a flash of light. In Chapter 2 we described how alien cat-like animals are often hard to identify, having features of other species such as dogs. One apparent black dog seen in Ireland (described more fully in Chapter 3) was not really identified completely by the witness as a dog. As it walked along in a shallow stream he could not tell whether it was a 'dog, panther, or what'.[22] All alien animals without exception are elusive. They usually appear when least expected, and rarely when watched for. We must not overlook the difficulty in tracking and catching 'real' animals, however.

. . . a crocodile was the subject of a large scale search in a small, shallow lake in Florida. This one was finally caught, but only after three weeks of Keystone Kops chases through the clear water, and the combined arsenal of grappling hooks, nets, electric shock and baited buoys. All of this was to no avail. Finally, the temperature dropped to 30 degrees, and the croc decided to end the game by leaving the water for a sun bath. Little wonder, then, that Nessie has avoided capture in the depths of Loch Ness, where the water even a few feet below the surface is nearly opaque with suspended particles of peat.[23]

So is it really surprising that these animals are not caught? They know their environment far better than we do. On the other hand, Jerome Clark and Loren Coleman give us the opposite viewpoint when they state:

Extraterrestrial spaceships simply could not be touring the earth in the massive numbers UFO sightings suggest . . . Neither could massive numbers of large unknown animals be roaming countrysides and city streets without long ago having been officially recognized and catalogued (and probably driven into extinction as well).

Moreover, they could not have done all this in such numbers without providing us with more conclusive physical evidence than they have given us so far. The 'physical evidence' is always just enough to suggest that the reported manifestation was not purely hallucinatory; it is never enough to prove that it was objectively real.[24]

It really sounds as though there is an intelligence behind the phenomenon which wishes to keep us guessing!

Many alien animals seem to be unaffected by gunfire. The reports of bullets fired at close range having no effect on them are inexplicable if they are normal physical creatures, but if they are considered as partially materialized phantoms, then we may be beginning to grapple with the problem. Some reports suggest that there are degrees of materialization ranging from the traditional ghost, which though appearing solid can rarely be touched (it usually fades away or always seems beyond the witness), right through to the completely physical which when injured will leave trails of blood, though the corpse is never discovered. Students of UFO reports will know that some of the entities reported have a greater than normal density, and bullets fired at point-blank range merely bowl them over, whilst knives glance off them as though their skins were made of steel. With water monsters it is rather more difficult to tell what effect gunfire has, because the beasts may have a particularly tough or thick hide which is not easily penetrated, and if a water monster submerges when shot at, it is impossible to know whether it is injured or only alarmed. A sea monster seen in Shetland Islands waters in 1881 was shot at from the fishing boat *Bertie*. The crew watched as a large creature gradually rose from the water near the boat.

The eyes could be seen very distinctly. These were extremely large and their glare gave the object an exceedingly fierce look. The creature headed straight for the boat, and as the men feared it would foul the lines they tried to frighten it off. One of the crew who had a rifle put in a double charge of powder and two balls. He fired at close range but the bullets were seen to glance off the huge slimy body . . . Ballast stones were thrown as well.

The men's frantic efforts only infuriated the brute. It raised its great tail and thrashed the water with a deafening noise, and at this stage it dived when quite close alongside, and the wash set up by the enormous body set the boat on her beam ends.

Much of their gear, oars and boxes of fish went overboard and the crew had to cut their lines. The monster (estimated to be considerably longer than their 45-foot boat) kept with them until night came.[25]

An account from the United States is relevant here, for as well as demonstrating the invulnerability of alien animals when shot at, it also includes other typical features – dogs' reluctance to chase it, and a shape-shifting ability.

People near Pevely, in Jefferson county, Missouri, tell of a ghostly white fox which has been seen by many farmers, and even by motorists on Highway 61, as recently as 1932. Albino foxes are not unknown in the Ozarks, but there was something very special about this one. It was quite tame and had been fired on many times at close range, but without result. Foxhounds seemed aware of its existence, but they would not chase it. Several persons believe that it could transform itself into a skunk at will; others say that they actually saw it turn into a short-haired black and white dog, with a stump tail.[26]

Also puzzling are those occasional reports which describe different kinds of alien animals being seen together. For example, an enormous dog seen near Orofino, California, in 1969 was thought to be running with the BHMs seen and frequently heard in the area;[27] and on 21 August 1978 Scott Patterson of Minerva, Ohio, saw two 'cougar-type felines' when he drove his car towards two pairs of large yellow eyes he had first seen reflected in torchlight. As he drove closer, his headlights on the animals, 'a large bipedal hairy creature stepped in front of the two cats as if to protect them. It then proceeded to lurch towards the headlights of Patterson's car.'[28]

There are so many similarities between UFOs, UFO entities and alien animals that there seems a strong possibility they are part of the same phenomenon; or at least are activated by the same stimulus. All that we have written about the elusiveness of alien animals applies, possibly even more so, to UFOs. UFO entities are a not inconsiderable part of the UFO phenomenon. Although many UFO reports feature only a craft or light in the sky, there are over 1,400 entity cases on record, and over 50 cases in which human witnesses have been abducted (and later returned) by UFO entities.[29] Sometimes these entities have incomplete lower limbs. They seem transparent as though only partially materialized, or their legs and feet are completely missing, or occasionally they are standing in long grass and the witness cannot see what their lower limbs are like.[30] It has also been noted[31] that water monsters even when seen on land always have part of their body obscured, which may suggest that this is incompletely formed. And on a few occasions incomplete BHMs have been reported (see page 166). A parallel to these incomplete materializations may perhaps be found in some experiments conducted with mediums earlier this century. The most gifted mediums were able to materialize limbs, heads, and even whole bodies, but sometimes imperfectly formed limbs were noted. This was especially so during the early 1920s when Dr Gustave Geley carried out experiments with the Polish medium Franek Kluski. He materialized hands which dipped themselves into hot paraffin wax and then dematerialized, leaving a wax 'glove' from which a cast could be made. Often these showed a variety of shapes and sizes of complete hands, but sometimes they were incompletely formed in some respect.[32] Also, as we remarked earlier, the traditional story of the headless ghost is confirmed by factual reports. We saw in Chapter 2 that the mysterious big cats often leave pawprints with claw marks typical of a dog, and the BHMs of Chapter 5, although often leaving footprints with the expected five digits, sometimes leave prints with only three; and even two-, four- and six-toed prints have been reported. A Cornish black dog sounded like a horse with clattering hoofs; and the weird winged Jersey Devil was sometimes seen to have horse's hoofs – two more examples of inaccurate extremities. Some witnesses have observed BHMs crossing a muddy area but have immediately afterwards been unable to find any footprints made by the creature. UFO entities often display the same ability to float or walk without actually touching the surface of the ground. The significance of the faulty materialization of extremities is not immediately apparent, but it may be that the creatures do not really need legs and feet, and only materialize them in order to 'complete the picture'; so they are not too concerned about getting the details exactly right, or even forming the extremities at all.

Another parallel between UFOs and alien animals is found in the speed with which they can all move, and the abrupt changes of direction which they can make. Water monsters are reported to have tremendous speed and manoeuvrability for a creature of massive size, and big cats and BHMs also can exhibit tremendous speeds when running. BHMs sometimes disappear in a flash of light, and the Jersey Devil of 1909 once vanished in an explosion. UFO entities also sometimes disappear before a witness, as happened on 30 September 1954 near Marcilly-sur-Vienne, Indre-et-Loire, France.

The witness said: 'Suddenly the strange man vanished, and I couldn't explain how he did, since he did not disappear from my field of vision by walking away, but vanished like an image one erases suddenly.'[33] The excitement or fear produced in animals, particularly dogs, by the close proximity of a UFO is well known among ufologists.[34] Similar odd reactions have appeared throughout our accounts of alien animals. Domestic animals are noted for their sensitivity and often show an awareness of hauntings and similar psychic happenings.

Vehicles seem to attract some alien animals, especially Mothman[35] and BHMs, as well as UFO entities. Many UFO sightings are made from cars, and those witnesses unfortunate enough to be abducted are often taken from cars. An encounter with a UFO entity on 14 November 1976 reported by Joyce Bowles of Winchester, Hampshire, took place while she and a friend were driving near the city. After seeing a UFO in the sky their car went off course in a lane and ended up on a wide grass verge. As the couple sat there, a 'man' emerged from a landed UFO close by and came over to the car. He placed one hand on the roof and looked inside at them for about two minutes, before moving away to the back of the car.[36] Compare this with the Yakima, Washington, BHM case of 19 or 20 September 1966 when a youth driving near the town at night saw a 7-foot hairy creature standing in the road ahead. He braked and stopped: 'It just stood there and looked at me right through the windshield of the car . . . He walked around behind my car and then turned around and came right back to the window and just bent over and looked in the window at me. I got my car started and took off.'[37] BHMs have also been accidentally hit by cars (but apparently not harmed too much) and have physically attacked cars on a number of occasions. Pumas too have a propensity for appearing near to or waylaying cars. Chapter 2 contains numerous examples of big cats running across a road in front of a car, sitting on the road and sometimes blocking the passage of a car, and on occasion even jumping at cars. On 29 July 1917 two married couples were motoring near Decatur, Illinois, when they saw a big animal by the roadside; it leapt 20 feet and crashed into the side of the car. During that month something called 'Nellie the Lion' had frequently been seen in the area, but was never caught. Thirty years later on 1 August 1948 near Quakertown, Indiana, game warden Clifford Fath had to swerve to avoid 'a varmint' that was sitting in the middle of the road. As he did so it leapt against the side of the car, crashed to the ground, and then raced off into the woods.[38]

Some researchers have gone even further in their linking of UFOs and alien animals, and have suggested that alien animals come from UFOs, which is somewhat different from the suggestion we made earlier, that alien animals and UFOs may be part of the same phenomenon, or triggered by the same stimulus. The following amazing case certainly suggests strongly that there is *some* kind of link between the two. Beginning in 1975, a series of UFO events was experienced by several people on a Rocky Mountain ranch in Colorado.[39] An untraceable humming sound was often heard; also noises as if someone was walking about outside; UFOs were often seen, both aerial and landed; entities were seen inside and outside the house; voices were heard; cattle mutilations (a recent large-scale phenomenon in the United States) were experienced; and 'Creatures who looked like "Big Foot" were seen in the woods.' Whether the BHM/UFO link demonstrated in this case was intentional or coincidental (i.e. that they were formed by the same stimulus but were otherwise unconnected) is not as yet clear. People who suspect that the link is intentional have suggested that BHMs are some form of experiment being conducted by UFO entities, perhaps to test our environment before they themselves land; or maybe they are exiles here from some other planet, or food animals being bred here for people on other worlds,[40] or even a genetic experiment being carried on before the UFO entities use them to colonize another planet, [41] as discussed in Chapter 5. We think a more likely possibility is that the BHMs (and also other alien animals) may *on occasions* be a form assumed by UFO entities, both to keep humans at a distance and to arouse their curiosity, because this may suit their intentions. (This is not necessarily to imply that the phenomenon has an extraterrestrial source.)

Other alien animals than BHMs have been seen in UFO-haunted areas, sometimes in close proximity to a UFO, as happened on 14 December 1963 in South Africa. Two men were driving in the small hours of the morning along the Potchefstroom to Vereeniging road when they saw something in the road 'that resembled a buck'. They turned back to investigate and saw that it 'appeared to be an exceptionally large dog'. As they turned their car to continue their journey the area became brightly illuminated, and

Suddenly a strange bright object appeared ahead of us and made straight for our car at a terrific speed. I was afraid that the object would hit our car, so I jumped out absolutely petrified. Mr Muller did likewise. Standing next to the car in the tarred road, we were astounded to see the object dive right over our car and ascend up into the sky.

It made another pass at the car, hovered over it for a couple of minutes, shot off, returned, and again dived low over the two men, repeating this performance several times more.[42] In 1968, around the time when they saw a UFO with entity hovering near their house, a Salem, Ohio, family often saw a large cat-like creature around the house, and they also believed a big black manlike creature had taken up residence in the nearby woods. On 9 September 1973 in Savannah, Georgia, 'ten big, black hairy dogs' were seen to come out of a landed UFO in a cemetery.[43] In England during 1964, Bushylease Farm, Crondall, Hampshire, was regularly visited by a strange animal (as already described in Chapter 2), and the farmer also saw a mysterious light moving around on the roofs of farm buildings. He could not trace its source, but he noticed that the puma-like animal appeared soon afterwards on each occasion.[44] In Chapter 4 we noted several correspondences between sightings of UFOs and of weird winged things. Mothman and Owlman in particular appeared when UFOs were around, but long before they came on the scene, a strange and possibly significant UFO sighting took place in the mountains between Mongolia and Tibet. Nicholas Roerich, archaeologist, anthropologist and painter, was camped in the area in the summer of 1927, and had set up a shrine dedicated to Shambhala. Shortly after its completion, several members of the party saw 'a remarkably big black eagle' flying overhead, and, high above it, 'something big and shiny reflecting the sun, like a huge oval moving at great speed.' It changed direction as they watched.[45] Morgawr, the Cornish sea monster, also appeared when UFOs were seen. For example, on Friday, 13 May 1977, Mr and Mrs Arthur Wood of Plymstock saw a bright orange and green ball of fire off Pendennis Point near Falmouth at 9 A.M.; half an hour later they both saw Morgawr in the water below the Point, heading out to sea.[46]

If UFOs and their occupants continue to remain as elusive as they have been since serious investigation into their behaviour first started, about thirty years ago, it may be some time before we discover the meaning of the alien animals/UFO link.

Of course not everyone takes seriously alien animals, UFOs, and the other untidy, because inexplicable, phenomena that persist despite debunking. Many an armchair critic will dismiss all the data with a wave of his little finger, putting it down, no doubt, to hysteria. Psychologists too will always be able to explain away such phenomena in terms of human aberration. There are only two 'explain away' theories which we feel may perhaps be relevant (but which should certainly not be used to dismiss the whole phenomenon). One says that people need and enjoy 'the unknown'. They may not be so interested in solving the mystery; they just like the uncertainty of not knowing what's out there! The other idea is that alien animals echo the conservationists' concern about this planet, and their view that civilization has gone too far along the road to destruction. The alien animal lives in harmony with its environment, and so it symbolizes freedom and security. However relevant such ideas may be in general, they still cannot seriously be used to deny the existence of the alien animals. It is more relevant to examine the reports, the witnesses, and the circumstances in which the events took place, which we shall do when discussing energy later in this chapter.

Before then, however, we must briefly describe a few more of the theories put forward to explain the presence of alien animals. Teleportation is a favourite one. This is, simply, when a living being or inert object is mysteriously transported from one location to another, often through solid matter, and usually instantaneously. Such an occurrence is thought to have happened in May 1906, at Furnace Mill, Lamberhurst, Kent, when a horse was discovered to be missing from its stall and was found by its owner in a nearby hay room. So far not too strange: horses like hay. But this hay room had a doorway 'barely wide enough for a man to enter', and a partition had to be knocked down to get the horse out. Poltergeist phenomena were also experienced at the mill.[47] Involuntary teleportation might be used to explain some 'out-of-place animals', in that they are suddenly, for reasons that are not understood, transferred from their everyday environment, be it a lion in Africa, to somewhere else in the world, such as Nottinghamshire, England. (We are not saying, however, that teleportation does necessarily explain the Nottinghamshire lion sightings, described in Chapter 2.) And then after a few days the beast is equally suddenly teleported either back to its home or to some other location. But such a theory could not be used to explain the presence of unknown or extinct species. The latter might be time-travellers; or phantoms of beasts which previously lived in the area they now haunt. R. J. M. Rickard and John Michell suggested this theory in regard to such aliens as the Surrey puma;[48] the Revd Dr W. D. Omand feels that this is the explanation for the Loch Ness Monster.[49] Unknown species are unlikely to be phantoms of that kind; they may teleport from other worlds, planes or dimensions – either intentionally or unintentionally. Whether such other worlds, planes or dimensions even exist is not known, only postulated. The idea is a useful one, because the presence of 'unknowns' on earth can be easily ascribed to it. Our world may be separated from the other world or worlds by a usually impenetrable barrier, but there may also be opening points or 'windows'[50] through which the unknowns emerge. The 'windows' are at certain points on the earth, which would explain why sightings of unknowns tend to cluster or be repeated at certain places. Or perhaps teleportation is not involved in this. It may simply be that when the conditions are right (increased radioactivity? increased psychic awareness?) the witness can see through the 'window' and catches a glimpse of an alien unknown, which really is in its own usual environment in some other world. Witnesses to UFO events, especially landings, often remark that all was silent in the area at the time, no birds sang, no vehicles passed along a normally busy road. This suggests that the normal passage of time we experience in this world was somehow temporarily suspended, and that the witness, for the duration of the event, exists somehow in another 'dimension'. This is pure speculation, a hypothesis put forward to encompass the strange facts. If it were true, it would indicate that the barrier between this dimension and others is a fragile one, easily penetrated if the conditions are right.

Another theory is that alien animals (and UFOs) are holograms. Holography, a relatively recent technique which has caught the public imagination, is a kind of lensless photography, and the resulting hologram is three-dimensional. Maybe alien animals and UFOs are merely holograms (but more advanced than those we can yet produce, for they move, utter sounds, feel solid when touched and leave traces), projected on to Earth by someone or something from elsewhere. An extension of the hologram theory is that reality itself is a hologram, and that each individual's understanding or seeing of it is only one narrow view of the whole. Sometimes, however, a person glimpses more of the total hologram, when an unusual phenomenon is perceived by him. In other words, such phenomena may be natural, but are rarely seen by man because his view of reality is so blinkered.[51]

One theory which we hope is not valid is that alien animals may be the result of black magic conjurations. According to Frank Hamel in *Human Animals*,[52] 'Books on ceremonial magic explain how it is possible to call up demons in the shape of beasts.' Among the creatures named are lions and other cats, monkeys, dogs, and birds or beasts of prey, and there are also 'compound monsters' – all prominent in our collection of alien animals. The Devil, too, can appear in any form he pleases, and did so appear to medieval witches, according to King James I in his *Daemonologie*: 'he [the Devil] obliges himself to appear at their [witches] calling upon him by such a proper name which he shows unto them, either in likeness of a dog, a cat, an ape, or suchlike other beast . . .' If black magic is involved in the manifestation of alien animals, they may have been intentionally created, or they may be the result of conjurations by the incompetent. The animals may now be on the loose, beyond the control of their creators. Data on such black magic conjurations is, not surprisingly, sparse, but it is known that the notorious magician Aleister Crowley conjured up Abra-Melin demons at Boleskine, his house on the shore of Loch Ness, which he chose because it was a potent psychic energy centre. According to John Symonds,[53] Crowley was successful in his conjurations and wrote: 'the lodge and the terrace soon became peopled with shadowy shapes'. But Crowley could not control them, and they began to cause misfortune, illness, madness and death in the house and environs. Could they also have strengthened the manifestations of the monster in Loch Ness? It is certain that the creature was in residence long before Crowley came on the scene (perhaps the earliest reference is to St Columba, who is said by his biographer Adamnan to have banished the monster in the sixth century) and so he could not have created it, but his magical practices could inadvertently have reinvigorated it. Crowley may also be partly responsible for the evil atmosphere which can be sensed in the area by some. This has been exorcized by the Revd Dr W. D. Omand, a practising exorcist for 40 years, who writes:

I never exorcised the monster, as is supposed, but Loch Ness and the land immediately round it. My reason was to overcome the spirit of evil which I have located in and around the various waterways in which monsters have been sighted. This spirit of evil was a danger not so much to local inhabitants as to strangers attracted to the locality in the hope of getting a viewing. People who so open themselves through curiosity are immensely receptive and therefore very easy to possess.

As a result of the success of the Loch Ness venture I repeated the operation in two other Highland lochs and also in Ireland, Sweden and Norway and the results were positive in each case.

It is true that on my annual visits to Scotland I invariably go by Loch Ness. I call on two highly educated men in the district who are checking developments on my behalf, as others are doing round the other lakes which I have exorcised. Results to date have been satisfactory and there has never been any question of repeating the proceedings.

You are right in thinking that 'Nessie', or whatever one chooses to call the phenomenon, is harmless, but evil often attaches itself to the innocent. I believe that what I and others have seen is a manifestation of something that was a physical reality in those waters centuries ago. Scotland has a number of psychical hangovers from previous ages which those of us who have inherited 'the gift' are privileged to behold.[54]

Dr Omand referred to the 'spirit of evil' which was the focus of his exorcism, and in a book about his work it is suggested that monsters can have 'a malevolent effect on human beings', causing unhappiness and tragedy in the vicinity of their haunts.[55] The 'psychic backlash' which has been experienced by Doc Shiels and others involved in invoking monsters may have the same origins. But there is a defence against it, as Doc tells when discussing 'the backlash problem'.

Monster raising can cause illness. This happened to several members of my 'Monstermind' team, and I know it happened to such stalwart hunters as Tim Dinsdale and Ted Holiday. Why? The simple answer is that, in all things magical, you pay for what you get. The very best protection against this disturbing type of psychic backlash is *humour*. The protection, in turn, has to be paid for. So, although my humorous wizardry is successful, it is not taken too seriously by the monster hunting establishment.[56]

However the truly alien animals (i.e. those that are non-physical) are initially created, be it at the instigation of an outside influence (e.g. UFO entities), by intentional or unintentional massed or individual thought power, by magic rituals, or whatever other stimulus, they seem to need energy to feed them. Some of the energy sources may even be responsible for actually triggering the alien animal manifestation, one such being electro-magnetic radiation.

The frequency of occurrences of alien animals and other phenomena in the area of microwave towers, electrical generating stations, nuclear power plants, and other similar structures has been noted by some researchers. It has been suggested that somehow the electrical interference patterns formed by the workings of the many electrical installations may be creating monsters,[57] or creating the conditions which enable them to penetrate into the physical world. So the majority of alien animals may be one of the unexpected offshoots of industrialization. Not only large power installations but even the domestic TV set and fluorescent tube emit radiation which disrupts the natural balance. Power lines, too, can produce ill effects; in Dorset the villagers of Fishpond have experienced all manner of unpleasant symptoms since a special high-voltage power line was placed through the village,[58] and an item published in *Science*[59] 'reveals that transmission of power by power lines disturbs the actual magnetic field of the earth.' More research definitely needs to be done to ascertain what are the real effects of today's massive energy outpourings and manipulations. It seems possible that one effect is the formation of alien animals, with electro-magnetic radiation directly responsible, or as one link in a chain of causes. If all the necessary conditions are fulfilled (and we do not of course know exactly what they are), an alien animal could appear anywhere, as indeed they have been doing.

An alternative idea is that alien animals are not actually produced by the effects of electro-magnetic radiation, but only feed on the energy given off, and are formed in some other way. That some alien animals *are* linked with electrical effects is indicated by an incident in the Monongahela National Forest, West Virginia, in October 1960 when a man driving his car saw an 8-foot hairy ape-like 'monster with long hair standing straight up'. His car stopped and the driver had to sit and wait. He commented: 'It seemed the monster was very much afraid of the bus [which was accompanying the witness, and backed up when its driver found he was no longer following] and dropped his hair and to my surprise, as soon as he did this, my car started to run again.' As he resumed his journey, the car again began to falter. 'I could see the sparks flying from under the hood of my car as if it had a very bad short. And sure enough, there beside the road stood the monster again. The points were completely burned out of my car.'[60] In another American car-stop case in Illinois (already described in Chapter 2), a man's car came to a stop and as he got out a black cat-like animal emerged from the shadows, almost as if it had deliberately caused the car's engine to fail. The sequence of 1. car fails, 2. witness gets out to check engine, 3. witness observes UFO nearby or is approached by a 'spaceman' figure, has been reported many times and is well known to UFO researchers. The cases above seem to be a new variant on it.

The fact that alien animals of all kinds are sometimes reported as appearing during electrical storms is also of significance. This would suggest that the creatures are enabled to manifest because of the increase in electrical energy available to them. Referring to the Black River water monster near Lyons Falls, New York, a report on recent sightings concluded with the sentence: 'The monster has been reported seen in this isolated section of northern New York three times in the past 10 years, but always when there was an electrical storm in progress.'[61] The black dog which wreaked havoc in Bungay and Blythburgh churches in Suffolk in 1577 appeared during a thunderstorm, and two similar occurrences, of strange animals appearing in churches during storms, were also described on page 90. The fires and explosions which sometimes occur during black dog manifestations (see page 94) may be caused by an outburst of the energy, maybe electrical, which the animal is using to materialize. Usable energy may also be created by the action of running water. Some alien animals, apart from the obvious water monsters, are often seen in or near water, BHMs and black dogs especially.

Among the other interesting ideas in their book *Space-Time Transients and Unusual Events*, Michael A. Persinger and Gyslaine F. Lafrenière discuss electric field columns produced by accumulating geological stress, and suggest that man could be affected by electrical currents produced in this way.[62] UFO incidents could be explained thus, they suggest, in that the witness's brain could be unnaturally stimulated and instead of seeing merely a luminous blob (the electrical field) he could experience a UFO landing with entities or even an abduction, depending on the richness of the material stored in his brain on which he could draw to create the event. It would be a 'waking nightmare'. This hypothesis could be extended to include the seeing of alien animals, and indeed to any visionary or apparitional experience.

Disturbances in the earth's magnetic field have also been suggested as a stimulus for all manner of Fortean events and psychic phenomena. It has been known for some time that an outburst of solar flares affects life on earth, and magnetic storms are apparently an associated event.[63] So this may be another feature that affects the manifestation of alien animals.

If relatively little is known about electrical field columns and geomagnetic anomalies and their effects on mankind, even less is known about the so-called 'earth currents' or 'earth energies' thought by many ley researchers to flow through or over the surface of the earth, a vital part of the earth's well-being comparable with the human body's intricate network of nerves. Research into leys and earth energies is actively being pursued,[64] and we have already written of possible links between black dog sightings and leys and the Owlman and leys. Unfortunately no data on leys are available from other parts of the world, for little research is being done other than in the UK, so we cannot extend our work on leys to non-British alien animals. However, while on this subject, we have also noted other possible ley/alien animal links in the UK, including a strange creature from the River Trent on the South Humberside/Lincolnshire border near Scunthorpe. There is a sharp bend in the river between Wildsworth and Owston Ferry known as Jenny Hurn, and this was widely known to be haunted. The apparition took at least two forms – 'a pygmy being, man-like, with long hair, and the face of a seal, that occasionally crosses the river from the eastern to the western side, embarked in a small craft resembling a large pie-dish.' He then crossed the road and browsed in a field. Or the 'thing' in the river had large eyes and long hair and tusks. It crawled out of the water and fed in the fields. In the old days the bend was avoided by local people on account of the 'Jinny On Boggard'.[65] Studying a large-scale map of the area, we have traced a possible ley passing through the bend: Epworth church (SE 781038) – Owston Ferry church (SE 805003) – Castle Hill (SE 805002) – Jenny Hurn (SE 816986) – Springthorpe church (SK 875897) (5 points in 11 miles on Ordnance Survey sheet 112, 1:50000).

A very short distance to the south of Jenny Hurn, again close to the river, is another haunting relevant to our theme. An abnormally large white cat was commonly seen at the end of the last century near Gunthorpe. Joe Jenkins told folklorist Ethel Rudkin, when she asked if he had ever seen it: 'Scores of times! It always crosses the road from the river and runs through the opening in the bank; it is white, and nearly as large as a pig.' One man who saw it on a snowy night kicked out at it, but it vanished, and next day when he went to the spot he saw his own bootprints, and the mark he made when kicking at the cat, but of a cat's prints there was no trace.[66] The cat's route was said to be along Commonpiece Lane, which suggests that this was a long-established trackway, and students of ley research will sense a ley here. Unfortunately we could not find one by reference solely to the map, and have not had time to try and trace it on the ground.

Another aspect of Britain's traditional lore which may be relevant here is dragons. We have already written about their possible links with earth currents in our book *The Secret Country*,[67] but they are worth mentioning again because they may easily have been a medieval alien animal, originating in the same way as today's alien animals and seen and feared by ordinary people.

Although there is enough evidence to suggest that some alien animals have a connection with earth energies, the exact link between the two is a matter for debate. Possibly their appearances are actually triggered by the earth energies, and are influenced by the apparent ebb and flow of the current, or perhaps the alien animals are formed independently and only obtain sustenance from the earth energies. Much more work needs to be done in the UK to establish in detail the nature of the relationship between leys/earth energies and alien animals.[68] The recent discovery of prehistoric stone structures in Loch Ness may possibly be relevant too, though we appreciate that the theory we are about to outline is sheer surmise. The stones are located at Lochend and are in two sets, one described as 'a mother lode of stone circles – big ones and little ones; single circles and circles intertwined with others; circles laid out in a straight line and circles in no particular order'. The set in deeper water consists of circles connected by lines of rocks.[69] Bearing in mind the theories about leys and earth energies and the fact that many prehistoric sites are thought to have been constructed for purposes connected with the manipulation of earth energies, we suggest that the Loch Ness complex of stone circles could have been erected either to originate or to control the monster by giving the builders control over the earth energies it utilized. Or perhaps, as a result of the building of the structures for other purposes, the energies so formed created the monster, which became uncontrollable. Perhaps the stones are even now an active part of an energy network, and the monster still feeds upon the energy. It has been one of the contentions of the anti-monster school that there is not enough food in the loch to support one or a herd of monsters. Perhaps they do not need food of the kind that the sceptics are thinking of.

We mentioned earlier that the earth currents in leys are thought to ebb and flow, and this was also discussed in *The Secret Country*. If, as the evidence suggests, the current varies in intensity, and if some of our alien animals are dependent on the energy for their sustenance, then it is to be expected that they will only appear at those times when the current is at its strongest. There is a certain amount of evidence to support this. John Keel has remarked, in putting forward his theory of 'windows', that 'These creatures and strange events tend to recur in the same areas year after year, even century after century.'[70] Curt Sutherly noticed that a strange animal was seen in the area of Upper Pottsgrove Township, Pennsylvania, in 1973, 28 years after one was seen in the very same area.[71] Every five years on 9 October a ghostly white horse is said to gallop over the lawns of the Walton Hall Hotel in Stratford, Warwickshire[72] – ghosts traditionally reappear in the same place at a certain time.

Apart from there having to be a suitable energy supply before the alien animal can appear, it may also be helpful if the potential witness is psychic. When investigating cases of UFO sightings, especially close encounters, we have found that a surprising number of witnesses have had repeated experiences of a psychic nature – especially precognition, out-of-the-body experiences, seeing ghosts. Investigators of alien animal sightings usually do not think to ask the witnesses if they have had such experiences, but it is an important question which should be asked. A little probing into a witness's background can often be revealing. Jerome Clark and Loren Coleman remark in *Creatures of the Outer Edge* that people who see alien animals may also experience other types of paranormal phenomena, such as poltergeists, strange phone calls and visits, and have 'psychic "revelations" of an apocalyptic nature'.[73] It may be that the alien animals are attracted to people of a certain psychic type, or they may be feeding on the excessive psychic energy emitted by the witness, which enables them to materialize before him. All alien animals produce fear and sometimes terror in those who see them; they often chase them, but apparently without the intention of catching them, and on the rare occasions when they do catch them, they cause little real physical harm. Mary Crane was caught and held down by a big cat which then proceeded to lick her face; Mike

Busby wrestled for several minutes with another large beast, but its 2-inch claws were 'dull' and when he finally got clear he had suffered only torn clothing and superficial scratches. Curiously, for several days afterwards he experienced dizziness and fainting spells, symptoms which are not unknown to those who have had close encounters with UFOs and their personnel. It may be that the intention of the alien animal is not to obtain physical prey but rather to terrify its victim and absorb the emotional energies which he then emits so profusely. Even the mildest of these phantoms, the black dogs, often seem to enjoy walking in close proximity to humans.

Another type of human energy which alien animals may utilize is sexual energy, the relevance of which has already been shown in Chapters 4 and 5. We have noted in Chapter 5 several instances where BHMs showed an interest in courting couples, and the lonely 'lovers' lane' location has long been known to ufologists as a frequent site of manifestations of a psychic and ufological nature. The Cornish Owlman described in Chapter 4 has so far been seen only by young girls, and alien big cats, too, seem to appear more frequently than might be expected before young women. Interestingly, sexual energy is also thought to be involved in poltergeist attacks. Children reaching sexual maturity and possibly with a surplus of sexual energy are usually present at houses which experience such attacks. There are on record a number of poltergeist cases, too, where sightings of strange animals have been reported in the afflicted houses.

Blood may be another energy source. We automatically think of the horror-story vampire and its eternal thirst for human blood when vampirism is mentioned. Real-life vampire cases today are admittedly rare, but they may exist.[74] Dr Nandor Fodor recounts one such at length in his book *On the Trail of the Poltergeist*.[75] It took place in 1938 and involved a lady living in Thornton Heath, London. She was visited at night by something which by its fluttering sounded like a bird. It pressed on her neck and left puncture marks. This happened more than once, and she recalled that it came when she was menstruating – a significant link with our earlier mentions of sexual energy and the appearance of alien animals. In the early 1920s a vampire-type phenomenon was experienced in Scotland, by a poacher in the mountains of Tayside. He and a companion had arrived at a bothy at Fealaar but it was locked and they had to climb in and out through a window. It was dark and they needed water, so one man agreed to fetch some. He put one leg over the windowsill and then began to scream, calling out that ' "some fiend" had got hold of his leg and was tearing it and sucking his blood.' He managed to pull himself free and, frightened, the two searched outside the bothy, but could see nothing. In the distance, however, they saw 'white winged objects and faint blue lights which kept changing their position in the darkness.'[76] We can surmise that energy-seeking entities were around that night, and that the poacher's blood would have met their needs. Sometimes UFO entities abduct people, take them inside their 'craft', and subject them to apparent medical examinations. Are they perhaps extracting blood or other vital energies? Antônio Villas Boas had blood extracted from his chin by the entities which took him aboard their UFO,[77] and other abductees have reported that samples of blood were extracted from their fingertips.

It seems to be blood that the cattle mutilators are after, too. During the 1970s there was a big increase in the number of cattle found dead and mutilated with surgical precision in the United States. Their blood has often been drained, and certain organs (especially the reproductive organs) removed. So far no culprit has been identified, but many people suspect that UFO entities are involved. The mutilations usually happen in isolated areas, far from any roads, and no footprints or tracks are left on ground where they would be expected. Local police forces are at a loss how to deal with the mysterious attacks and government agencies label everything as 'predators'.[78] Alien big cats kill animals, but whether they are doing so for food, for blood, or for sport is difficult to decide. It becomes stranger when animals are apparently just killed and dropped, as has happened from time to time in connection with American big cats and BHM sightings. We have a number of cases like this on file, and we wonder if the big cat or BHM has perhaps utilized the blood of these unfortunate creatures. This seems to have happened in Florida, where investigator Mike Corradino has reported findings of 'Dead animals, chicks, rabbits, racoons, with their heads bitten off and always the blood completely drained from the body.' This is in areas where the 'skunk ape', Florida's name for the BHM, has been seen.[79] Stan Gordon speculates that the blood is needed for its salt content,[80] but we suspect that its value to the alien animal is rather more subtle than that.

There are many questions we have been unable to answer in this book, and some that we have not even attempted to answer, such as: Why do alien animals appear in such a multiplicity of forms? Why are they materializing at all? Is there an intelligence behind them? But we hope we have at least indicated the complexity of the subject, and presented a few leads which will be more thoroughly investigated by those with the necessary knowledge. We are convinced that in most cases witnesses do see what they report. Whether they are seeing what is really there is another question. Our suspicion is that many alien animals are non-physical, in some way linked to the witness, and needing a suitable energy source to help them materialize and to sustain them. The only thing of which we can be completely sure, however, is that alien animals are appearing in their hundreds, even their thousands, all over the world.

Appendix 1
A few hints for monster watchers

What to do when you see a . . .

WATER MONSTER

On sighting a water monster – freeze! Do not attempt to get closer, or to a better sighting position. Do not shout or slam car doors. Try to stop dogs and children from making a noise. The creatures are timid and any noise or movement is likely to startle them and cause them to submerge.

When beside or on a stretch of water known to be the haunt of a monster, carry a loaded camera at all times, and do not forget to use it if a monster is sighted. Take one shot as quickly as possible; then check exposure and focusing before taking more.

BIG CAT

If you see a big cat on the loose, do not move. Movement can cause felines to attack. (Birds which 'freeze' in the face of an attack by a domestic cat are more likely to survive.) 'Alien' big cats are rarely known to attack people, but it could happen, so if you see one, do not try to run away. The motionless reaction also has the advantage that the cat might ignore you sufficiently to carry on doing whatever it was doing, and you might learn something interesting about it. Only try taking photographs if you are in a safe place (a car), or are sure the cat cannot see you and will not be attracted by your movement.

BLACK DOG

A black dog is unlikely to hurt you physically, but its sudden appearance may scare you. Keep your wits and observe the animal as closely as possible. Try and take photographs (though it will probably be dark and the use of a flash is likely to cause the black dog to disappear, so do not attempt this until you have fully observed it for some while). Also try and touch the dog, in a friendly manner by giving it a pat on the head, and see if it reacts and if it feels solid.

WINGED THING

If you see a 'big bird', it is likely to be in the sky. Note as many details as possible, and try to photograph it, including some recognizable object in the picture if you can, to help determine the bird's size. Do not get too close to any 'big bird' on the ground. Their reaction is unpredictable, and it might want to kidnap you. Try and take a picture, if in a safe place. A Mothman- or Owlman-type creature is somewhat different, its intentions towards us being completely unknown, so if you do see one, keep your distance and your nerve, and observe keenly. Try and take a photograph, and also try speaking to it. No one has tried this yet, and the creature might just answer. If it does, ask it where it comes from and what it wants.

BHM

On sighting a BHM, *if it has not seen you*, freeze and observe its behaviour, taking photographs if possible. If it has seen you, act according to its behaviour. That is, if it approaches aggressively, make your escape. If it approaches timidly, appearing curious, stay where you are and try to establish a friendly relationship (if you have the nerve!) and speak calmly to it, keeping your camera out of sight (it might annoy the BHM). *Do not fire guns at it or otherwise attack it, unless absolutely necessary to preserve your life*. The same applies to all the alien animals.

If you have seen an alien animal

Any reader who has seen an alien animal is invited to send the details to the authors c/o Fortean Picture Library, at the address given below.

The Fortean Picture Library would also be very interested to see any photographs of alien animals. Please send them, carefully packed (remove colour slides from protective glass before posting), to Fortean Picture Library, Melangell House, Princes Street, Montgomery, Powys, SY15 6PY, United Kingdom. Or write in the first instance, giving details.

Appendix 2
A listing of 300 lake monsters around the world

We have not included sea monsters in this listing, because there are so many reports.[1] Also, as the seas are so vast and likely to contain many life forms never seen by man, there is a good chance that many sea monsters seen may be 'new' species. Therefore monster reports from inland lakes, cut off from the sea, are potentially more exciting because of the apparent impossibility of such large creatures remaining unknown for so long. Occasionally, however, there is some overlap because some lakes are connected to the sea (especially in Scotland), and also many rivers. We have included reports from many sources, so long as we have no reason to doubt the source. But such a listing as this can never be comprehensive, because no one has a record of all the lake monsters ever seen.

Some lake monsters have been given names, and where we know these we have added them in brackets.

AFRICA

Junction of Bamingui and Koukourou Rivers, Central African Republic; Lake Bangweulu, Zambia; Dilolo marshes, Zaïre; dam at Grootvlei pumping station near Vereeniging, South Africa; Ingruenfisi River, South Africa; Mamfe Pool, Upper Cross River, Cameroun; Mara River, Tanzania; Lake Mweru, Zaïre/Zambia; Lake Nyasa, Malawi; Orange River, South Africa; Ouémé River, Benin; Lake Tanganyika, East Africa; Vaaldam reservoir, South Africa; Lake Victoria, Tanzania/Uganda/Kenya; swamps at sources of White Nile River.

AUSTRALIA

Australian Capital Territory Molonglo River
New South Wales Lake Bathurst; Cowal Lake; Edward River (Tnata); Fish River; Lake George; Hawkesbury River headwaters; Hunter River (Yaa-Loo); lagoon north of Lismore; Macquarie River; Midgeon Lagoon near Narrandera; Murray River (also in South Australia);

Murrumbidgee River; Lake Paika; Lake Tala; Tuckerbil swamp near Leeton
Northern Territory Gudgerama Creek (Mannie; the Maningrida Monster)
Queensland near Dalby; Diamantina River (the Kuddimudra); Nerang River, Mirramac Plains
South Australia Lake Alexandrina (the 'moolgewanke'); Crystal Brook; lagoon near Mount Gambier
Tasmania Lake Echo; Great Lake; Jordan River; Lake Tiberias
Victoria Barwon River; Lake Burrumbeet; Lake Corangamite; Eumeralla River; Euroa; reservoir at Malmsbury; Port Fairy district; Port Phillip district (the 'tunatpan'); Lake Werribee/Modewarre

BHUTAN

a northern lake

CANADA

Alberta Battle River
British Columbia Bennet Lake; Boiling Lake; Chadburn Lake; Cowichan Lake, Vancouver Island (Tsinquaw); Harrison Lake; Kamloops Lake; Lake Kathlyn; Kootenay Lake; Martin's Lake; Lake Okanagan (Ogopogo); Osoyoos Lake; Shuswap Lake (Ta-Zum-A; Sicopogo; Shuswaggi); Skaha Lake; Somenos Lake; Lake Tagai (Tag); Williams Lake
Manitoba Cedar Lake; Lake Manitoba/Lake Winnipegosis/Dauphin Lake (Manipogo); Red River; Lake St Martin
New Brunswick Lake Utopia
Newfoundland Lake Crescent; Dildo Pond; Gander Lake; Great Gull Lake; Lond Pond; Swangler's Cove (Maggot)
Nova Scotia Lake Ainslie
Ontario Lake of Bays; Berens Lake; Lake Deschenes/Ottawa River (also in Quebec); Lake Erie; Lake Huron; Lake Mazinaw; Lake Meminisha; Muskrat Lake (Hapyxelor; Mussy); Nith River (Slimy Caspar); Lake Ontario (Metro Maggie); Rideau Canal; Lake Simcoe (Igopogo; Kempenfelt Kelly); Lake Superior
Prince Edward Island O'Keef's Lake
Quebec Aylmer Lake; Brompton Lake; Lake Champlain (Champ); Lake Decaire (Lizzie); Lake Phenegamook/Moking Lake (Ponik); Lake Remi; Lake of St Francis; St Lawrence River

Saskatchewan Saskatchewan River (Powsaswop); Turtle Lake
Yukon Teslin Lake (also in British Columbia)

DENMARK

Christianshavn moat, Copenhagen; Farrisvannet

ENGLAND

We know of no English lakes or rivers (except the Thames estuary)
where water monsters have been sighted. However, some of the
traditional dragon legends may have been based on water monsters,
for example: Worm of Spindleston Heugh (Northumberland); Pol-
lard worm (Durham); St Leonard's Forest dragon (West Sussex);
the Knucker (West Sussex); Bures dragon (Suffolk); Lambton worm
(Durham); Sockburn worm (Durham); Ludham dragon (Norfolk);
Walmsgate dragon (Lincolnshire); Nunnington/Loschy Hill worm
(North Yorkshire); Mordiford dragon (Herefordshire); Worm of
Sexhow (North Yorkshire); Dragon of Aller (Somerset); Worm of
Shervage Wood (Somerset); Henham dragon (Essex), and many
others.[2] Sea monsters have been seen all around England's long
coastline, the most recent being Morgawr (Falmouth Bay, Corn-
wall; see pages 33–6).

FINLAND

Lake Loukusa

ICELAND

The Lagarflot; The Thorskafjord

IRELAND

County Clare Lough Graney
County Cork Lough Attariff
County Donegal Lough Keel; Lough Muck
County Galway Lough Abisdealy; Lough Auna; Ballynahinch Lake;
Lough Claddaghduff; Lough Crolan; Lough Derg; Lough Derrylea;
Lough Dubh; Lough Fadda; Lough Glendalough; Lough Gowlan;

Lough Inagh; Lough Kylemore; Lough Mask; Maumeen Lough; Lough Nahillion; Lough Nahooin; Lough Neagh; Lough Ree; Lough Shanakeever; Lough Waskel
County Kerry Lough Brin; Lough Geal; Lough Lackagh; Lough Looscaunagh
County Limerick Lough Auna
County Mayo Carrowmore Lake; Keel Lough, Achill Island; Lough Nacorra; Straheens Lough, Achill Island
County Monaghan Lough Major
County Waterford Counfea Lough
County Wicklow Lower Lough Bray; Lough Nahanagan

ITALY

Lake Maggiore

JAPAN

Lake Chuzenji, Honshu; Lake Ikeda, Kyushu; Kuccharo Lake, Hokkaido (Kussie)

JAVA

Lake Patenggang

MALAYA

Lake Chini

MEXICO

Lake Catemaco

NORWAY

Bergso; Jolstravatnet; Krovatnet; Krodern; Lundevatnet; Lake Mjösa; Mosvatnet; Odegardskilen; Ormsjoen; Oyvanna; Repstadvanet; Ringsjoen; Rommen; Sandnesvatnet; Seljord, Telemark; Skodje; Lake Snasa; Sogne; Sorsasjoen; Sor Somna; Storevatn; Lake Suldal, Rogoland; Tinnkjodnet; Torfinnsvatnet; Tyrifjorden

PAPUA NEW GUINEA

Lake Dakataua, New Britain

SCOTLAND

Borders Cauldshiels Loch
Central Loch Lomond (also in Strathclyde); Loch Venachar
Highland Loch Alsh; Loch Arkaig; Loch Assynt; Loch na Beiste;
Loch Brittle, Isle of Skye; Loch nan Dubhrachan, Isle of Skye; Loch
Duich; Loch Eil; Loch Hourn; Loch Linnhe; Loch Lochy; Loch
Morar (Morag); Loch Ness (Nessie); Loch Oich; Loch Quoich;
Loch Scavaig, Isle of Skye; Loch Shiel; Loch Treig
Strathclyde Loch Awe
Tayside Loch Rannoch; Loch Tay; River Tay
Western Isles Loch Duvat, Isle of Eriskay; inland loch near Leurbost,
Isle of Lewis; Loch Suainaval, Isle of Lewis; Loch Uraval, Isle of
Lewis

SOUTH AMERICA

Argentina mountain lake in the Esquel region, Patagonia; Lake
Lacar; Lake Nahuel Huapi; lake in Santa Cruz; River Tamango;
White Lake, Patagonia
Bolivia swamps in the forests of the Madidi
Brazil Amazon River
Paraguay Paraguay River, Gran Chaco

SWEDEN

Lake Bullare; Lake Fegen, Halland/Jönköping; Lilla Källsjö;
Myllesjön; Slagnässjön, Blekinge; Lake Storsjö, Jämtland; Lake
Tingstäde, Gotland

UNITED STATES OF AMERICA
(*This is a partial listing. Loren Coleman's* Mysterious America *lists 153
lake and river monsters in the United States.*)

Alaska Iliamna Lake
Arkansas Lake Conway; White River (Whitey)
California Elizabeth Lake; Lake Elsinore; Lake Folsom; Lafayette
Lake; Lake Tahoe

Colorado Lake Katherine; Twin Lakes
Connecticut Lake Kenosha; Lake Pocotopang
Florida St Johns River; St Lucie River
Idaho Payette Lake (Slimy Slim/McCall Monster/Sharlie)
Illinois Stump or Flat Pond, Du Quoin
Kentucky Harrington Lake; Kentucky Lake
Michigan Narrow Lake; Paint River
Minnesota Great Sandy Lake
Mississippi Mississippi River near Natchez
Missouri Lake of the Ozarks
Montana Lake Chelan; Flathead Lake; Missouri River; Lake Waterton
Nebraska Alkali Lake
Nevada Pyramid Lake; Walker Lake
New Jersey Old Mill Pond, Trenton
New York Black River; Mazinaw Lake; Lake of the Woods
Oregon Hollow Block Lake; Wallowa Lake
South Dakota Lake Campbell
Utah Bear Lake (also in Idaho); Utah Lake
Vermont Lake Champlain (also in New York) (Champ)
Wisconsin Browns Lake; Delavan Lake; Elkhart Lake; Lake Geneva; Lake Keonsa; Maidson Four Lakes; Lake Mendota; Lake Michigan; Lake Monona; Oconomowoc Lake; Pewaukee Lake; Red Cedar Lake; Rock Lake; Lake Waubesa; Lake Wingra

USSR

Lake Khaiyr, Siberia; Lake Kok-kol, Kazakhstan; Lake Labynkyr, Siberia; Lake Vorota, Siberia

WALES

Dyfed Llyn Eiddwen; Llyn Farch
Gwynedd Llyn yr Afanc, River Conwy; Llyn Cynwch; Llyn-y-Gadair; Glaslyn Lake; Marchlyn Mawr; Llyn Tegid/Bala Lake
Powys Llangorse Lake

Bibliography

Bord, Janet and Colin, *Bigfoot Casebook*, London: Granada Publishing, 1982; Harrisburg, PA: Stackpole Books, 1982

—— *The Evidence for Bigfoot and other Man-Beasts*, Wellingborough: The Aquarian Press, 1984

Burton, Maurice, *The Elusive Monster*: An Analysis of the Evidence from Loch Ness, London: Rupert Hart-Davis, 1961

Byrne, Peter, *The Search for Bigfoot:* Monster, Myth or Man? Washington: Acropolis Books, 1975; New York: Pocket Books, 1976

Campbell, Elizabeth Montgomery, with David Solomon, *The Search for Morag*, London: Tom Stacey, 1972

Clark, Jerome and Loren Coleman, *Creatures of the Outer Edge*, New York: Warner Books, 1978

Coleman, Loren, *Mysterious America*, London: Faber & Faber, 1984; Winchester, MA: Faber & Faber, 1983

Costello, Peter, *In Search of Lake Monsters*, London: Garnstone Press, 1974; St Albans: Panther Books, 1975; New York: Berkley Pub., 1975

Dinsdale, Tim, *Loch Ness Monster*, London: Routledge & Kegan Paul, 1961, fourth edition 1982; Boston: Routledge & Kegan Paul, 1976

—— *The Leviathans*, London: Routledge & Kegan Paul, 1966; London: Futura Publications, 1976

—— *Project Water Horse*: The True Story of the Monster Quest at Loch Ness, London: Routledge & Kegan Paul, 1975; Boston: Routledge & Kegan Paul, 1975

Eberhart, George M., *Monsters*: A Guide to Information on Unaccounted For Creatures, Including Bigfoot, Many Water Monsters, and Other Irregular Animals, New York & London: Garland Publishing, 1983

Francis, Di, *Cat Country*: The Quest for the British Big Cat, Newton Abbot: David & Charles, 1983

Gould, Rupert T., *The Loch Ness Monster and Others*, London: Geoffrey Bles, 1934; Secaucus, New Jersey: Citadel Press, 1976

Green, John, *The Sasquatch File*, Victoria, British Columbia: Cheam Publishing (1299 Tracksell Avenue, Victoria, B.C., V8P 2C8, Canada), 1973

—— *On the Track of the Sasquatch* (incorporating *On the Track of the Sasquatch* and *Year of the Sasquatch*), New York: Ballantine Books, 1973; published individually by Cheam Publishing, B.C.

—— *Sasquatch: The Apes Among Us*, Victoria, B.C.: Cheam Publishing, 1978; Seattle: Hancock House Publishers, 1978

Heuvelmans, Bernard, *On the Track of Unknown Animals*, New York: Hill & Wang, revised edition 1965; St Albans: Paladin Books, 1970

—— *In the Wake of the Sea-Serpents*, London: Rupert Hart-Davis, 1968; New York: Hill & Wang, 1968

Holiday, F. W., *The Great Orm of Loch Ness*, London: Faber & Faber, 1968; New York: Norton, 1969

—— *The Dragon and the Disc*, London: Sidgwick & Jackson, 1973; London: Futura Publications, 1974

Hunter, Don, with René Dahinden, *Sasquatch*, Toronto, Ontario: McClelland & Stewart, 1973; Scarborough, Ontario: New American Library of Canada, 1975

Joyner, Graham C., *The Hairy Man of South Eastern Australia*, booklet published 1977 by the author and available from him at P.O. Box 253, Kingston ACT 2604, Australia

Keel, John A., *Strange Creatures from Time and Space*, Greenwich, Connecticut: Fawcett Publications, 1970; London: Neville Spearman, 1975; London: Sphere Books, 1976

McCloy, James F. and Ray Miller, Jr, *The Jersey Devil*, Wallingford, Pennsylvania: The Middle Atlantic Press, 1976

Mackal, Roy P., *The Monsters of Loch Ness*, London: Macdonald and Janes, 1976; London: Futura Publications, 1976; Chicago: Swallow, 1976

—— *Searching for Hidden Animals*, Garden City, NY: Doubleday & Company, 1980

Markotić, Vladimir and Grover Krantz (eds), *The Sasquatch and Other Unknown Hominoids*, Calgary, Alberta; Western Publishers, 1984

Meredith, Dennis L., *Search at Loch Ness*: The Expedition of The New York Times and the Academy of Applied Science, New York: Quadrangle/The New York Times Book Co., 1977

Michell, John, & Rickard, Robert J. M., *Living Wonders*: Mysteries and Curiosities of the Animal World, London: Thames and Hudson, 1982

Moon, Mary, *Ogopogo*: The Okanagan Mystery, Vancouver: J. J. Douglas, 1977 (available in UK from Canongate Publishing, 17 Jeffrey Street, Edinburgh EH1 10R)

Napier, John, *Bigfoot*: The Yeti and Sasquatch in Myth and Reality, London: Jonathan Cape, 1972; London: Abacus Books, 1976; New York: Dutton, 1973

O'Reilly, David, *Savage Shadow:* The Search for the Australian Cougar, Perth: Creative Research, 1981

Oudemans, A. C., *The Great Sea Serpent*, London: Luzac & Co., 1892; Leiden: E. J. Brill, 1892

Sanderson, Ivan T., *Abominable Snowmen:* Legend Come to Life, Philadelphia: Chilton Book Co., 1961; New York: Jove Publications, revised abridgement 1977

Shackley, Myra, *Wildmen*: Yeti, Sasquatch and the Neanderthal Enigma, London: Thames and Hudson, 1983; New York: Thames and Hudson, 1983 (title *Still Living?*)

Slate, B. Ann and Alan Berry, *Bigfoot*, New York: Bantam Books, 1976

Smith, Steven, *The Tasmanian Tiger – 1980*, Tasmania: National Parks and Wildlife Service, 1981

Sprague, Roderick and Grover S. Krantz (eds), *The Scientist Looks at the Sasquatch,* Moscow, Idaho: The University Press of Idaho, 1977

Tchernine, Odette, *The Snowman and Company*, London: Robert Hale, 1961

—— *The Yeti*, London: Neville Spearman, 1970

Whyte, Constance, *More Than a Legend*: The Story of the Loch Ness Monster, London: Hamish Hamilton, 1957

Witchell, Nicholas, *The Loch Ness Story*, Lavenham: Terence Dalton, 1974; London: Penguin Books, revised edition 1975; New York: Penguin, 1976

Wright, Bruce S., *The Eastern Panther*: A Question of Survival, Toronto and Vancouver: Clarke, Irwin & Company, 1972

Wylie, Kenneth, *Bigfoot*: A Personal Inquiry into a Phenomenon, New York: Viking Press, 1980

Zarzynski, Joseph W., *Champ – Beyond the Legend*, USA: Bannister Publications, 1984

The following magazines regularly publish reports of alien animal sightings:

Bigfoot Co-op, 14602 Montevideo Drive, Whittier, CA 90605, USA

Champ Channels, Lake Champlain Phenomena Investigation, P.O. Box 2134, Wilton, NY 12866, USA

Cryptozoology, Interdisciplinary Journal of the International Society of Cryptozoology, P.O. Box 43070, Tucson, AZ 85733, USA

Fate, 170 Future Way, Marion, OH 43302, USA

Fortean Times, 96 Mansfield Road, London NW3 2HX

Forteana News, Route One, Box 220, Plumerville, AR 72127, USA

INFO Journal, P.O. Box 367, Arlington, VA 22210–0367, USA

The ISC Newsletter, address as *Cryptozoology* above

Nessletter, Huntshieldford, St Johns Chapel, Bishop Auckland, Durham, DL13 1RQ

Pursuit (the journal of the Society for the Investigation of the Unexplained), SITU/PURSUIT, P.O. Box 265, Little Silver, NJ 07739, USA

Notes

Where only author and book title are given, publication details can be found in the Bibliography. The book page references relate to the first edition listed in the Bibliography, unless otherwise noted.

The sources given here are usually those sources most accessible to the reader who wishes to investigate further, and not necessarily the primary sources. For instance, if we have taken a case report from a published book, that book is given here as the source. The case may be one investigated by that author, or if not, he may have noted the source of his information. Where the primary source is not available to us, we have used only data from researchers and authors who are known to us personally or by reputation.

1. ELUSIVE LAKE MONSTERS

1. Campbell, *The Search for Morag*, p. 139.
2. Holiday, *The Great Orm of Loch Ness* (hereinafter *TGOOLN*), ch. 6.
3. Mackal, *The Monsters of Loch Ness*, p. 84 Futura edn.
4. Holiday, *The Dragon and the Disc* (hereinafter *TDATD*), p. 56.
5. ibid., p. 57.
6. ibid., p. 62.
7. Moon, *Ogopogo*, p. 45.
8. ibid., p. 47.
9. *Pursuit*, vol. 5 no. 3 (July 1972) p. 63.
10. *Fate*, vol. 25 no. 3, issue 264 (March 1972) p. 30.
11. ibid., loc. cit.
12. *Pursuit*, vol. 5 no. 3 (July 1972) p. 63.
13. According to an undated (1970s) report, 'The Lake Champlain Monsters', by Joseph W. Zarzynski.
14. *Fate*, July 1967 (UK edn) p. 11.
15. Information on Flathead Lake sightings from Tim Church, 'The Flathead Lake Monster: A Preliminary Report', published 21 March 1975; reprinted in *Pursuit*, vol. 8 no. 4 (Oct. 1975) pp. 89–92.

16. Moon, op. cit., p. 134.
17. *Fate*, March 1971 (UK edn) p. 14.
18. Mackal, op. cit., p. 118.
19. Dinsdale, *The Leviathans* (hereinafter *TL*), p. 44 Futura edn.
20. ibid., pp. 45–6.
21. G. Rokosuev, 'The Mystery of Lake Khaiyr', *Komsomol'skaya Pravda*, 21 Nov. 1964, quoted in Dinsdale, *TL*, p. 47; see also Costello, *In Search of Lake Monsters*, pp. 291–3 Panther edn.
22. This sighting was reported in a number of papers including *Sunday Express, Sunday People, Sunday Times* and *South China Morning Post*, all of 30 Jan. 1977, and *The Times* and *Yorkshire Post* of 2 Feb. 1977.
23. Letters from Ivar Anderson to the authors; he obtained his information on Lake Myllesjön from Rune Aronson who was 'born and raised close to the lake'.
24. Costello, op. cit., p. 221.
25. Dinsdale, *TL*, pp. 51–2.
26. Costello, op. cit., p. 219.
27. ibid., loc. cit.
28. Information on the last two cases supplied by Bertil Falk, to whom also our thanks for the translations.
29. Dr Jacques Vallee speaking at the *Fate* International UFO Congress, June 1977, Chicago, USA.
30. Witchell, *The Loch Ness Story*, p. 137 Penguin edn.
31. Quoted in ibid., loc. cit.
32. Mackal, op. cit., p. 118.
33. Costello, op. cit., p. 78.
34. Mackal, op. cit., p. 117.
35. The media often see their function more as entertainers than informers, and are usually ready to give space to self-appointed clowns who thereby find it easy to obtain publicity and notoriety with which to feed their egos. These people have been evident in UFO research from the earliest years and to a lesser extent are also present in water monster research.
36. Witchell, op. cit., pp. 39–42.
37. ibid., p. 136.
38. ibid., p. 97.
39. ibid., loc. cit.
40. Mackal, op. cit., p. 17.
41. ibid., p. 15.

42. ibid., p. 119.
43. ibid., loc. cit.
44. ibid., p. 16.
45. ibid., p. 132.
46. ibid., p. 32; Witchell, op. cit., p. 115.
47. Mackal, op. cit., p. 111.
48. ibid., loc. cit.
49. *MIT Technology Review*, vol. 78 no. 5 (Mar./Apr. 1976).
50. ibid.
51. ibid.
52. *Nessletter*. 29 (Aug. 1978) p. 2.
53. *Nessletter*. 59 (Aug. 1983) p.2.
54. *Falkirk Herald*, 24 June 1978, reprinted in *Forteana News* (Aug. 1978) p. 16.
55. *Fortean Times* (hereinafter *FT*), no. 22 (summer 1977) pp. 23–4.
56. *Falmouth Packet*, 17 Sept. 1976.
57. David Clarke, 'The Myth & Mystery of Morgawr, the Helford Monster', in *Cornish Life*, vol. 4 no. 1 (1977) pp. 13–15.
58. *FT*, no. 19 (Dec. 1976) p. 14.
59. *FT*, no. 19 (Dec. 1976) pp. 12–17, and no. 22 (summer 1977) pp. 18–19.
60. *Sunday Mirror*, 16 Mar. 1975; *Merioneth Express*, 7 Mar. 1975; *The News* (now *FT*) no. 10 (June 1975) pp. 18–20.
61. *The News* (now *FT*) no. 15 (Apr. 1976) pp. 12–13.
62. ibid., p. 13.
63. ibid., loc. cit.
64. *The Cambrian* (Merioneth and Caernarfon), 29 Aug. 1975.
65. ibid.
66. *The News* (now *FT*) no. 11 (Aug. 1975) p. 22, quoting *Nature*, vol. 27 (1883) pp. 293, 315, 338, 366.
67. *Western Mail*, 8 March 1975.
68. Mackal, op. cit., Table 2, p. 263.
69. F. W. Holiday, 'The Monster of the A85', *Flying Saucer Review* (hereinafter *FSR*) (address: West Malling, Maidstone, Kent) vol. 19 no. 2 (Mar./Apr. 1973) pp. 24–5.
70. Mackal, op. cit., p. 183.
71. This catalogue of failure from Holiday, *TDATD*, pp. 184–5.
72. ibid., p. 24.
73. Costello, op. cit., p. 152.
74. Dinsdale, *TL*, p. 114.

75. ibid., p. 217.

76. Moon, op. cit., p. 160.

77. Holiday, *TDATD*, p. 182.

78. Mackal, op. cit., pp. 94–6; Whyte, *More Than a Legend*, pp. 2–4.

79. Mackal, op. cit., p. 96; Whyte, op. cit., pp. 6–7.

80. *Nessletter*, no. 23 (Aug. 1977) p. 2.

81. Holiday, *TDATD*, p. 183.

82. ibid., loc. cit.

83. F. W. Holiday, 'A Brief Taste of Fairyland', *FSR*, vol. 20 no. 6 (Apr. 1975) p. 9.

84. *FT*, no. 22 (summer 1977) p. 24.

85. Mackal, op. cit., p. 290.

86. Witchell, op. cit., p. 145, fn.

87. Holiday, *TGOOLN*, p. 113 and *TDATD*, p. 186.

88. Moon, op. cit., p. 84.

89. *ISC Newsletter* (winter 1983) vol. 2 no. 4 p. 3 & (summer 1984) vol. 3 no. 2 pp. 7–9.

90. Costello, op. cit., p. 198.

91. Translation by Stephen Jones, quoted in Holiday, *TDATD*, pp. 85–6.

92. Moon, op. cit., p. 24; Costello, op. cit., p. 241.

93. An extract from an article by Dr S. K. Klumov in *Priroda*, August 1962, quoted in Dinsdale, *TL*, pp. 44–5.

94. Costello, op. cit., pp. 148–9.

95. From John Morgan, *Life and Adventures of William Buckley*, Hobart 1852; quoted in W. Fearn-Wannan, *Australian Folklore: A Dictionary of Lore, Legends and Popular Allusions* (Landsdowne Press, 1970) p. 106.

96. Dinsdale, *TL*, p. 27.

97. Holiday, *TGOOLN*, p. 188.

98. ibid., p. 52; and Dinsdale, *Loch Ness Monster* (hereinafter *LNM*), p. 96.

99. Holiday, 'A Brief Taste of Fairyland', op. cit., p. 9.

100. Holiday, *TDATD*, pp. 37–8.

101. Mackal, op. cit., p. 135; Dinsdale, *LNM*, p. 154.

102. Holiday, *TGOOLN*, p. 139.

2. CATS THAT CAN'T BE CAUGHT

1. R. J. M. Rickard, 'If you go down to the woods today . . .' (a useful catalogue of UK big cat sightings covering the years

1962–73, from which much of our data is taken for this chapter) *INFO Journal*, vol. IV no. 1, issue 13 (May 1974) pp. 3–18; R. J. M. Rickard, 'The "Surrey Puma" and Friends: More Mystery Animals' (a list supplementing that in *INFO Journal*, no. 13), *The News* (now *Fortean Times*, hereinafter *FT*) no. 14 (Jan. 1976) pp. 3–8.

2. John Michell and Robert J. M. Rickard, *Phenomena*: A Book of Wonders (Thames and Hudson, 1977) p. 124.

3. Maurice Burton, 'Is This the Surrey Puma?', *Wildlife*, no. 260 (Nov. 1966).

4. *Kentish Mercury*, 19 July 1963; London *Evening News*, 18 and 19 July 1963.

5. *Kentish Mercury*, 26 July 1963.

6. *Daily Telegraph*, 20 Feb. 1964, quoted in *Flying Saucer Review* (hereinafter *FSR*) vol. 10 no. 4 (July/Aug. 1964) pp. 21–2; Charles Bowen, 'Mystery Animals', *FSR*, vol. 10 no. 6 (Nov./Dec. 1964) pp. 15–17.

7. Bowen, op. cit.

8. ibid., loc. cit.

9. *Reveille*, 5 Nov. 1964.

10. Burton, op. cit.

11. *Reveille*, 5 Nov. 1964.

12. ibid., and Victor Head, 'Trailing the Surrey Puma', *The Field*, 8 Apr. 1965.

13. *Reveille*, 5 Nov. 1964.

14. *The Observer*, 11 Oct. 1964; *Sunday Telegraph*, 20 Dec. 1964.

15. Head, op. cit.

16. *The Observer*, 11 Oct. 1964; Head, op. cit.

17. *Daily Mirror*, 26 Sept. 1964.

18. Head, op. cit.

19. London *Evening News*, 24 Oct. 1964.

20. London *Evening News*, 28 Oct. 1964.

21. *Sunday Telegraph*, 20 Dec. 1964.

22. ibid.

23. Head, op. cit.

24. ibid.

25. *Sunday Telegraph*, 20 Dec. 1964.

26. Head, op. cit.

27. Report in newspaper, name unknown, 12 Feb. 1965.

28. *Evening News & Star*, 3 Feb. 1965, quoted in *FSR*, vol. 11 no. 2 (Mar./Apr. 1965) p. 24.

29. London *Evening Standard*, 4 Feb. 1965; *FSR*, vol. 11 no. 2 (Mar./Apr. 1965) p. 24.

30. *London Life*, 30 July 1966.

31. Wright, *The Eastern Panther*, p. 31.

32. *The Times*, 5 July 1966.

33. Rickard, 'The "Surrey Puma" . . .', op. cit., p. 5.

34. *Western Times*, 20 June 1969, quoted in *FSR*, vol. 15 no. 5 (Sept./Oct. 1969) p. 36.

35. *Aldershot News*, 27 Jan. and 10 Feb. 1970.

36. *Aldershot News*, 23 June 1972.

37. *Aldershot News*, 15 Sept. 1972.

38. *Aldershot News*, 22 Sept. 1972.

39. *Bournemouth Evening Echo*, 11 Sept. 1972.

40. Report in newspaper, name unknown, 10 Feb. 1972.

41. *Folkestone Herald*, 10 Jan. 1973.

42. *Folkestone Herald*, 27 Jan. 1973.

43. *Aldershot News*, 3 Apr. 1973.

44. *Farnborough News*, 22 and 29 June 1973.

45. *Bournemouth Evening Echo*, 7 Apr. 1974, quoted in *The News* (now *FT*) no. 9 (Apr. 1975) pp. 19–20.

46. *The Sun*, 16 Jan. 1975, quoted in *The News* (now *FT*) no. 9 (Apr. 1975) p. 17.

47. *West Sussex County Times*, 7, 14 and 21 Mar. 1975; *The Sun*, 7 Mar. 1975; quoted in *The News* (now *FT*) no. 9 (Apr. 1975) p. 18.

48. *Daily Mirror*, 5 May 1975.

49. *Daily Mirror*, 7 and 21 Nov. 1975.

50. *Daily Express*, 10 Apr. 1976.

51. *Daily Mirror*, 16 Sept. 1976.

52. *Sunday Express*, 26 Sept. 1976.

53. *Bath Chronicle*, 27 Oct. 1976; *Daily Mirror*, 28 Oct. 1976.

54. *Daily Press* (Newport News, VA), 28 Oct. 1976.

55. *The Sun*, 14 Jan. 1977.

56. Burton, op. cit.

57. Head, op. cit.

58. ibid.

59. Burton, op. cit.

60. *Nottingham Evening Post*, 29 July 1976.
61. London *Evening News*, 29 July 1976.
62. *Nottingham Evening Post*, 30 July 1976.
63. *Nottingham Evening Post*, 31 July 1976.
64. BBC Radio news bulletin.
65. All details of the Normanton sighting from *Nottingham Evening Post*, 2 Aug. 1976, *Leicester Mercury*, 2 Aug. 1976, *The Guardian*, 3 Aug. 1976.
66. *Nottingham Evening Post*, 3 Aug. 1976.
67. *Nottingham Evening Post* and *Leicester Mercury*, 4 Aug. 1976.
68. *Nottingham Evening Post*, 5 Aug. 1976.
69. *Nottingham Evening Post*, 6 Aug. 1976.
70. *Yorkshire Evening Post*, 10 Aug. 1976.
71. *Yorkshire Evening Post* and *Daily Mail*, 11 Aug. 1976.
72. R. J. M. Rickard in *FT*, no. 20 (Feb. 1977) p. 19.
73. Sighting made 12 Feb. 1975 from a distance of 20 yards. *Yorkshire Evening Press*, 13, 14 and 17 Feb. 1975, reprinted in *The News* (now *FT*) no. 9 (Apr. 1975) p. 16.
74. *Scunthorpe Evening Telegraph*, 21 Sept. 1976, quoted in *FT*, no. 20 (Feb. 1977) p. 20.
75. *Runcorn Weekly News*, 30 May 1974.
76. *Liverpool Echo*, 23 Oct. 1976, quoted in *FT*, no. 20 (Feb. 1977) p. 20.
77. *Sunday Express*, 16 June 1974; *Sunday Mirror*, 23 June 1974; quoted in *The News* (now *FT*) no. 6 (Sept. 1974) p. 3, and no. 7 (Nov. 1974) p. 2.
78. *Bath Chronicle*, 28 Aug. 1976.
79. *The Complete Books of Charles Fort* (New York: Dover Publications, 1974) pp. 643, 645.
80. *Glasgow Sunday Post*, 15 Aug. 1976.
81. *Daily Telegraph*, 29 Sept. and 1 Oct. 1977; *Sunday Express*, 2 Oct. 1977.
82. All information on Sutherland sightings from *Evening Express* (Aberdeen), 14 Dec. 1977, quoted in *FT*, no. 25 (spring 1978) p. 34; *The Press and Journal* (Aberdeen), 15 Dec. 1977.
83. *The Press and Journal* (Aberdeen), 7 Feb. 1978.
84. *The Complete Books of Charles Fort*, p. 600, quoting *Daily Express*, 14 Jan. 1927.
85. *Aberdeen Evening Express*, 8 Feb. 1978.

86. Quoted in Colin Clair, *Unnatural History* (London: Abelard-Schuman, 1967) p. 57.

87. Quoted by Harold T. Wilkins in *Mysteries Solved and Unsolved* (London: Odhams Press, 1959) p. 197.

88. *The News* (now *FT*), no. 14 (Jan. 1976) p. 8.

89. William Cobbett, *Rural Rides* (first published 1830).

90. An excellent book detailing the sightings and habits of the remaining wild big cats is Bruce S. Wright's *The Eastern Panther*. It should be read by all who are interested in studying this matter in depth, as the witnesses' sighting reports give a clear insight into the difference between the behaviour of the 'natural' big cats still living in the wild and the alien behaviour of the creatures we are writing about.

91. pp. 122–3.

92. *New York Times*, 28 Dec. 1877, and described in Clark and Coleman, *Creatures of the Outer Edge* (hereinafter *COTOE*) p. 123; Jerome Clark and Loren Coleman, 'On the Trail of Pumas, Panthers and ULAs', Part 1, *Fate*, vol. 25 no. 6, issue 267 (June 1972) pp. 73–4.

93. Clark and Coleman, *COTOE*, p. 131.

94. Jerome Clark and Loren Coleman, 'On the Trail of Pumas, Panthers and ULAs', Part 2, *Fate*, vol. 25 no. 7, issue 268 (July 1972) p. 94.

95. Clark and Coleman, 'On the Trail . . .' Part 2, p. 95.

96. Clark and Coleman, 'On the Trail . . .' Part 1, p. 75.

97. Clark and Coleman, 'On the Trail . . .' Part 2, p. 96.

98. Letter from Jim Miles in *Fate*, vol. 31 no. 12, issue 345 (Dec. 1978) pp. 128–9.

99. Loren Coleman, 'Phantom Panther on the Prowl,' *Fate*, vol. 30 no. 11, issue 332 (Nov. 1977) pp. 62–7; Loren Coleman, 'Phantom Panther on the Prowl Again', *Res Bureaux Bulletin*, no. 20 (14 July 1977) pp. 1–3.

100. *Anomaly Research Bulletin*, no. 6 (June 1977) pp. 9–10.

101. *Washington Star*, 23 Jan. 1978, quoted in *Res Bureaux Bulletin*, no. 30 (2 Mar. 1978) p. 4.

102. Loren E. Coleman, 'Mystery Animals in Illinois', *Fate* (July 1971).

103. Clark and Coleman, *COTOE*, p. 136.

104. ibid., loc. cit., quoting Bruce S. Wright's *The Ghost of North America*.

105. Clark and Coleman, 'On the Trail . . .' Part 1, p. 72.
106. Clark and Coleman, *COTOE*, p. 122, quoting from *New England Farmer*, 3 Aug. 1823.
107. ibid., loc. cit.
108. *Sunday Express*, 2 Mar. 1969, quoted in *The News* (now *FT*), no. 6 (Sept. 1974) p. 3; B. L. Owens, 'The Strange Saga of the Emmaville Panther', *Australian Outdoors and Fishing*, April 1977, pp. 17–19.
109. *The Australian*, 5 and 6 June 1978; there is also an interesting chapter on 'The Queensland Marsupial Tiger' (ch. 8) in Heuvelmans, *On the Track of Unknown Animals*.

3. MYSTERIOUS BLACK DOGS

1. Alasdair Alpin MacGregor, *The Ghost Book* (London: Robert Hale, 1955) p. 163.
2. Ethel H. Rudkin, 'The Black Dog', *Folk-Lore*, vol. 49 (1938) p. 125.
3. Stephen Jenkins, *The Undiscovered Country* (Sudbury: Neville Spearman, 1977) p. 177.
4. Rudkin, op. cit., p. 118.
5. D. A. MacManus, *The Middle Kingdom*: The Faerie World of Ireland (Gerrards Cross: Colin Smythe Ltd, 1972), p. 68.
6. Rudkin, op. cit., p. 123.
7. Ivan Bunn, 'Black Dogs and Water', *Fortean Times* (hereinafter *FT*) no. 17 (Aug. 1976) p. 12.
8. Jenkins, op. cit., p. 177.
9. MacManus, op. cit., p. 68.
10. Personal communication to the authors.
11. Doris Jones-Baker, *The Folklore of Hertfordshire* (London: B. T. Batsford, 1977) p. 118.
12. Ivan Bunn, 'Black Shuck, part one: Encounters, Legends and Ambiguities', *Lantern*, no. 18 (summer 1977) p. 4, quoting from 'Tales and Traditions of Old Yarmouth', *Yarmouth Mercury*, 7 Jan. 1893.
13. Patricia Dale-Green, *Dog* (London: Rupert Hart-Davis, 1966) p. 56.
14. Theo Brown, 'The Black Dog', *Folk-Lore*, vol. 69 (1958), p. 181.
15. Enid Porter, *The Folklore of East Anglia* (London: B. T. Batsford, 1974) p. 89.

16. R. L. Tongue, *Somerset Folklore* (London: The Folk-Lore Society, 1965) p. 109.

17. *Notes and Queries*, vol. 2 no. 34 (22 June 1850) pp. 52–3.

18. Frank Hamel, *Human Animals* (Wellingborough: The Aquarian Press, new edition 1973) p. 239.

19. Jenkins, op. cit., p. 177.

20. See, for example, the report of a white hound with red ears seen near Priddy, Somerset, quoted in K. M. Briggs, *The Fairies in Tradition and Literature* (London: Routledge & Kegan Paul, 1967) p. 75.

21. Roy Palmer, *The Folklore of Warwickshire* (London: B. T. Batsford, 1976) p. 79.

22. MacGregor, op. cit., pp. 57–61.

23. John Harland and T. T. Wilkinson, *Lancashire Folk-Lore* (Manchester and London: John Heywood, 1882; Wakefield: E. P. Publishing, 1973) p. 91.

24. Wirt Sikes, *British Goblins* (London: Sampson Low, 1880; Wakefield: E. P. Publishing, 1973) p. 171.

25. R. Macdonald Robertson, *Selected Highland Folk Tales* (Oliver & Boyd, 1961) p. 86.

26. Marie Trevelyan, *Folk-Lore and Folk-Stories of Wales* (London, 1909; Wakefield: E. P. Publishing, 1973) p. 52.

27. Ivan Bunn, 'Black Shuck' part two, *Lantern*, no. 19 (autumn 1977) p. 4.

28. Hone's *Everyday Book*, vol. 111, p. 655, quoted in Katharine Briggs, *A Dictionary of Fairies* (hereinafter *ADOF*) (London: Allen Lane, 1976) pp. 16–17.

29. A letter received by Ivan Bunn from the witness, quoted in his 'Black Shuck' part one, p. 6.

30. Rudkin, op. cit., pp. 118 and 123.

31. ibid., p. 124.

32. MacManus, op. cit., p. 74.

33. L. F. Tebbult, 'A Buckinghamshire Black Dog', *Folklore*, vol. 56 (1945) p. 222.

34. Ralph Whitlock, *The Folklore of Devon* (London: B. T. Batsford, 1977) p. 60.

35. Described in a letter to Ruth E. St Leger-Gordon, and mentioned in her book *The Witchcraft and Folklore of Dartmoor* (London: Robert Hale, 1965; Wakefield: E. P. Publishing, second edition 1973) p. 188.

36. MacManus, op. cit., pp. 74–5.

37. MacGregor, op. cit., p. 66.

38. Letter to the editor of *Eastern Daily Press*, 16 Nov. 1971, mentioned in Bunn, 'Black Shuck' part one, p. 6.

39. Rudkin, op. cit., p. 125.

40. All from Vance Randolph, *Ozark Superstitions* (Columbia University Press, 1947; New York: Dover Publications, 1964) pp. 224–5.

41. Rudkin, op. cit., p. 114.

42. Bunn, 'Black Shuck' part one, p. 4, quoting Morley Adams, *In the Footsteps of Borrow and Fitzgerald*, 1914.

43. Trevelyan, op. cit., p. 52.

44. Briggs, *ADOF*, p. 183.

45. Harland and Wilkinson, op. cit., p. 91.

46. Told by witness to Ivan Bunn and repeated in his 'Black Shuck' part one, p. 5.

47. R. Chambers, *The Book of Days*, ii (1888) p. 434, quoted in Brown, op. cit., p. 180.

48. Told by the witness to R. L. Tongue and noted in her op. cit., p. 108.

49. Newbell Niles Puckett, PhD., *Folk Beliefs of the Southern Negro* (The University of North Carolina Press and Oxford University Press, 1926).

50. From Eric Swift, *Folktales of the East Midlands* (London: Thomas Nelson, 1954), quoted in Paul Devereux & Andrew York, 'Portrait of a Fault Area', *The News* (now *Fortean Times*) no. 12 (Oct. 1975) p. 11.

51. Ruth L. Tongue, 'Traces of Fairy Hounds in Somerset', *Folklore*, vol. 67 (1956) pp. 233–4.

52. Robertson, op. cit., p. 86.

53. See Helen Creighton, *Folklore of Lunenburg County, Nova Scotia* (National Museum of Canada Bulletin no. 117, 1950) p. 41 fn. 2, and Brown, op. cit., p. 180.

54. Brown, op. cit., p. 180.

55. Bunn, 'Black Shuck' part one, p. 4, quoting from 'Tales and Traditions of Old Yarmouth' in the *Yarmouth Mercury*, 7 Jan. 1893.

56. Bunn, 'Black Shuck' part two, p. 4.

57. Rudkin, op. cit., p. 121.

58. MacGregor, op. cit., p. 71.

59. Peter Moss, *Ghosts over Britain* (London: Elm Tree Books, 1977), p. 160.
60. Porter, op. cit., pp. 91–2.
61. Palmer, op. cit., pp. 78–9.
62. Creighton, op. cit., p. 41.
63. Robertson, op. cit., p. 86.
64. See, for example, Brown, op. cit., p. 186, and Dale-Green, op. cit., pp. 66–9, 76–7.
65. MacManus, op. cit., p. 70.
66. Hamel, op. cit., p. 240.
67. MacGregor, op. cit., p. 162.
68. Bunn, 'Black Shuck' part one, p. 5, quoting *Eastern Daily News*, 15 Mar. 1965.
69. *Eastern Daily Press*, 27 Apr. 1972.
70. Moss, op. cit., p. 34.
71. Harland and Wilkinson, op. cit., p. 91.
72. Tebbult, op. cit., p. 222.
73. Harland and Wilkinson, op. cit., p. 91; see also Brown, op. cit., p. 182.
74. 'West Hertfordshire Notes and Queries', 2 December 1911, p. 3, quoted in Jones-Baker, op. cit., pp. 117–18.
75. Devereux and York, op. cit., p. 11.
76. Rudkin, op. cit., p. 116.
77. Tongue, *Somerset Folklore*, op. cit., p. 109.
78. Whitlock, op. cit., p. 60.
79. *A Relation of Apparitions of Spirits, In the County of Monmouth, and the Principality of WALES ... England,* &c., by the late Rev. Edmund Jones, of the *Tranch* (Newport, 1813) pp. 70–1.
80. Revd Elias Owen, *Welsh Folk-lore* (Oswestry & Wrexham: Woodall, Minshall & Company, 1896; Wakefield: E. P. Publishing, 1976) p. 157.
81. Leonard H. Stringfield, *Situation Red, the UFO Siege!* (New York: Doubleday & Company, 1977) p. 63.
82. Bunn, 'Black Shuck' part one, p. 4.
83. Quoted in The Lady Eveline Camille Gurdon, *County Folk-Lore, Suffolk* (London: Folk-Lore Society, 1893) pp. 85–8.
84. All from Harold T. Wilkins, *Mysteries, Solved and Unsolved* (London: Odhams Press, 1959) pp. 205–8.
85. MacManus, op. cit., pp. 67–8.
86. MacGregor, op. cit., pp. 66–7.

87. Personal letter to the authors; witness's name and address on file.

88. Forby, *Vocabulary of E. Anglia*, vol. ii, p. 238, quoted in Gurdon, op. cit.

89. *Eastern Daily Press*, 2 July 1894, quoted in Bunn, 'Black Shuck' part one, p. 3.

90. 'Tales and Traditions of Old Yarmouth' in *Yarmouth Mercury*, 7 Jan. 1893, quoted in Bunn, 'Black Shuck' part one, p. 4.

91. Dale-Green, op. cit., p. 56.

92. ibid., pp. 55–6.

93. Both from Tongue, *Somerset Folklore*, op. cit., p. 108.

94. All three cases from Rudkin, op. cit., pp. 116, 117 and 126.

95. Tongue, *Somerset Folklore*, op. cit., p. 108.

96. All in Briggs, *ADOF*, pp. 207–8 and 301.

97. ibid., p. 301.

98. Quoted from J. Wentworth Day by MacGregor, op. cit., p. 71.

99. Hamel, op. cit., p. 239.

100. Both from MacManus, op. cit., pp. 69–70.

101. John H. L'Amy, *Jersey Folk Lore* (Jersey: J. T. Bigwood, 1927) p. 116.

102. MacGregor, op. cit., p. 70.

103. See, for example, Dale-Green, op. cit., pp. 70–5.

104. Tebbult, op. cit., p. 222.

105. All three from Rudkin, op. cit., pp. 113 and 118, and there are many other examples in this article.

106. *Eastern Counties Magazine*, 1, 3 (1901) pp. 170–1, quoted in Porter, op. cit., p. 89.

107. Brown, op. cit., p. 183.

108. ibid., loc. cit.

109. ibid., loc. cit.; Rudkin, op. cit., pp. 118 and 126; and the Buckinghamshire farmer case quoted earlier.

110. Rudkin, op. cit., pp. 119 and 122.

111. 'Willie Sled's dog', a white 'boggle', haunted the meeting of four roads at Brigham, Humberside – John Nicholson, *Folk Lore of East Yorkshire* (London, 1890; Wakefield: E. P. Publishing, 1973) p. 79.

112. Brown, op. cit., p. 176.

113. ibid., p. 185; Jones-Baker, op. cit., p. 117.

114. Brown, op. cit., pp. 176 and 182.

115. All from Rudkin, op. cit., pp. 113, 117, 124 and 125.

116. Jacqueline Simpson, *The Folklore of the Welsh Border* (London: B. T. Batsford, 1976), p. 89.

117. Tongue, *Somerset Folklore*, op. cit., p. 107.

118. Randolph, op. cit., p. 225.

119. Robertson, op. cit., p. 86.

120. Both from Rudkin, op. cit., pp. 113 and 124–5.

121. Edward Moor, *Suffolk Words and Phrases* (1823), quoted in Bunn, 'Black Shuck' part one, p. 3.

122. Ella Mary Leather, *Folk-Lore of Herefordshire* (Hereford: Jakeman & Carver, 1912; Wakefield: S. R. Publishers, 1970) p. 38.

123. Harland and Wilkinson, op. cit., p. 91.

124. All from Rudkin, op. cit., pp. 118, 119 and 121.

125. MacManus, op. cit., p. 72.

126. *Eastern Daily Press*, 17 Jan. 1968, quoted by Bunn, 'Black Shuck' part one, p. 3.

127. Tongue, *Somerset Folklore*, op. cit., p. 109.

128. MacManus, op. cit., p. 71.

129. Rudkin, op. cit., pp. 128–30.

130. Bunn, 'Black Dogs and Water', op. cit. He has also analysed his cases county by county – see Bunn, 'Black Shuck' part one, p. 3.

131. Steve Moore, 'Notes on Greenwich Phenomena', *Fortean Times*, no. 16 (June 1976) pp. 8–12.

132. For more information on leys see: Janet and Colin Bord, *Mysterious Britain* (London: Garnstone Press, 1972; St Albans: Paladin Books, 1974; New York: Doubleday & Company, 1973); Janet and Colin Bord, *The Secret Country* (London: Paul Elek Ltd, 1976; St Albans: Paladin Books, 1978; New York: Walker and Company, 1977; New York: Warner Books, 1978); Paul Devereux and Ian Thompson, *The Ley Hunter's Companion:* Aligned Ancient Sites – A New Study with Fieldguide and Maps (London: Thames and Hudson, 1979); Tom Graves, *Needles of Stone* (London: Turnstone Books, 1978); John Michell, *The New View Over Atlantis* (London: Thames and Hudson, 1983); Paul Screeton, *Quicksilver Heritage* (Wellingborough: Thorsons Publishers, 1974; London: Abacus Books, 1976); *The Ley Hunter*, a magazine edited by Paul Devereux (P.O. Box 13, Welshpool, Powys); Alfred Watkins, *The Old Straight Track*: Its Mounds, Beacons, Moats, Sites and Mark

Stones (London: Methuen & Co., 1925; London: Garnstone Press, 1970; London: Abacus Books, 1974).

133. Briggs, *ADOF*, pp. 74–5.

134. *Notes and Queries*, vol. 2 no. 34 (22 June 1850) pp. 52–3, and Harland & Wilkinson, op. cit., p. 92.

135. *Notes and Queries*, vol. 1 no. 29 (18 May 1850) p. 468.

136. Brown, op. cit., p. 179.

137. Both from Rudkin, op. cit., pp. 113 and 117.

138. Margaret Killip, *The Folklore of the Isle of Man* (London: B. T. Batsford, 1975) p. 151.

139. MacGregor, op. cit., p. 71.

140. All from Bunn, 'Black Shuck' part one, p. 4.

141. Aubrey L. Parke, 'The Folklore of Sixpenny Handley, Dorset', *Folklore*, vol. 74 (autumn 1963) p. 486.

142. Leslie V. Grinsell, *Folklore of Prehistoric Sites in Britain* (Newton Abbot: David & Charles, 1976) p. 142.

143. ibid., p. 103; Tongue, *Somerset Folklore*, op. cit., p. 110.

144. Tony Deane and Tony Shaw, *The Folklore of Cornwall* (London: B. T. Batsford, 1975) p. 110.

145. Jones-Baker, op. cit., p. 32.

146. Bord, *The Secret Country*, p. 183.

147. Sikes, op. cit., p. 168.

148. Alasdair Alpin MacGregor, *The Peat-Fire Flame* (Edinburgh and London: The Moray Press, 1937) p. 286.

149. Grinsell, op. cit., pp. 191, 221 and 223.

150. Brown, op. cit., p. 184.

151. Both from Rudkin, op. cit., pp. 119 and 122.

152. Porter, op. cit., p. 89.

153. Theo Brown, 'The Black Dog in Devon', *Transactions* of the Devonshire Association, vol. XCI (1959) pp. 41–2; Theo Brown, 'The Folklore of Devon', *Folklore*, vol. 75 (autumn 1964) p. 160.

154. Both from Kathleen Wiltshire, *Ghosts and Legends of the Wiltshire Countryside* (Salisbury: Compton Russell, 1973), p. 12.

155. Andrew Lang, *The Book of Dreams and Ghosts* (London: Longmans, Green & Co., 1897) pp. 145–54.

156. Jacqueline Simpson, *The Folklore of Sussex* (London: B. T. Batsford, 1973) p. 49.

157. Brown, 'The Black Dog', op. cit., p. 186.

158. See *The Secret Country*, pp. 147–9 of Elek edn.

159. Augustus J. C. Hare, *In My Solitary Life* (London: George Allen & Unwin, 1953) p. 251.

160. Rudkin, op. cit., p. 113.

161. ibid., p. 117.

162. ibid., loc. cit.

163. ibid., p. 125.

164. Both from ibid., pp. 118 and 123.

165. MacManus, op. cit., pp. 73–4.

166. Pierre van Paassen, *Days of Our Years* (London: William Heinemann, 1939) pp. 237–40.

167. Tongue, *Somerset Folklore*, pp. 107–8.

168. See, for example, Charlotte S. Burne, *Shropshire Folk-Lore* (London: Trübner & Co., 1883; Wakefield: E. P. Publishing, 1974) p. 105; Trevelyan, op. cit., pp. 158 and 182.

169. Hamel, op. cit., p. 243.

170. Herbert Thurston, *Ghosts and Poltergeists* (London: Burns, Oates & Washbourne, 1953) p. 166.

171. Dale-Green, op. cit., p. 58.

172. Marc Alexander, *To Anger the Devil* (Sudbury: Neville Spearman, 1978) pp. 46–51.

173. Owen, op. cit., pp. 155–7.

174. Brown, 'The Black Dog', op. cit., p. 192.

175. Rudkin, op. cit., pp. 128–31.

176. *Northern UFO News*, no. 42 (Nov. 1977) pp. 4–5.

177. Coventry *Evening Telegraph*, 3 May 1977, and *Western Telegraph*, 19 Aug. 1976, quoted, along with other instances not mentioning black dogs, in *Fortean Times*, no. 23 (autumn 1977) pp. 3–5.

178. MacManus, op. cit., pp. 67–8.

4. GIANT BIRDS AND BIRDMEN

1. F. A. Pouchet, *The Universe* (1890) p. 255 fn.

2. Heuvelmans, *On the Track of Unknown Animals*, p. 316 Paladin edn.

3. Pouchet, op. cit., loc. cit.

4. Anon., *The Zoologist*, 26 (July 1868) p. 1295, reprinted in *Strange Life*, vol. B-1 of The Sourcebook Project (see n. 79 on page 241 for further details), p. 209.

5. Keel, *Strange Creatures from Time and Space*, p. 203.

6. *The New York Times*, 12 September 1880, reprinted in Jerome Clark and Loren Coleman, 'Winged Weirdies', *Fate*, vol. 25 no. 3, issue 264 (March 1972) p. 82.

7. Curtis K. Sutherly, 'Strange Creatures of the Keystone State', *Pennsylvania Illustrated* (Dec.–Jan. 1976–77) p. 38.

8. Full story in 'Thunderbirds Again – and Again', *Pursuit*, vol. 5 no. 2 (Apr. 1972) pp. 40–1.

9. Reprinted in *Res Bureaux Bulletin* (hereinafter *RBB*) no. 5 (2 Sept. 1976) p. 2.

10. Details from the *St Louis Globe Democrat*, 24 Feb. 1895, reprinted in *RBB* no. 8 (4 Nov. 1976) pp. 1–2.

11. V. K. Arsenyev, *V. gorach Sichote-Alinya* (Vladivostok, 1947) p. 52. An extract was sent to *Flying Saucer Review* (hereinafter *FSR*) in the form of a letter by Yuri B. Petrenko, Kharkov, USSR, and published in *FSR* vol. 19 no. 2 (Mar./Apr. 1974) p. 29.

12. The full story can be found in McCloy and Miller, *The Jersey Devil*, from which the details of the 1909 cases are also taken.

13. *Cornish Echo*, 4 June 1926, reprinted in A. Mawnan-Peller, *Morgawr, the Monster of Falmouth Bay* (a booklet published by Morgawr Productions, *c.* 1976).

14. New Jersey cases from McCloy and Miller, op. cit., p. 90.

15. Robert Lyman, *Amazing Indeed* (Coudersport, PA: The Potter Enterprise, *c.* 1976).

16. Curt Sutherly, 'Pterodactyls and T-Birds', *Pursuit*, vol. 9 no. 2 (Apr. 1976) p. 35.

17. Jerome Clark and Loren Coleman, 'Unidentified Flapping Objects', *Oui* (Oct. 1976) pp. 95–106. Indian pictographs of Thunderbirds and details of Thunderbird lore are given in Garrick Mallery, *Picture-Writing of the American Indians* (first published 1893; republished by Dover Publications, 1972) pp. 483–7.

18. More information on the Piasa rock can be found in Mallery, op. cit., pp. 77–80, and in 'The Piasa', a booklet produced in the 1970s at Alton, IL.

19. *Pursuit*, vol. 11 no. 3, issue 43 (summer 1978) p. 87.

20. All 1948 IL and MO reports from Clark and Coleman, 'Winged Weirdies'.

21. 'Homens Alados em Pelotas', *SBEDV Bulletin*, no. 112/115 (Sept. 1976/Apr. 1977).

22. Reported in the Houston *Chronicle*; our details taken from John Keel's report in Keel, op. cit., pp. 207–8.

23. *Fate*, vol. 9 no. 12, issue 81 (Dec. 1956) p. 12.

24. Clark and Coleman, 'Winged Weirdies', p. 88.

25. Keel, op. cit., p. 210.

26. Clark and Coleman, 'Winged Weirdies', p. 88.

27. Details from Sutherly, 'Pterodactyls and T-Birds' and the New Zealand *Star*, 7 July 1975.

28. 9 Feb. 1856, p. 166, quoted in *RBB*, no. 9 (25 Nov. 1976) p. 1.

29. *FSR*, vol. 10 no. 2 (Mar./Apr. 1964) p. 11.

30. *Deseret News*, 18 July 1966.

31. *New York Times*, 27 Nov. 1966.

32. Last three reports from John Keel, 'West Virginia's Enigmatic "Bird"', *FSR* vol. 14 no. 4 (July/Aug. 1968) p. 13.

33. E. P. Dutton & Co., 1975; published in the UK under the title *Visitors from Space* (St Albans: Panther Books, 1976).

34. All accounts from Keel, *The Mothman Prophecies*, op. cit., and Keel, 'West Virginia's Enigmatic "Bird"'.

35. Don Worley, 'The Winged Lady in Black', *FSR Case Histories*, supplement 10 (June 1972) pp. 14–16.

36. Marie Trevelyan, *Folk-Lore and Folk-Stories of Wales* (London: Elliot Stock, 1909; Wakefield: E. P. Publishing, 1973) p. 65.

37. Johannes C. Andersen, *Myths and Legends of the Polynesians* (London: George G. Harrap & Company, 1928) pp. 126–31.

38. Richard Barker and Anne Riches, *A Dictionary of Fabulous Beasts* (New York: Walker & Company, 1972) pp. 125–6; Colin Clair, *Unnatural History* (London: Abelard-Schuman, 1967) pp. 156–7.

39. Trevelyan, op, cit., pp. 141–3.

40. Katharine Briggs, *A Dictionary of Fairies* (London: Allen Lane, 1976) p. 34.

41. Clair, op. cit., pp. 149–50.

42. Richard Carrington, *Mermaids and Mastodons* (London: Chatto & Windus, 1957) pp. 80–2.

43. More information on the Tengu can be found in F. Hadland David, *Myths and Legends of Japan* (London: George G. Harrap & Company, 1912) pp. 352–5, and Carmen Blacker, *The Catalpa Bow* (London: George Allen & Unwin, 1975) pp. 182–5.

44. *Portsmouth News*, 1 and 4 Aug. 1969.

45. Sutherly, 'Strange Creatures of the Keystone State', p. 38.

46. Details from a local paper, name unknown, dated 14 Aug. 1970.

47. *Middlesex Advertiser and Gazette*, 5 Sept. 1974.

48. *County Times & Express* (Powys), 28 Sept. 1974.

49. Keel, *The Mothman Prophecies*, p. 37.

50. Sebastian Robiou Lamarche, 'UFOs and Mysterious Deaths of Animals', *FSR*, vol. 22 no. 5 (Feb. 1977) pp. 15–18.

51. All 1976 reports up until this point are given in great detail in Clark and Coleman, *Creatures of the Outer Edge*, pp. 165–88; also consulted was Clark and Coleman, 'Unidentified Flapping Objects', and Don Berliner, 'Big Bird', *INFO Journal*, vol. VI no. 3, whole no. 25 (Sept./Oct. 1977) pp. 15–16.

52. *Fortean Times* (hereinafter *FT*) no. 16 (June 1976) p. 19.

53. *FT*, no. 17 (Aug. 1976) pp. 17–18.

54. *Falmouth Packet*, 9 July 1976; *FT*, no. 17 (Aug. 1976) p. 18. Thanks are due to Doc Shiels for talking to the witnesses where possible and getting them to draw what they saw.

55. Palestine *Herald Press*, 19 Dec. 1976, reprinted in *Anomaly Research Bulletin* (hereinafter *ARB*) no. 4 (Jan. 1977) pp. 17–18.

56. Palestine *Herald Press*, 22 Dec. 1976, reprinted in *Shadows*, no. 4 (Jan. 1977) p. 3.

57. Palestine *Herald Press*, 22 Dec. 1976, reprinted in *Shadows*, no. 5 (Feb. 1977) p. 3.

58. Lima *News* (OH), 18 May 1977, reprinted in *ARB*, no. 7 (Sept. 1977) p. 8.

59. Jerry Coleman, 'Notes on the Illinois Big Bird', *ARB*, no. 7 (Sept. 1977) pp. 8–9.

60. *ARB*, no. 7 (Sept. 1977) p. 9.

61. Gilbert J. Ziemba, 'Mysterious "Giant Bird" Invades Central Illinois', Page Research Library *Newsletter*, no. 20 (18 Sept. 1977) pp. 14–16.

62. *Daily Pantagraph* (Bloomington-Normal Illinois), 29 July 1977, reprinted in *The Seeker*, vol. 1 no. 11 (10 Oct. 1977) p. 5.

63. Ziemba, op. cit., p. 15.

64. *The News Gazette* (Champaign-Urbana), 31 July 1977; Ziemba, op. cit., p. 15; Berliner, op. cit., pp. 15–16.

65. Jiemba, op. cit., pp.15–16.

66. *Washington Post*, 9 June 1978, reprinted in *INFO Journal*, vol. VII no. 1, whole no. 25 (May/June 1978). Steve Hicks'

interview with the jogger, Richard Lees, is quoted verbatim in *INFO Journal*, vol. VII no. 3, whole no. 31 (Sept./Oct. 1978).

67. *Leicester Mercury*, 1 June 1978.
68. *The Daily Telegraph*, 10 February 1978.
69. *FT*, no. 27 (autumn 1978) p. 45, quoting from letters from Doc Shiels dated 19 June and 6 Aug. 1978. Doc's thoughts about Owlman are also published in the same issue of *FT* – 'To Wit! To Woo?', pp. 44–6.
70. *ISC Newsletter* (winter 1983) vol. 2 no. 4 pp. 8–9.
71. Oliver L. Austin, *Birds of the World* (London: Paul Hamlyn, 1962) p. 33.
72. Heuvelmans, op. cit., ch. 18.
73. ibid., ch. 9.
74. Ivan T. Sanderson, *Investigating the Unexplained* (Englewood Cliffs, NJ: Prentice-Hall, 1972) ch. 3.
75. Peter Underwood, *A Gazeteer of British Ghosts* (London: Souvenir Press, 1972; London: Pan Books, 1973) pp. 264–5 Pan edn.
76. Aubrey L. Parke, 'The Folklore of Sixpenny Handley, Dorset', *Folklore*, vol. 74 (autumn 1963) p. 486.

5. MAN OR MANIMAL?

1. Quoted from a letter printed in the *Antioch Ledger*, a California newspaper, 16 Oct. 1870; discovered by Jim McClarin and reprinted in *Bigfoot News* (hereinafter *BN*), no. 27 (Dec. 1976) p. 2.
2. William Roe, quoted from his affidavit dated 26 Aug. 1957, describing his encounter with a BHM in British Columbia, Canada, in 1955. This sighting is described fully later in this chapter.
3. This creature was seen in Point Isabel, OH, in 1964, and the quotation is taken from Leonard H. Stringfield, *Situation Red, The UFO Seige!* (New York: Doubleday & Company, 1977) p. 65.
4. Tchernine, *The Yeti*, pp. 173–81.
5. *The Australian*, 3 Oct. 1978 and *The Guardian*, 4 Oct. 1978, quoted in *Fortean Times*, no. 27 (autumn 1978) p. 48. For more details of sightings of hairy creatures in South America, Africa and Sumatra, consult Heuvelmans, *On the Track of Unknown Animals*.

6. For the whole story read 'Preliminary Description of the External Morphology of What Appeared to be the Fresh Corpse of a Hitherto Unknown Form of Living Hominid' by Ivan T. Sanderson. Part 1 in *Pursuit*, vol. 8 no. 2 (Apr. 1975) pp. 41–7, and Part II in *Pursuit*, vol. 8 no. 3 (July 1975) pp. 62–7. See also Napier, *Bigfoot*, pp. 98–114, Cape edn.

7. *San Francisco Chronicle*, 18 and 26 July 1974, reporting a Nepalese News Agency story.

8. Sanderson, *Abominable Snowmen* (hereinafter *AS*) pp. 294–7 Jove edn.

9. *The Queanbeyan Observer*, 30 Nov. 1894, p. 2, and *The Cooma Express*, 30 Nov. 1894, p. 3, quoted in Joyner, *The Hairy Man of South Eastern Australia*, p. 9.

10. *The Sydney Morning Herald*, 23 Oct. 1912, p. 15, or 24 Oct. 1912, p. 4, quoted in Joyner, op. cit., pp. 15–16.

11. *The Sun* (Sydney), 10 Nov. 1912, p. 13, quoted in Joyner, op. cit., pp. 19–20.

12. Rex Gilroy, 'Apemen in Australia', *Psychic Australian* (Aug. 1976) pp. 23–4.

13. Rex Gilroy, 'Eastern States Yowies', *Paranormal and Psychic Australian*, vol. 3 no. 4 (Apr. 1978) p. 15.

14. *Paranormal and Psychic Australian*, vol. 3 no. 4 (Apr. 1978) p. 5.

15. ibid., p. 4.

16. *The Northern Star* (Lismore, NSW), 17 Aug. 1977.

17. Also wodehouse, wodwose, wodewose, wodewese, wodwos, wudéwásá.

18. An interesting study of the woodwose appears in Ivan T. Sanderson, *'Things'* (New York: Pyramid Books, 1967), ch. 10 'The Wudéwásá', pp. 107–21.

19. Both from John Michell and R. J. M. Rickard, *Phenomena: A Book of Wonders* (London: Thames & Hudson, 1977) p. 111.

20. D. Parry-Jones, *Welsh Legends and Fairy Lore* (London: B. T. Batsford, 1953) pp. 112–15.

21. Revd Elias Owen, *Welsh Folk-lore* (Oswestry & Wrexham: Woodall, Minshall & Co., 1888; Wakefield: E. P. Publishing, 1976) pp. 152–3.

22. Quoted in Affleck Gray, *The Big Grey Man of Ben MacDhui* (Aberdeen: Impulse Books, 1970) pp. 3–4, which book provides a comprehensive account of the phenomenon.

23. ibid., p. 11.
24. ibid., p. 18.
25. Marie Trevelyan, *Folk-Lore and Folk-Stories of Wales* (London: Elliot Stock, 1909; Wakefield: E. P. Publishing, 1973) p. 69.
26. Gray, op. cit., p. 101.
27. Byrne, *The Search for Bigfoot*, p. 113.
28. See Loren E. Coleman and Mark A. Hall, 'Some Bigfoot Traditions of the North American Tribes', *INFO Journal*, vol. II no. 3, whole no. 7 (winter 1970) pp. 2–10; and Wayne Suttles, 'On the Cultural Track of the Sasquatch' in Sprague & Krantz, *The Scientist Looks at the Sasquatch,* pp. 39–76.
29. See Ivan T. Sanderson's discussion of this case in Sanderson, *AS*, pp. 85–95.
30. All quotations are from Albert Ostman's account of his experiences, quoted in full in Green, *On the Track of the Sasquatch*, pp. 21–34.
31. Byrne, op. cit., pp. 1–3.
32. See R. S. Lambert, *Exploring the Supernatural* (London: Arthur Barker, n.d. (*c.* 1954)) pp. 178–9; Moon, *Ogopogo*, pp. 144–5; Suttles, op. cit., passim.
33. Sanderson, *AS*, p. 68.
34. ibid., p. 184.
35. The story, as told by a Kirghiz called Saikbaia Karalaein, is given in ibid., p. 323.
36. This quotation comprises the major part of Roe's affidavit sworn on 26 Aug. 1957, given in full in ibid., pp. 108–11.
37. Hunter, *Sasquatch*, p. 43.
38. ibid., pp. 42–4; Green, op. cit., pp. 135–8.
39. Byrne, op. cit., pp. 22–8.
40. Sanderson, *AS*, pp. 102–3.
41. Hunter, op. cit., pp. 84–5.
42. Green, op. cit., p. 113.
43. For the full story see Sanderson, *AS*, pp. 63–7.
44. See Clark and Coleman, *Creatures of the Outer Edge*, p. 29.
45. Green, op. cit., p. 188.
46. Grover S. Krantz, 'Anatomy of the Sasquatch Foot' in Sprague & Krantz, op. cit., pp. 79 and 90.
47. Otto Ernest Rayburn, *Ozark Country* (New York: Duell, Sloan & Pearce, 1941) pp. 313–14, reprinted in *INFO Journal*, no. 1 (spring 1967) p. 48.

48. Louisville, KY, *Courier-Journal*, 24 Oct. 1878, reprinted in Keel, *Strange Creatures From Time and Space*, p. 117.

49. Sanderson. *AS*, pp. 298–9.

50. See Sprague & Krantz, op. cit., pp. 12–13.

51. Extracts from his report are given in Green, op. cit., pp. 147–56.

52. The story of the Patterson film, what effect it had, and the various specialist reports on it would fill a book. For further information see 'The Patterson Affair', *Pursuit*, no. 3 (June 1968) pp. 8–10; Dmitri D. Donskoy, Chief of the Chair of Biomechanics, Physical Culture Institute of the USSR, 'The Patterson Film; an Analysis', *Pursuit*, vol. 7 no. 4 (Oct. 1974) pp. 97–8; Ivan T. Sanderson, *More 'Things'* (New York: Pyramid Books, 1969) ch. 5 'Wandering Woodspersons', pp. 65–79; Napier, op. cit., pp. 89–95; Green, op. cit., pp. 70–4; Hunter, op. cit., pp. 116–28, 180–6, 199–202; Byrne, op. cit., pp. 115–55, 167–8.

53. Stan Gordon, 'UFO's, in Relation to Creature Sightings in Pennsylvania', a paper presented to the MUFON UFO Symposium 1974, pp. 144–5.

54. Full story of the Roachdale events in Jerome Clark, 'Anthropoid and UFO in Indiana', *Flying Saucer Review*, vol. 20 no. 3 (1974) pp. 17–18, from where the quotations are also taken. See also Jerome Clark, 'On the Trail of Unidentified Furry Objects', *Fate*, vol. 26 no. 8, issue 281 (Aug. 1973) pp. 56–64.

55. Clark and Coleman, *Creatures of the Outer Edge*, p. 89.

56. Keel, op. cit., p. 107.

57. *News Observer* (Crossett, AR), 29 June 1978, reprinted in *Forteana News* (July 1978) p. 18.

58. *Fate*, Jan. 1961, reprinted in Sanderson, *AS*, p. 164.

59. Allen V. Noe, 'ABSMal Affairs in Pennsylvania and Elsewhere', *Pursuit*, vol. 6 no. 4 (Oct. 1973) pp. 84–9.

60. Great Falls, MT, *Tribune*, 20 Aug. 1977, mentioned in *Anomaly Research Bulletin*, no. 8 (spring 1978) p. 12.

61. Bigfoot/Sasquatch Information Service *Newsletter*, vol. 1 no. 9 (Dec. 1977) p. 2.

62. *Fate*, vol. 30 no. 6, issue 327 (June 1977) p. 32.

63. *National Enquirer*, 8 Oct. 1972.

64. *INFO Journal*, vol. V no. 6, whole no. 22 (Mar. 1977) p. 15.

65. Green, op. cit., pp. 156–7.

66. p. 117.
67. For more details read Grover S. Krantz, 'The Anatomy of the Sasquatch Foot' and 'Additional Notes on Sasquatch Foot Anatomy' in Sprague & Krantz, op. cit.
68. Gordon, op. cit., p. 138.
69. ibid., pp. 136–7.
70. Sanderson, *AS*, pp. 99–102.
71. Clark and Coleman, op. cit., p. 116.
72. Slate and Berry, *Bigfoot*, p. 62.
73. Gordon, op. cit., p. 137.
74. *Forteana News* (Aug. 1978) p. 16.
75. Gordon, op. cit., pp. 146–7.
76. Keel, op. cit., p. 104.
77. ibid., p. 113.
78. ibid., p. 106.
79. An article by J. K. Parrish in *Old West* (autumn 1969), reprinted in *Strange Life* Sourcebook vol. B1, compiled by William R. Corliss, The Sourcebook Project, Glen Arm, MD 21057 (1976) p. 21 – write for a complete list of Sourcebooks available.
80. *The Chronicle* (Wilkesboro, NC) 5 Feb. 1902, reprinted in *INFO Journal*, vol. V no. 4, whole no. 20 (Nov. 1976) p. 13.
81. Isabel Davies and Ted Bloecher, *Close Encounter at Kelly and Others of 1955* (Evanston, IL: Center for UFO Studies, 1978) pp. 171–2.
82. Sanderson, *AS*, pp. 134–7.
83. ibid., p. 143.
84. Keel, op. cit., p. 106.
85. Green, op. cit., p. 163.
86. *Sunday Gazette* (McCurtain, OK) 9 July 1978, reprinted in *Forteana News* (Sept. 1978) p. 16.
87. Green, op. cit., p. 187.
88. Quotations from Tawani Wakawa, 'Encounters with the Matah Kagmi', *Many Smokes*, National American Indian Magazine (autumn 1968), reprinted in *INFO Journal*, vol. II no. 2, whole no. 6 (spring 1970) pp. 39–40.
89. S. N. Mayne, 'The Wantage Event', *Pursuit*, vol. 10 no. 4, whole no. 40 (autumn 1977) pp. 124–7.
90. p. 205.
91. See, for example, Heuvelmans, *On the Track of Unknown Animals*, pp. 281–3 (surviving *Australopithecus* in Africa?); Sanderson,

AS, passim; Napier, op. cit., ch. 7, pp. 173–92; J. Richard Greenwell, 'Further Notes on the Origin of Bigfoot', *INFO Journal*, vol. VII no. 2, whole no. 30 (July/Aug. 1978) pp. 14–16; Sprague & Krantz, op. cit., pp. 20–3.

92. *The National Tattler*, 19 Aug. 1973; and a letter to the authors from Jun-Ichi Takanashi, Japan.

93. The sighting allegedly took place in Pennsylvania, in Sept. 1973, and is reported in Gordon, op. cit., p. 142.

94. Reported in ibid., pp. 142–4. Gordon himself was at the scene only three hours after the events. Also see the comprehensive report by Berthold Eric Schwarz, MD, 'Berserk: A UFO-Creature Encounter', *Flying Saucer Review*, vol. 20 no. 1 (July 1974) pp. 3–11.

95. B. Ann Slate, 'Does the Earth Really Belong to Man?', *Saga UFO Report* (Oct. 1977) beginning p. 32. Also see Brad Steiger, *Mysteries of Time and Space* (London: Sphere Books, 1977) pp. 117–19. The Wyatt story he quotes is intriguing, but sounds too 'pat'.

96. Stringfield, op. cit., pp. 64–5.

97. Jim Brandon, *Weird America* (New York: E. P. Dutton, 1978) p. 199.

98. Sprague & Krantz, op. cit., p. 47.

99. Stringfield, op. cit., p. 65.

100. Gordon, op. cit., p. 140.

101. Clark and Coleman, op. cit, p. 80.

102. According to ibid., p. 92.

103. Gordon, op. cit., p. 140.

104. ibid., loc. cit.

105. See several examples cited earlier in this chapter.

106. All attractions noted by Gordon, op. cit., p. 140.

107. R. Martin Wolf, 'Coherence in Chaos', *Pursuit*, vol. 11 no. 1, whole no. 41 (winter 1978) pp. 28–39.

6. ANIMALS THAT AREN'T

1. See, for example, David Fideler and Loren Coleman, Kangaroos from Nowhere', *Fate*, vol. 31 no. 4, issue 337 (Apr. 1978) pp. 68–74.

2. John J. Dunne, *Haunted Ireland* (Dublin: Appletree Press, 1977) pp. 92–3.

3. Charlotte S. Burne, *Shropshire Folk-Lore* (London: Trübner & Co., 1883; Wakefield: E. P. Publishing, 1974) pp. 106–7, who had the story direct from the witness's employer a few weeks after the event.

4. Enid Porter, *Cambridgeshire Customs and Folklore* (London: Routledge & Kegan Paul, 1969) p. 149.

5. D. A. MacManus, *The Middle Kingdom:* The Faerie World of Ireland (Gerrards Cross: Colin Smythe Ltd, 1972), pp. 133–5.

6. Richard Curle, *Caravansari and Conservation*, quoted in Affleck Gray, *The Big Grey Man of Ben MacDhui* (Aberdeen: Impulse Books, 1970) pp. 58–9.

7. Ethel H. Rudkin, *Lincolnshire Folklore* (Gainsborough: Beltons, 1936; Wakefield: E. P. Publishing, 1973) p. 30.

8. R. L. Tongue, *Somerset Folklore* (London: The Folk-Lore Society, 1965), p. 13.

9. Jim Brandon, *Weird America* (New York: E. P. Dutton, 1978) p. 199.

10. Green, *On the Track of the Sasquatch*, p. 163 Ballantine edn.

11. Florence Carré, *Folklore of Lytchett Matravers, Dorset*, West Country Folklore no. 8 (Guernsey: The Toucan Press, 1975) p. 10.

12. F. W. Holiday, *The Great Orm of Loch Ness*, p. 155.

13. Theo Brown, 'Living Images', *Folklore*, vol. 73 (spring 1962) pp. 25–40.

14. 1936 Penguin edition, pp. 278–85.

15. The BHM as a psychological phenomenon is interestingly discussed by Dr Delwin D. Cahoon in 'The Psychological Hypothesis Defended', *INFO Journal*, vol. VII no. 2, whole no. 30 (July/Aug. 1978) pp. 11–13.

16. Letter to the authors from Doc Shiels, 17 Nov. 1978.

17. *Falmouth Packet*, 14 May 1977, quoted in *Fortean Times* (hereinafter *FT*) no. 16 (June 1976) p. 18.

18. Information from a letter from Doc Shiels to the authors, 3 Nov. 1978; more details of participants and sightings are in *FT*, no. 21 (spring 1977) pp. 27–8.

19. Letter from Doc Shiels to the authors, 3 Nov. 1978.

20. Lyall Watson, *The Romeo Error* (London: Hodder & Stoughton, 1974; London: Coronet Books, 1976) p. 175 Coronet edn.

21. Green, op. cit., p. 63.

22. MacManus, op. cit., p. 67.
23. *Pursuit*, vol. 7 no. 2 (Apr. 1974) p. 43.
24. Clark and Coleman, *Creatures of the Outer Edge*, p. 196.
25. Extracts from a letter to author Tim Dinsdale from John Nicolson who had the details from a man on the boat, quoted in Dinsdale, *The Leviathans*, pp. 79–80 Futura edn.
26. Vance Randolph, *Ozark Superstitions* (Columbia University Press, 1947; New York: Dover Publications, 1964) p. 226.
27. Green, *Sasquatch: The Apes Among Us*, p. 289, quoting from a 1971 *Bigfoot Bulletin* report by Russ Gebhart.
28. Report No. 9 of Para-Hominoid Research, Ohio UFO Investigators League, 1979, p. 1.
29. Letter from Dave Webb of the CUFOS Humanoid Study Group, USA, in *Flying Saucer Review* (hereinafter *FSR*) vol. 22 no. 6 (Apr. 1977) p. 23.
30. See section 'Missing, transparent or indistinct extremities' in Luis Schönherr, 'The Question of Reality', *FSR*, vol. 17 no. 2 (Mar./Apr. 1971) p. 23.
31. F. W. Holiday, *The Dragon and the Disc*, p. 187.
32. Dr Gustave Geley, *Clairvoyance and Materialisation* (London: T. Fisher Unwin, 1927).
33. Quoted in Jacques Vallee, *Passport to Magonia*: From folklore to flying saucers (Chicago: Henry Regnery Company, 1969; London: Neville Spearman, 1970) p. 68 Regnery edn.
34. Gordon Creighton, 'A New FSR Catalogue – The Effects of UFOs on Animals, Birds and Smaller Creatures', *FSR*, vol. 16 no. 1 (Jan./Feb. 1970) p. 26, and subsequent issues.
35. 11 out of 26 cases in John Keel, 'West Virginia's Enigmatic "Bird"', *FSR*, vol. 14 no. 4 (July/Aug. 1968) p. 13.
36. Leslie Harris, 'UFO and Silver-Suited Entity Seen Near Winchester', *FSR*, vol. 22 no. 5 (Feb. 1977) pp. 3–6.
37. Green, *On the Track of the Sasquatch*, p. 81 Ballantine edn.
38. Both cases from Jerome Clark and Loren Coleman, 'On the Trail of Pumas, Panthers and ULAs', *Fate*, vol. 25 no. 6, issue 267 (June 1972) pp. 77 and 79.
39. Their names and the exact location are on record with the investigators concerned who are known to be reliable and experienced, but have not been published in order to save them harassment from the media and sensation-seekers. Source: John S. Deer, Ph.D. and R. Leo Sprinkle, Ph.D.,

'Multiple Phenomena on Colorado Ranch', *APRO Bulletin*, vol. 27 no. 1 (July 1978) pp. 5–8.

40. Brad Steiger, *Mysteries of Time and Space* (London: Sphere Books, 1977) pp. 117–19.

41. B. Ann Slate, 'Does Earth Really Belong to Man?' *Saga UFO Report* (Oct. 1977) pp. 32–5.

42. Philipp J. Human, 'On the Road to Vereeniging', *FSR*, vol. 10 no. 3 (May/June 1964) p. 27.

43. Both cases from Clark and Coleman, op. cit., pp. 17–18 and 23.

44. Charles Bowen, 'Mysterious Animals', *FSR*, vol. 10 no. 6 (Nov./Dec. 1964).

45. The 5 August entry in Nicholas Roerich, *Altai-Himalaya*, quoted in Geoffrey Ashe, *The Ancient Wisdom* (London: Macmillan, 1977) p. 187.

46. Information from Doc Shiels, printed in *Fortean Times*, no. 21 (spring 1977) p. 28.

47. *Daily Mail*, 28 May 1906, reported in Charles Fort, *Wild Talents*, from *The Complete Books of Charles Fort* (New York: Dover Publications, 1974) p. 915.

48. John Michell and R. J. M. Rickard, *Phenomena:* A Book of Wonders (London: Thames & Hudson, 1977) p. 125.

49. Donald Omand, *Experiences of a Present Day Exorcist* (London: William Kimber & Co., 1970) p. 164.

50. John Keel's term – see, for example, Keel, *Strange Creatures from Time and Space*, pp. 15–16.

51. Based on ideas on pp. 30–1 of R. Martin Wolf's article 'Coherence in Chaos', *Pursuit*, vol. 11 no. 1, whole no. 41 (winter 1978).

52. First published by Rider & Co.; Wellingborough: The Aquarian Press, reissued 1973 – see ch. XXIV, 'Animal Spirits in Ceremonial Magic'.

53. In *The Great Beast* (London: Macdonald & Co., 1971; London: Mayflower Books, 1973) pp. 42–3 Mayflower edn.

54. A private communication to the authors dated 7 June 1978. There is also a detailed account of the Loch Ness exorcism of 2 June 1973 in Marc Alexander, *To Anger the Devil* (Sudbury: Neville Spearman, 1978) ch. 6.

55. Alexander, op. cit., p. 80.

56. From an interesting article by Doc Shiels, 'Words from the

Wizard', in which he relates some of the stranger aspects of monster-hunting, including telekinesis, cosmic jokery, and psychic backlash. *Fortean Times*, no. 23 (autumn 1977) pp. 20–2.

57. See Wolf, op. cit., for more details.

58. *Undercurrents*, no. 26 (Feb. 1978).

59. By C. G. Park and R. A. Helliwell, both of Stanford University, USA, issue 4343 (19 May 1978). Helliwell is professor of electrical engineering. The main details are summarized in *Journal of Geomancy*, vol. 2 no. 4 (1978) p. 85.

60. Clark and Coleman, op. cit., p. 45.

61. Ivan T. Sanderson, *'Things'* (New York: Pyramid Books, 1967) p. 29.

62. (Chicago: Nelson-Hall, 1977) pp. 206–8.

63. Livingston Gearhart, 'Geomagnetic Storms and Fortean Events', *Pursuit*, vol. 8 no. 2 (Apr. 1975) pp. 38–40.

64. See, for example, Tom Graves, *Needles of Stone* (London: Turnstone Books, 1978) and Paul Devereux and Ian Thompson, *The Ley Hunter's Companion*: Aligned Ancient Sites – A New Study with Fieldguide and Maps (London: Thames & Hudson, 1979).

65. Rudkin, op. cit., pp. 34–5.

66. ibid., pp. 30–1.

67. And see also Paul Screeton, *The Lambton Worm and Other Northumbrian Dragon Legends* (London: Zodiac House Publications, 1978).

68. Our hypothesis on the link is confirmed by Colin H. Bloy in his article 'Telluric Lines', *Journal of Geomancy*, vol. 3 no. 1 (1978) pp. 9–13.

69. Details from Meredith, *Search at Loch Ness*, pp. 144–5.

70. Keel, op. cit., p. 15.

71. 'The "thing" of Sheep's Hill', *Pursuit*, vol. 9 no. 1 (Jan. 1976) pp. 9–10.

72. Roy Palmer, *The Folklore of Warwickshire* (London: B. T. Batsford, 1976), p. 80.

73. Clark and Coleman, op. cit., pp. 198–9.

74. See Martin V. Riccardo, 'Vampire Reports in Modern History', *Anomaly Research Bulletin*, no. 23 (1978) pp. 15–20.

75. (New York: The Citadel Press, 1958) ch. XX, 'Vampire Visitations'.

76. R. Macdonald Robertson, *Selected Highland Folk Tales* (Oliver & Boyd, 1961) pp. 64–5.

77. In Brazil in 1957; see Charles Bowen (ed.), *The Humanoids* (London: Neville Spearman, 1969) p. 212.

78. For more information on 'mutes', see Roberta Donovan & Keith Wolverton, *Mystery Stalks the Prairie* (Montana: T.H.A.R. Institute, 1976) and Frederick W. Smith, *Cattle Mutilation, the Unthinkable Truth* (Cedaredge, CO: Freedland Publishers, 1976).

79. *INFO Journal*, vol. VII no. 2, whole no. 30 (July/Aug. 1978) p. 9.

80. Stan Gordon, 'UFOs in Relation to Creature Sightings in Pennsylvania', a paper presented to the MUFON UFO Symposium, 1974, p. 140.

APPENDIX 2: A LISTING OF 300 LAKE MONSTERS AROUND THE WORLD

1. A chronological table of sightings of sea monsters can be found in Heuvelmans, *In the Wake of the Sea-Serpents*, pp. 575–85; 167 Canadian sea monster reports from the years 1583 to 1976 are listed in *Res Bureaux Bulletin*, no. 33 (4 May 1978), and a further 37 covering 1656–1956 in issue no. 39 (28 Sept. 1978).

2. See also Bord, *The Secret Country* (London: Paul Elek Ltd, 1976; St Albans: Paladin Books, 1978; New York: Walker & Company, 1977; New York: Warner Books, 1978); Paul Screeton, *The Lambton Worm and Other Northumbrian Dragon Legends* (London: Zodiac House Publications, 1978); Jacqueline Simpson, *British Dragons* (London: B. T. Batsford, 1980).

Index

Abdin Rock, 71
abduction by BHM, 146–50
'Abominable Snowman', 137
Abominable Snowmen: Legend Come to Life (Sanderson), 159
Academy of Applied Science, 30–31, 42
Adamnan, 187
Aepyornis, 125, 134
Africa, 45, 137, 199; *see also* South Africa, West Africa
Agnagna, Marcelin, 45
Ahool, 134
Alabama, 119
Alaska, 203
Albany (Ky), 158
Albany (Or), 156
albatross, 134
Alberta, 200
Aldeburgh, 96
Aldershot, 57
Alfriston, 101
Algarkirk, 97, 100, 103
Alkham, 59
alligators, out-of-place, 170
'Almas', 137
Alton, 116, 118
Amlwch, 100
An Carn Mor, 100–1
Anderson, Ivar, 22–3
Anderson, Julie, 36
Anderson, R. A., 36
Anderson, Sven, 22
Andover, 91
Anglesey, 38, 100
Annales Francorum Regum, 90
Ape Canyon, 152
Archaeopteryx, 121
Argentina, 203
Argyll, 101, 125
Arizona, 111
Arkaig, Loch, 14

Arkansas, 153, 156, 203
Armington, 132
Armstrong, P. A., 117
Arnold, Christabel, 53
Arnold, Fred, 59
Arrowan common, 131
Asen, P. E., 23
Ash Ranges, 57
Aspinall, John, 61
Atlanta, 78
Australia, 46–7, 78–9, 139–43, 199–200
Australian Capital Territory, 199
Austria, 80
Avon, 68
Aylesbury, 94
Ayrshire, 67

Babb, Veryl, 118
Back, David, 50
Bacon, Les, 118
Bagshot, 58, 178
Baker, Dr Peter F., 30
Ballageich Hill, 67
Ballaghadereen, 88, 96
Ballygar, 96, 98
banshee, 125
Bardsey Sound, 37
Barfoot, W., 38
'Barguest', 80, 83, 87
Barham, 88
Barmouth, 37
Barnby, 98
Barrmill, 67
Barvas, 101
Barwon River, 47
bat, giant micro-, 134
Bath Slough, 97
Bavaria, 105
Bayamón, 128
Bay Springs, 75
bear, 65

Beauterme, Monsieur, 72
Beaver Pond, 115
Beech Hills, 156
Belfast, 61
Belle Hole Farm, 89
Belyea, Herman, 77
Bemboka, 140
Benin, 199
Bennett, Marcella, 124
Bennett, Marjorie, 37–8
Bennett, Vernon 37–8
Bentley, David, 62–3
Berkshire, 87
Berry, Clive, 78
Bertie, 179
Bertin, 90
Bethel, 131
Bettyhill, 69, 70
Bewdley, 81
BHM ('big hairy monster'), 136–68,
    178, 180, 189, 195, 198; abduction of
    humans, 146–50; absence of remains,
    153; attack people, 159–60; attraction
    to cars, 159, 182; attraction to houses,
    158; attractions, 167; captured, 152–3;
    disappearance of, 155, 166; dislike of
    dogs, 160; electro-magnetic energy,
    167, 189–90; eyes, 156, 165; food, 147,
    150, 154; footprints, 154, 157–8, 159,
    166; gentler side of, 160–61;
    identification of, 163; insubstantiality
    of, 156, 166, 172, 180–81;
    invulnerability to gunfire, 156, 166;
    killed, 138, 152–3; smell of, 157, 164;
    UFO link, 165–6, 182–3; weather,
    importance of, 167
Bhutan, 200
Big Bend National Park, 120
'Bigfoot', 137, 146–68
Bigfoot (Napier), 157, 162
Big Grey Man of Ben MacDhui, 144–5,
    163
bird, giant, 111–12, 117–18, 120, 122–3,
    126–9, 131–5, 184, 198
Birdlip Hill, 95
birdmen, 110–11, 113, 118–20, 123–5,
    129–31, 133, 198
birdwoman, 124–6
Birmingham (UK), 133

Birmingham (USA), 119
Birstall, 86, 89
Björks, Ragnar, 25
black dog, 65, 80–108, 178, 181, 190,
    197; and UFOs, 183–4; as death
    omen, 95; as protector, 94–5;
    behaviour of, 83–8; breath of, 83, 93;
    coat, 81; disappearance of, 88–90;
    eyes, 83, 91; headless, 82; injury
    caused by, 94; location of sightings of,
    96–101; names of, 80; reaction of other
    animals to, 104–5; size of, 81; sound
    of, 83
Black Forest (Pa), 115–16
Black River, 190
Blackley, 61
'Black Shuck', 80, 86, 88, 90, 93, 96, 97,
    100
Blairgowrie, 101
Blanks, Edward, 52–3
Blickling Hall, 102
Bliss, Rennee, 17
Blue Mountains, 139
Bluff Creek Valley, 152, 154
Blyborough, 85
Blythburgh church, 83, 90, 96, 100, 190
Boas, Antônio Villas, 195
Boeger, Lewis, 114
Boleskine House, 69, 187
Bolivia, 203
Bombala, 140
Boobrie, 125–6,
Borders Region, 203
Borlum Bay, 33
Bourne Wood, 97
Bowen, Charles, 52
Bowlby, David, 65
Bowles, Joyce, 182
'Bozo', 138
Braeraich, 145
Braggadocio, 97
Braithwaite, Dr Hugh, 30
Bramley, 58
Branksome, 60
Brazil, 118–19, 203
Brechfa, 66
Breckland, 101
Bredon, 81, 92
Brenin Llwyd, 145

Brigg, 98
Bristol (USA), 113
British Columbia, 17–18, 41, 44, 46, 146, 149, 150, 152, 158, 166, 173, 178, 200
British Museum, 15
British Museum of Natural History, 27, 28, 31
Brittany, 101
Brooklyn, 110
Brooks Green, 60
Brothers, Glenn, 74
Brown, Theo, 100, 105, 174
Brownsville, 128, 129
Bruce, Police Sergeant Donald, 70–71
Bryant, Patricia, 129
Buckinghamshire, 54, 84, 94, 96, 172
Buckland, 126
Buckley, William, 46
Budleigh Hill, 89, 98
'Buggane', 80
Buinaksk, 153
bullets, invulnerability to, *see* gunfire, invulnerability to
Bungay, 92; church, 90, 96, 100, 190
Bunker, 85
Bunn, Ivan, 98
bunyip, 46–7
Burdine, Carter and Junior, 156
Burgh, 97
Burkholder, Sherwood, 75
Burnley, 106
Burns, J. W., 149
Burton, Dr Maurice, 14, 27, 61
Busby, Mike, 77, 193–4
Bushylease Farm, 52–3, 54, 184
Butterworth, Alan, 41–2
Buxton Lamas, 100
Byrne, Peter, 146

Cadney church, 103
Cairngorms, 144–5
Caisteal a Choin Dubh, 101
Caledonia, 117
California, 19, 39, 136, 137, 146, 152, 154, 158, 160, 180, 203
calls, big cat, 62
Cambridge, 171
Cambridgeshire, 95, 96, 171
Camden, 114

Cameron County, 111
Cameroun, 199
Campbell, Elizabeth, 13
Campbell, Howard, 115
Campbell, Sheri, 17
Canada, 17–18, 41, 44, 46, 55, 72, 77, 80, 87, 95, 105, 116, 117, 137, 145, 146–9, 150, 152, 166, 173, 178, 200
Canton Township, 74
'Cappel', 80
Carberry, Georgina, 48
carcases, sea monster, 39
Cardigan Bay, 36–7
Carmarthenshire, 82
Carnac, 101
Carr, Vic, 58
Carroll, John S., 139
Cascade mountains, 146
Cashton, 157
Castell Coch, 125
Castle Hills, 103
cat, ghost, 191–2
Catamount, *see* puma
Catfish Creek, 131
Cator, 84
Caucasus, 137, 138
Cave of Owen Lawgoch, 144
Central African Republic, 199
Central Region, 203
'Champ', 18
Champaign County, 74
Champlain, Lake, 18
Champlain, Samuel de, 18
Chapman, Sally, 129–30
Chappell, John and Wanda, 132
cheetah, 50, 51
Cheshire, 66
Chester, 66
Chesterfield, 159
Chetco River, 160
Chiddingfold, 55
Chief Cornstalk Hunting Grounds, 120, 124
Chile, 110
China, 102, 138
Chippenham, 100
Chisholm, Dr John, 63
Chittyville, 159
Christopher, Charlie, 59–60

Chronicon Saxonicus, 91
'Chuchuna', 137
City of Polson, 19
Clare, County, 201
Clark, Jerome, 129, 178, 193
Clarke, David, 35, 42
Clayton, 114
Clipstone, 63
Clopton Hall, 87
Coast Salish, 166
Cobbett, William, 72
Cock, John, 34
Coleman, E. M., 118
Coleman, Loren, 129, 178, 193
Collie, Professor Norman, 144–5
Colorado, 183
Columba, Saint, 187
condor, 132, 134
Coney Island, 111
Congo, 45
Connecticut, 204
Conon Bridge, 70
Conser Lake, 156
Conuma River, 149
Cookson, Peter, 59
Copalis Beach, 151
Copiapo, 110
Copplestone, 101
Cork, County, 201
Cornhill, 91
Cornish Life, 35, 42
Cornwall, 32, 33–6, 42, 48, 82, 88, 96,
    100, 115, 129–31, 133, 175–6, 181, 184
Corradino, Mike, 195
Costello, Peter, 24, 27
Cot Moor, 100
Coudersport, 116
cougar, *see* puma
Covellat, 132
Coventry, 107
Coyne, Stephen, 15–16
Craignish, 101
Cranborne Chase, 135
Crane, Bill, 60
crane: crowned, 127; sandhill, 134;
    whooping, 134
Crane, Mary, 73, 193
Cranleigh, 54, 55
Cranmer, H. M., 119

Crask, 69
Creag an Ordain, 82, 86, 88, 97
Creasey, Dr D. J., 30
Creatures of the Outer Edge (Clark and
    Coleman), 129, 193
Croatia, 80
crocodiles, 178; out-of-place, 170
Cromer, 85, 96
Cromley, William, 114
Cron brothers, 59
Cron, Mrs L. M., 59
Crondall, 52, 53, 54, 62, 184
Crosby, 94
Crowley, Aleister, 69, 187
Crowley, Tom, 145
Crowther, David, 62
cu sith, 80, 82
Culdethel, 69
Culmont, 121
Cumbria, 68, 81, 95
Curle, Richard, 171
Currickbilly mountain range, 140
Currie, James, 44
Cynwch Lake, 46

Da Nang, 124
Daemonologie (James I), 187
Dagestan, 153
Dahinden, René, 151
Daily Express, 58
Daily Mail, 27
Dale-Green, Patricia, 105
Dan, Frank, 152
Dartmoor, 81, 84, 89
David-Neel, Alexandra, 175, 177
Davis, Jackie, 128
Day, Jeff, 60
Decatur, 182
Delamere Forest, 66
Delavan, 132
Delex, Marie, 109
Denmark, 201
Dent's Run, 111
Derbyshire, 88, 95
Derry, 158
Deseret, 122
Deverell, Joan, 58
Devil, the, 87, 88, 106, 187
Devil's Den, 100, 101

Devil's Nags, 89, 100
Devon, 56–7, 84, 89, 101
Dinsdale, Tim, 20, 24, 29, 41, 47, 188
Ditchingham, 92
Dixon, Joseph, 76
Doghill barrow, 100
Dog o' Mause, 101
Dolezal, Dr Kristine, 118
Donegal, County, 201
Dorset, 60, 100, 135, 173, 189
dragons, 177, 192, 201
Drew, Samuel, 96
Drogheda, 170
Dubbo, 141
Duich, Loch, 44
'Duligahl', 139
Dun a Choin Dubh, 101
Dun Borbe, 101
Dunn, Mary and Charles, 118
Dunsfold, 154
Dunthorne, John, 63
Dyfed, 66, 89, 100, 107, 204

eagle, 109, 112; American bald, 109, 133,
    134; golden, 134
Eagle Pass, 129
Eanaich, Glen, 145
earth energy, *see* energy, earth
East Africa, 199
Eastcombe, 135
Eastern Panther, The (Wright), 73
East Runton, 51
East Sussex, 101
Edgerton, Harold E., 31
electro-magnetic energy *see* energy,
    electro-magnetic
Elfers, 159
Elmdon Airport, 133
Elsinore, Lake, 19–20, 39
'El Sisemite', 149
Elusive Monster, The (Burton), 27
Emmaville, 78
energy: earth, 99–102, 191–3;
    electro-magnetic, 167–8, 189–90;
    human, 193–5; sources of, 188–95
England, 33–6, 49–66, 80–108, 122,
    126–7, 129–31, 133, 135, 143, 171,
    172–3, 176, 181, 182, 184, 185, 191–2,
    194, 201

Ennerdale, 68
Epitaph, 111–12
Epsom, 61
Epworth church, 191
Erial, 115
Essex, 94
Evans, Mr and Mrs Nelson, 114
Everest, Mount, 138
Ewhurst, 55
Ewshot, 52
Exmoor, 57
exorcism, 187–8
experiments in monster-raising, 176–7,
    188
Expressen, 24
eyes, glowing, 68–9, 75, 81, 83, 91, 95,
    110, 123, 126, 130, 155, 156, 165, 178

Fadda, Lough, 48
fairies, 177
fairy dog, 80
Falkirk Herald, 32
Falmouth Bay, 32, 33–6, 42, 48, 176
Falmouth Packet, 34, 35, 48
Farley, 55
Farley Mount, 54
Farnborough, 59
Farnham, 57, 72
Faroe Islands, 145
Farr, 69
Fath, Clifford, 182
Fealaar, 194
Fear Liath Mór, 145
Feliciano, Juan Muñiz, 128
feng-shui, 100
Fideler, David, 132
Field, The, 61
Fiji, 125
Finland, 201
Fishpond, 189
Fitch, Helen, 70
Flathead Lake, 19
Fleet, 58
Fleming, Abraham, 90
Flintshire, 144
Florida, 159, 178, 195, 204
Flying Saucer Review, 52
Fodor, Dr Nandor, 194
Folden, Arthur, 44–5

folklore, *see* legends
food supply, 17, 18, 61, 147, 150, 154
footprints: big cat, 49, 50, 53–4, 59, 61, 70, 181; Bigfoot, 154, 157–8, 159, 166, 181; black dog, 82; Kaptar, 138–9; water monster, 37; Yeti, 137, 138; Yowie, 140
Ford, Libby and Deany, 129
Fortean Picture Library, 7, 198
Fortean Times, 49
fox, ghost, 171, 180
France, 71–2, 80, 90–91, 101, 104, 121, 181
Francis, Di, 66
Freeport, 118
Frere, Richard, 145
Furnace Mill, 185
Fyfield, 100

Gainsborough, 60
Gallipolis Airport, 123
'Gallytrot', 80, 86
Galway, County, 96, 98, 201
Gartshore, P. C. Jock, 66
Garuda, 126
Garveston, 80, 97
Geldeston, 85, 100
Geley, Dr Gustave, 181
geomagnetic anomalies, 190–91
Georgia, 61, 74, 78, 159, 184
Germany, 80
Gévaudan, Wild Beast of, 71–2
ghost: animals, 170–74, 180, 181, 193; birds, 135
Ghost Book, The (MacGregor), 92
ghosts, headless, 172–3
Gibson, Wilfred, H., 41
Gigantopithecus, 163
Gilbert, Joan, 60
Gill, Walter, 95
Gilmour, Hugh, 67
Gilroy, Rex, 139
Gimlin, Bob, 154
Gladkikh, N. F., 21
Glamorgan, 82, 86; South, 125; Vale of, 82, 86; West, 66
Glenfarg, 68
Glentworth, 103; church, 103
Gloucester City (USA), 114

Gloucestershire, 95, 100
Gobilli, River, 113
Godalming police, 49–50, 53
Gold Coast, 139, 142
Goodbody, W. U., 173
Goonhilly Downs, 131
Gordon, Dr, 85
Gordon, Stan, 167, 195
Gorleston, 87, 88, 94
Grampian Region, 144
Grant, Arthur, 28, 39
Grant, Graham, 88
Grant, U. S., 19
Grassington, 83, 87
Gray, George, 141
Gray, Hugh, 42
Grayingham church, 103
Gray's Harbor County, 151
Great Badminton, 68
Great Bealings, 87
Great Notch, 128
Great Orm of Loch Ness, The (Holiday), 44
Great Snoring, 85
Great Torrington, 101
Great Yarmouth, 82
Grebe Beach, 35
Green, Jim, 51
Green, John, 151, 153, 160
Green, Mrs Robert A., 18
Greenwood, Jane, 130
Griffith, Mrs R., 37
Grimaldo, Armando, 128
Grýla, 145
Guajardo Alvérico, 128
Guatemala, 149
Guernsey, 101
gunfire, invulnerability to, 78, 179–80
Gunthorpe, 85, 191
'Guytrash', 80
Gwent, 89, 92
Gwrach-y-rhibyn, 125
'Gwyllgi', 80
Gwynedd, 204

Hackett, Theodore D., 115
Haddon Heights, 114
Haines, Colonel, W. A. C., 56
'Hairy Jack', 80
Hamel, Frank, 187

Hamm, A. V., 77
Hampshire, 50, 51, 54, 55, 56, 57, 58–60, 61, 91, 126, 182, 184
Hangley Cleeve barrows, 172
Harada, Mrs Reiko, 164
Harlingen, 128, 133
Harmondsworth, 127
Harper, Charles, 140
Harper, John, 50
Harpswell, 103; church, 103
Harpy, 126
Harrison River, 149
Hascombe, 54
Hatfield Peverell, 94
hawk, crooked-leg, 133
Head, Victor, 61
headless: black dog, 82; ghosts, 172–3
Heathy Park Reservoir, 50
Helford River, 176
Hemswell church, 103
Henderson, John, 70
Hennelly, Francis, 118
Hereford and Worcester, 97; *see also* Worcestershire
Hergest Court, 97
Hernandez, Homer and Marie, 129
heron, great blue, 134
Herrington, Verlin, 151–2
Hertfordshire, 61, 81, 89, 100
Heuvelmans, Dr Bernard, 109, 138
Hiba Heights, 163–4
'Hibagon', 163–4
Hibayama National Park, 164
Highland Region, 203
Hilgay, 87
Hindhead Common, 54
Hiroshima Prefecture, 163
hoaxes, 27–8, 157–8
Hobbs, Leonard, 53
Hoe Benham, 87
Holiday, F. W., 15, 16, 40, 43, 47, 174, 188
Holinshed, Ralph, 71
Holmes, Mr, 37
holography, 186–7
Hoopa Valley, 158
'Hooter', 80
Hopson, Keith, 58
hornbill, Abyssinian ground, 134

horse, ghost, 170
Horsham, 60
Houston, 119
Howletts Park, 61
Hoy, 88
Huachuca mountains, 111
Hudson River Valley, 120
Huffer, 'Texas John', 132
Hughes, Edna, 58
Human Animals (Hamel), 187
Humberside, 191
Hundred Stream, 98
Huntington, 74
Hurtwood Common, 55
hyena, 71
Hythe, 122

Iceland, 201
Idaho, 146, 159, 204
Illinois, 72, 74, 76, 77, 116, 117, 118, 131–2, 159, 182, 189, 204
Illustrated London News, 121
India, 126, 176
Indiana, 72, 73–4, 155, 167, 182
Indians, American, 116–17, 146, 166; Ojibway, 116
Indonesia, 134
Indre-et-Loire, 181
Ingalic Creek, 157
Inverness-shire, 69–70
Ireland, 15–17, 39, 48, 80, 84, 88, 96, 98, 104, 170, 171, 178, 188, 201–2
Italy, 80, 202

'Jacko', 152
Jackson, John, 67
Jackson-Parr, Stephen, 61
James I, 187
Jamieson, Dr Alec, 65
Japan, 126, 163–4, 202
JARIC, *see* Joint Air Reconnaissance Intelligence Centre
Java, 202
Jeannette, 157
Jefferson County, 180
Jellet, Ernie, 50
Jenkins, Joe, 191–2
Jenkins, John, 69
Jenkins, Stephen, 81

Jenkyns, Mr and Mrs R., 43, 47
Jenny Hurn, 107, 191
Jepsom, Tony, 59
Jersey, 80, 96
Jersey Devil, 113–15, 117, 121, 181
Jersey Pines, 115
Jinden, 139
Johannsson, Mr and Mrs A. M., 24
Johnson, Bruce, 17
Johnson, Gwen, 17
Johnston, Margaret, 170
Johnston, Scott, 69
Joint Air Reconnaissance Intelligence
    Centre, 29
Jones, Carys, 36
Junkins, Landy, 112
Jurmut River, 138

kangaroos, out-of-place, 170
'Kang-mi', 137
Kansas City, 133
'Kaptar', 137, 139
Karapetyan, V. S., 153
Karr, Dr James, 132
Kazakhstan, 21
Keel, John, 123, 193
Kenney, Jemmie, 110
Kent, 59, 61, 122, 185
Kentucky, 76, 78, 123, 131, 153, 158,
    160, 204
Kenya, 137, 199
Kern, James, 19
Kerry, County, 202
Kettle Creek, 126
Kettleness, 105
Khaiyr, Lake, 21
Kidbrooke, 51
Kielar, Alan, 31
Kinchafoonee Creek, 159
Kings Somborne, 154
Kirton, 89, 103; church, 103
Kish-Kiik, 149
Klumov, Dr S. K., 20
Kluski, Franek, 181
Knaith, 87
Knapdale, 101
Kok-kol, Lake, 21, 41, 176
Konsomol'skaya Pravda, 21

Kookaburra, 141
Kristianstad, 127

Labynkyr, Lake, 21, 46
Lafayette, 75
Lafrenière, Gyslaine, F., 190
lake monsters, 13–48, 181, 186, 190, 197,
    199–204
Lamberhurst, 185
Lambert-St Louis Field, 118
Lancashire, 80, 82, 95, 97, 100, 106
Langham, 60
Langlois, Mr and Mrs Charles, 18
Languedoc, 71–2
Larsson, Rolf, 24–5
Laugharne, 82
Launceston, 100
Lawndale, 132
Lawson, Douglas, 120
Lawson, Tracey, 128
Lee, Sam, 77
legends, 41, 45–7, 75, 116, 125–6, 143–4,
    145, 146, 173
Leicestershire, 80, 86, 89
Leiston churchyard, 100
Lemmon Creek, 178
Leontiev, Professor V. K., 138–9
leopard, 61
Leverton, 96, 97
Lewis, David, 55
Lewis, Michael, 55
leys, 99–104, 131, 191–3
Lilla Källsjö, 22
Lincoln (USA), 132
Lincolnshire, 60, 65–6, 80, 81, 83, 85, 87,
    89, 94, 97, 98, 99, 100, 101, 102–3,
    104, 171, 172, 191
lion, 50, 51, 60, 61, 62–5, 69, 71, 74
Little Eagle, 157
Little Snoring, 85
Littleworth Common, 54
Llanaber, 37
Llandudno, 38
Llangurig, 66
Lock Morar Survey, 14, 41
Loch Ness Investigation Bureau, 14, 27,
    30, 40, 41
Loch Ness Monster, 14–15, 20, 27–33,
    40–44, 47, 50, 173–4, 176, 178, 186,

187–8, 192–3; cine film of, 20, 27, 29, 44; explanations for, 14, 28, 31, 48; photographs of, 30–31, 32–3, 42; seen on land, 28, 39, 47; underwater photography of, 30–31, 42
Lochy, Loch, 14
Locks Heath, 126
Lofton, Mike, 156
London, 50–51, 54, 91, 194
Londonderry, County, 91
Long, Dennis, 58
Long Stone, 100
Lothian, Lord and Lady, 102
Louisiana, 157
Louth, County, 170
Lowdham, 63
Lowe, Marlon, 132
Lowell, 123
Lower Quinton, 87
Lowestoft, 87
Lyman, Henry, 30
Lyman, Robert, 115
Lympne, 59
lynx, 66, 68, 70
Lyons Falls, 190
Lytchett Matravers, 173

Mabe church, 131
McArthur, Ian, 40
McCullough, Joe, 76
MacDhui, Ben, 144–5
MacDonnell, Duncan, 13
MacGregor, Alasdair Alpin, 92
Maciver, Roderick, 40
Mackal, Dr Roy P., 18, 27, 28–9, 30, 39
Mackay, Hugh, 70
Mackenzie, Donald, 69
Mackenzie, James, 69
McLean, Alistair, 70
MacLeod, Dr Kenneth, 43
MacManus, D. A., 91, 171
McRae, Dr, 44
McWilliams, Johnnie, 139
Madagascar, 125, 134
Magallanez, Francisco, 129
magic, black, 187–8
Magnusson, Irene, 24–5
Major, James, 132

Malawi, 199
Malaya, 41, 202
Mallette, Mr and Mrs Steve, 123
Malmesbury, Third Earl of, 46
Mamquam, 173
Man, Isle of, 80, 95, 100
Manaccan church, 131
Manchester, 61
Manitoba, 200
'Man-Monkey', 171, 172
Mansi, Sandra, 18
Manton, 98, 101
Maoris, 125
Marcilly-sur-vienne, 181
Marlow, F. J., 38
Marquette, Jacques, 116
Marrero, Pellin, 128
Marrington, Thomas, 66
Marshall, 156
Marten, Murray, and Mr and Mrs Pat, 17
Martin, Ollis, 76
'Mary F.', 34, 48
Mason, 158
Matah Kagmi, 160–61
materialisations, mediumistic, 175, 180–81; faulty, 181
Maven, Max, 44
Mawnan, 35, 129; church, 130–31, 133, 176
Mayo, County, 98, 104, 202
Maysville, 123
Medstead, 60
melanism, 73
Melling, June and Vicky, 129
Mesopotamia, 71
Mexico, 176, 202
Mica Mountain, 150
Michell, John, 99, 186
Michigan, 74, 76, 156, 159, 204
Middle Kingdom, The (MacManus), 91
Middlesex, 127, 135
Miller, Mr and Mrs R. H., 17
Minchinhampton, 100
mind power, 175, 177
Minerva, 180
Minnesota, 138, 204
Minster, E. W., 113
Mississippi, 75, 80, 86, 204

Missouri, 80, 85, 97, 110, 118, 133, 157, 180, 204
moa, 134
Moca, 128
'Moddey Dhoo', 80, 100
Modewarre, Lake, 47
Moel Offrum, 46
Mokele-Mbembe, 45
Monaghan, County, 202
Monarch, 157
Mongolia, 137, 184
Monongahela National Forest, 189
Monroe, 159
'Monstermind' experiments, 176–7, 188
Montalba, 131
Montana, 19, 157, 204
Monument City, 74
Moon, Mary, 17
Moore, Steve, 98
Moorman, Ed, 74
Moortown Hall, 83, 97, 103, 104
'Morag', 13–14, 41–2, 176
Morar, Loch, 13–14, 41–2, 176
Morgan, John, 46
'Morgawr', 32, 33–6, 42, 48, 129, 130–31, 176, 184
Morris Creek, 152
Morrison, Earl, 124
Morristown, 159
'Mothman', 120, 123–4, 178, 182, 184
Mothman Prophecies, The (Keel), 123
Mott, F. T., 38
Mountain Fork River, 160
mountain lion, *see* puma
Mount Hawke, 115
Muchalat Harry, 149
Munstead, 53–4
Murray, Fred. 111
mutilations, cattle, 106–7, 127, 183, 195
Myatt, Barbara, 88–9
Myllesjön, Lake, 23

Nahooin, Lough, 15–16
Nanhwynan, 143–4
Napier, John, 157, 162
Nare Point, 131
Nature, 30
Naver, River, 69
Nebraska, 204

'Nellie the Lion', 182
Nepal, 138
Nesbaum, Elmer, 75
Ness, Lock, 14, 16, 20, 23, 27–33, 39–44, 47, 69, 173, 176, 187–8, 192–3
'Nessie', *see* Loch Ness Monster
Nettlebed, 54
Nevada, 204
New Brunswick, 72, 77, 200
Newfield, 114
New forest, 55, 57, 59
Newfoundland, 200
New Jersey, 111, 113–15, 128, 159, 161–2
New Scientist, 30
New South Wales, 78, 139–41, 199–206
Newstead Priory, 103
New York State, 18, 110, 190, 204
New Zealand, 125, 134
Ngani-vatu, 125
Ngutu-lei, 125
Nihiser, Rube, 112
Noble, L., 50
Norfolk, 51, 60, 63, 80, 82, 85, 87, 88, 92, 94, 95, 97, 101, 102
Norley, 66
Normanton on the Wolds, 63–4
North Carolina, 156
Northchapel, 155
Northern Ireland, 61, 91
Northern Territory, 200
North Kelsey, 103
Northorpe, 100, 103
North Yorkshire, 65, 80, 83, 105
Norway, 188, 202
Nottinghamshire, 62–5
Nova Scotia, 80, 87, 200
Nowata, 167
Nuthall, 64

Odiham, 51
Odin, 132
'Ogopogo', 17–18, 46; cine film of, 44–5
Ogopogo (Moon), 17
O'Grady, Richard, 67
Ohio, 75, 76, 123, 166, 180, 184
Okanagan Lake, 17–18, 41, 44, 46
Oklahoma, 160, 167
Olive Branch, 77

Olmito, 129
Olsson, Karin, 24
Olsson, Marta, 24
Olsson, Dr Peter, 23
Omand, Revd Dr Donald, 105, 186, 187–8
On the Trail of the Poltergeist (Fodor), 194
Ontario, 116, 117, 200
Oregon, 146, 156, 160, 204
Orestimba Peak, 136
Orkneys, 88
Orofino, 180
Ostman, Albert, 146–9, 151
Outer Hebrides, 101
Overland, 118
Overstrand, 85, 100
Owl Head Mountain, 112
'Owlman', 126, 129–31, 133, 176, 178, 184, 194
Owston Ferry, 191; church, 191
Oxfordshire, 54, 105
Ozarks, 180

Paassen, Pierre van, 104
Packer's Swamp, 140
'Padfoot', 80
Palmer, Colin, 37
Pana, 77
Panama, 153
panther, *see* puma
Papua New Guinea, 203
Paradise, 74
Paraguay, 203
Parke-Fountain County line, 156
Patterson, Roger, 154
Patterson, Scott, 180
Peak District, 88
Pease Pottage, 60
Pechersky, Anatoly, 21–2, 41
Peddar's Way, 101
Peel Castle, 100
pelican, white, 134
Pelotas, 118
Pembroke Dock, 107
Pembrokeshire, 89, 100, 107
Pendennis Point, 33, 184
Peniscot County, 85
Penmaenpool toll bridge, 37

Pennsylvania, 80, 89, 111, 113, 114, 115, 119, 126, 154, 157, 158, 159, 165, 166, 193
Perry, Barbara, 129–30
Persinger, Michael A., 190
Perthshire, 68, 101
Pestell, Alan, 65
Pevely, 180
Philadelphia, 114
Philadelphia Record, 114
photographic difficulties and missed opportunities, 36, 40–43, 45, 127
piasa, 116–17
Pine Barrens, 115
Pleasantville, 115
plesiosaur, 48
Point Isabel, 166
Point Pleasant, 123
Poland, 80
poltergeists, 105, 123, 177, 185, 194
Pomerania, 80, 105
Pontoon, 98, 104
Porshnev, Professor, 153
Porter, Officer J. F., 78
Porthtowan, 115
Potchefstroom, 183
Poteet, 128
poua-kai, 125
Powys, 66, 127, 204
Pray, Bonnie, 20
Price, Mr and Mrs Robert, 117
Prince Edward Island, 200
psychic backlash, 176, 188
psychokinesis, 177
Pteranodon, 122, 129
pterodactyl, *see* pterosaur
pterosaur, 120–22
Puckett, N. N., 86
Puerto Rico, 127–8
puma: alien, 49–79, 178, 180, 182, 184, 186, 193–4, 197; behaviour of in natural state, 55–6, 61–2; natural escapees, 60–61; similarity to black dog, 107
Pursuit, 111

Quakertown, 182
Quantocks, 94
Quebec, 105, 200–1

Queens County, 77
Queensland, 78, 139, 142, 200
Quoich, Loch, 14

Rabbit Hash, 131
radiation, as cause of monsters, 164
Ramore, 117
Ramsey, 95
Rao, Chandra, 176
Raymondville, 128
Razdan, Rikki, 31
Real, Luiz do Rosário and Lucy
    Gerlach, 119
Redbourne, 103; church, 103
Red Sky, James, 116
Red Wharf Bay, 38
Rendon, David, 129
Renfrewshire, 67
Renovo, 119
Rexville, 128
Reynolds County, 85
Rice Hope Plantation, 77
Richards, Bill, 57
Richland Township, 75
Richmond, 73
Rickard, R. J. M., 49, 186
Riley, Mr, 33
Rines, Dr Robert H., 30–31, 42
Ringgold, 61
Rio Grande do Sul, 118
Risca, 89
Rising Sun, 73
Roachdale, 155–6
Roberts, Richard, 144
roc, 125
Rockland, 94
Rocky Mountains, 183
Roe, William, 150–51
Roerich, Nicholas, 184
Rogers family, 155
Rogers, Troy T., 77
Roosevelt, Theodore, 159
Roscommon, County, 88, 96
Ross-shire, 70
Roumeguere-Eberhardt, Jacqueline, 137
Rous's Brook, 87
Ruby Creek, 158
Ruddington, 63
Rudkin, Ethel H., 98, 101, 103, 106, 191

rukh, 125
Rural Rides (Cobbett), 72
Russelville, 78
Russia, 20–21, 41, 46, 113, 137, 138–9,
    153, 176, 204
Ryan, Margo, 84–5

St Anthony church, 131
St Blazey, 82
St Elian church, 100
St James Chronicle, 71
St Louis, 118
St Martin-in-Meneage, 131
Salem, 184
Saline County, 153
San Antonio, 122, 129
San Benito, 129
Sanderson, Ivan T., 134, 138, 159, 160
Sandling Park, 122
Santee River, 77
Saskatchewan, 201
'Sasquatch', 137, 146–68
Savannah, 184
Sazawa, Mr, 164
Scarberry, Mr and Mrs Roger, 123
Schwarz, Dr Berthold, 128
Science, 189
Scotland, 13–15, 27–33, 40–44, 46–7,
    66–71, 80, 82, 86, 88, 97, 101, 125–6,
    144–5, 171, 176, 187–8, 192, 194–5,
    203
Scott, Mrs, 33
Scotter, 98, 101; church, 103
Scotton church, 103
Scunthorpe, 94, 191
Seaford, 101
Secret Country, The (Bord), 101, 192, 193
'Shag Dog', 80, 86, 89
shape-shifting, 87, 166, 173, 180
Shasta, Mount, 152, 161
Shasta-Trinity National Forest, 160
Sharpsville, 167
Shawnee National Forest, 77
Shawville, 105
Shelbyville, Lake, 132
Shelton, Sheriff Robert, 74
Sherpani, Lakpa, 138
Shetland Islands, 179
Shiel, Loch, 14, 176

Shiels, Christine, 35
Shiels, Doc, 32–3, 35–6, 44, 130, 176–7, 188
Shooters Hill, 50
Short, Mrs H. P., 59
Shropshire, 81
Siberia, 20–21, 137
Siegmund, Walter, 117
Siggers, Freda, 57
Sikhote-Alin mountains, 113
similarities: between the various alien animals, 177–80; between UFOs and alien animals, 180–84
Simpson, William, 13
Sites family, 161–2
Six Hills, 100
Sixpenny Handley, 100
'Skeff', 80, 97; *see also* 'Black Shuck'
Skegness, 65–6
Skerray, 70
Skipwith Common, 65
'Skriker', 80, 82, 86, 89, 97, 100
Slagesnässjön, 22–3
Slate, B. Ann, 166
smell: BHM, 157, 164; puma, 52
Smith, Mr and Mrs Clyde C., 118
Smith, Chief Inspector John, 64
Smith, Philip, 115
Smith, Mr and Mrs Richard, 32
Snitterfield, 82
Snowball, 139
Society for the Investigation of the Unexplained, 111, 161–2
Somerset, 57, 82, 86, 89, 94, 95, 97, 98, 100, 101, 105, 172
sonar in Loch Ness, 29–31, 42
Soulbury, 84, 96
South Africa, 106, 183–4, 199
South America, 55, 110, 118–19, 137, 203
South Australia, 200
South Carolina, 77
South Crossett, 156
South Dakota, 157, 204
South Kelsey, 97, 103
Space-Time Transients and Unusual Events (Persinger and Lafrenière), 190
Spicer, George, 47
Springbrook, 142
Springer, Arthur, 172

Springthorpe church, 191
Sproughton, 143
Squires, David, 141
Staffordshire, 80, 171
Staines reservoir, 127
Stevenage, 61, 100
Stewart, John, 67
Stewkley, 84, 96
Stithians church, 131
Stockbridge, 74
Stogursey, 97
Stoke Poges, 54
stork: Jabiru, 134; Marabou, 134; Wood, 134
storms, animals appear during, 96, 101–2, 190
Storsjö, 22, 23–6
'Storsjöodjuret', 24–5
Stowe, John, 91
Stratford, 193
Strathclyde Region, 203
Strathnaver, 69
'Straunge and Terrible Wunder, A', 90
Stuart, John, 46
Suffolk, 80, 81, 82, 86, 87, 88, 90, 92, 95, 97, 98, 100, 143, 190
Summerell, George, 140
Sunday Express, 63
Surfleet church, 103
Surrey, 51–5, 56, 58, 61, 72, 126, 178
'Surrey puma', 49
Sussex, 81; *see also* East Sussex, West Sussex
Sutherland, 69–70, 82, 86, 88, 97
Sutherly, Curt, 116, 193
Suttles, Wayne, 166
Swadley, Peter, 112
Sweden, 22–5, 127, 188, 203
Switzerland, 109
Sydney Cove, 139
Symonds, John, 187

Tabor City, 156
Talerddig, 127
Taney County, 85
Tanzania, 199
Tasek Bera, 41
Tasmania, 78, 200
Tasmanian marsupial wolf, *see* thylacine

Tay, Loch, 101
Tay, River, 39
Taylor, G. E., 27
Tayside Region, 101, 194, 203
Tchan de Bouôlé, Le, 80, 96
telekinesis, 42–3
teleportation, 185–6
Telle, Lake, 45
Tengu, 126
Tete Jaune Cache, 150
Texas, 119, 120, 122, 128–9, 131, 133
Thomas, P. C. Anthony, 60
Thompson, James, 133
Thompson, Stanley, 132
Thomson, Frank, 32
Thorganby, 65
Thornton Heath, 194
Three Brothers of Grugwith, The, 131
Thunder Bay, 116
Thunderbird, 111, 116
thylacine, 60, 78–9
Tibet, 137, 149, 175, 184
Ticonderoga, S. S., 18
tiger, 51, 71
Till, River, 98
Tingewick, 172
Tippah County, 110
Toba Inlet, 146
Todd, Thomas, 69
Tollerton, 62
Tombstone, 111
Tongham, 126–7
Tonmawr, 66
Trares, James, 117
'Trash', 80, 82, 86, 89, 97, 100
Trellech, 97
Trent, River, 191
Trenton, 114
Trier, 90–91
Trimble County, 160
Tucker, Professor D. Gordon, 29
Tulelake, 160
tulpa, 175–6, 177
Turner, Arthur, 73–4
Turner, Howard, 73–4
Tverdokhlebov, 20
Tyrol, 105
Tytton Hall, 103

Udehe-men, 113
UFO entities, 180, 182, 183, 195
UFOs, 26–7, 28, 51, 68, 106, 118, 122, 124, 129, 155, 156, 165–6, 169, 172, 177, 179, 180–84, 186, 190, 193–4, 195
Uganda, 199
Uniontown, 89, 154–5, 165, 166
United States of America, 18–20, 56, 61, 72–8, 80, 85, 86, 89, 97, 106, 110–21, 122–4, 128–9, 131–4, 136–7, 138, 145–67, 170, 176, 180, 182, 189–90, 195, 203–4
Uplyme, 86
Upper Potsgrove Township, 193
Upton, 66
Urabhal, Loch, 40
Uralla, 78
Urquhart Bay, 32, 33, 40
Ury, Thomas, 123
USSR, *see* Russia
Utah, 122, 204

Valais, the, 109
Vallee, Dr Jacques, 26–7
vampirism, 68, 175, 177, 194–5
van Acker, Christine, 159
Vereeniging, 183
Vermont, 18, 204
Vestigia, 146
Victoria, 47, 78, 200
Vietnam, 124
Vinnicombe, George, 34
Vladivostock, 113
Vorota, Lake, 20, 21
vulture, 133; black, 134; turkey, 132, 134

Wakefield, 80
Wales, 36–8, 45–6, 66, 80, 86, 89, 100, 105, 107, 125, 127, 143–4, 145, 204
Walker, Hilda, 119
Walls, Willie, 17
Walton Hall Hotel, 193
Wambarrows, 101
Wantage, 161–2
Warden, Clifford, 118
Ware, Ron, 55
Warwickshire, 80, 82, 87, 193
Washington, DC, 76

Washington State, 146, 151, 152, 157, 182
Wasso, William, 114
water monsters, *see* lake monsters
water, significance of, 97–8, 190
Waterford, County, 202
Watkins, Alfred, 99
Watson, Lyall, 177
Wavell, Stewart, 41
Waverley Abbey, 72
Webster County, 112
Wellington, 86
Wendel, Phillip, 38
werewolves, 177
West Africa, 134
West Bridgford, 62–3
West Briton, 35
West Drayton church, 135
Western Australia, 79
Western Isles, 203
Western Morning News, 34
West Kennet long barrow, 100, 101
West Midlands, 107, 133
Westmorland, 80
Westport, 119
West Sussex, 55, 60
West Virginia, 112, 120, 123–4, 189
Whaley, Joseph, 159
Whetstone, 111
White, Allan, 35
White, Mrs J. H., 114
White, Sally, 35
Whiteborough, 100
Whiteland, Ernest, 92
Whiteway, Felicity, 55
Whitney, 158
Wicklow, County, 84, 202
Wilderness Hunter (Roosevelt), 159–60
Wildlife, 61
Wildsworth, 191
Willingham, 98
Willoughton, 81, 83, 95, 97, 99, 101, 103, 104, 171
Wilson, R. K., 42
Wiltshire, 55, 95, 100, 101, 143
Winchester, 182
Windsor Safari Park, 127

winged men, *see* birdmen
Winsford, 100
Winsford Hill, 82
Winsor, 59
Wisconsin, 157, 204
Wisdom River, 159
Wisdom, George, 54
witches, 87, 97, 173, 176
Witch Tree, 97
Witheridge, 56
With Mystics and Magicians in Tibet (David-Neel), 175
Wolf, R. Martin, 167
Wood, Mr and Mrs Arthur, 184
Woodcutts, 100
Woodenbong, 142
Woodlands, 59
Woodseaves, 171
Woodstock, 105
Woodstown, 115
woodwose, 143
Woolpit, 82
Worcestershire, 81, 92
Worley, Don, 124
Wrangle, 96, 97
Wright, Bill, 32
Wright, Bruce, 73
wyvern, 46

X, Mr, 112

'Yahoo', 139
Yakima, 182
Yale, 152
'Yeti', 137–8
Yorkshire, 80
Young, Robin, 56
'Yowie', 139–43, 163
Yukon, 201
Yugoslavia, 80

Zaïre, 199
Zambia, 199
Zarzynski, Joseph W., 18
Zeuglodon, 18
Zigler, Mr and Mrs, 19
Zoological Society of London, 15, 58